THE DIALECTICS
OF SOCIAL LIFE

T H E
DIALECTICS
O F
SOCIAL LIFE:

*Alarms and Excursions in
Anthropological Theory*

ROBERT F. MURPHY

BASIC BOOKS, INC. PUBLISHERS

New York London

TO MY WIFE

Yolanda

G N
320
M 85

© 1971 by Basic Books, Inc.
Library of Congress Catalog Card Number 72–147015
SBN 465–01643–X

Manufactured in the United States of America

Preface

Anthropological theories are spun from the mind but forged in practical life. Many of the substantive ideas that I present in this book were stimulated by other writers, and proper acknowledgement is made to them. It is far more difficult, however, to sort out from the residue of experience those influences that have caused me to question and reformulate the very bases of a discipline within which I have spent half my life. But I can be certain that much of the book is a refraction of my attempts to understand and account for the social phenomena that I observed among the Múndurucu of Amazonian Brazil and the Tuareg of the southern Sahara Desert. They taught me the remarkable complexity of social life; they demonstrated that social reality is shifting and ineluctable; and they told me that underlying the veneer of cultural differences, there is a primordial humanity that must be accounted for as well as respected.

My book, then, emerged in the first place from a series of empirical studies in which I found orthodox theories inadequate, and was forced to turn to new and innovative works and to return to older bodies of social thought that shared my outlook. The catalyst of the book was the mood of profound social unrest and pessimism that began in the mid-1960s and has not yet seen either its end or its culmination. The regnant theories

of the social sciences, which are the official social philosophies
of our times, offered poor understanding of what was happening
to Western culture, and orthodox radicalism rose to the occasion
with tired slogans. My own attempts to comprehend disorder
brought me back to my fieldwork and those contemporary
writers, who include Claude Lévi-Strauss, Edmund Leach and
Herbert Marcuse, whose work had compelled me to ask new
questions. These questions again proved to me the continuing
vitality of the ideas of Sigmund Freud and the German sociologist Georg Simmel. The total yield of these diverse influences is
the present attempt toward a theoretical synthesis that will, I
hope, find pertinence to all societies and not just our own.

The book has been kept short, because I believe that excessive length may not only breed but bespeak unclarity. An anthropologist or sociologist will find sections in which he might
wish for more complete discussion, just as the lay reader may
occasionally feel that he has been told more than he wanted to
know. I have, however, tried to be selective in my sources and
to keep close to my topic.

The research and thought that went into the work spanned
many years, but it was mostly written during the academic year
of 1968–1969. Support during this period was given me by the
John Simon Guggenheim Memorial Foundation, which gen-
erously designated me a Fellow, and by a sabbatical leave
kindly granted me by Columbia University. I am grateful to both
institutions also for the total freedom given me to pursue my
interests.

The scope and subject matter of the book are so broad that
it is difficult to acknowledge all the students, teachers and colleagues who have helped to shape it. It is a summing up;
associates from many years past will see snippets of our con-
versations in its pages. I must then restrict myself to expressing
my debt to those who have read and criticized the manuscript,
or upon whose knowledge I drew during the writing. They include George Bond, Malcolm Brown, Morton Fried, Marvin

Harris, Allen Johnson, Harvey Pitkin, Carl Resek, Abraham Rosman, Paula Rubel, David M. Schneider and Joan Vincent. The preparation of the manuscript benefited greatly from the attentions of Mrs. Jessie Malinowska and Mrs. Virginia Brown. My thanks to them all.

Finally, my wife Yolanda read and criticized the work in its various stages of development and cheerfully tolerated the disruptions of life that go with authorship. Without her encouragement and sustenance, it would never have been written.

ROBERT F. MURPHY

New York City
February 1971

Contents

PART
II
The Negative Attitude

PART
III
Structures

PART
I

The Positive Attitude

I

Contemporary Social Anthropology

Social thought, unlike natural science, tends to be cyclical, returning to its roots periodically for sustenance, reassessment and reformulation. The study of man is passing through such a period now; social scientists are in seeming disarray, doubling their goals, methods, objectivity and even their motives. Traditional perspectives have failed at exactly the point in history that demands fullest understanding. Marxism has become bureaucratized by a tedious class analysis, its materialism reduced to an economic determinism that is belied by its own history. And the comfortable assumption of the social sciences that human activity functions to assure the continuity and stability of the structures of society has fallen victim to the evidence of the recent past. The failure of this idea—the structural-functional approach of anthropology and sociology—and the renaissance of an alternate vision of the human condition are the subjects of this book.

It is only a little over thirty years ago that the sociologist Talcott Parsons asked who killed Herbert Spencer and, with him, sociological utilitarianism (Parsons 1937). The evolution of the discipline was found, rhetorically, to be the answer, and Parsons proceeded to analyze the intellectual strains that contributed to the demise of this simple faith. In my own accounting of the passing of the new day that Parsons then celebrated, I will similarly outline the theories, past and contemporary, that have been supplanting functionalism, but the reader is cautioned that the story is incomplete. Like Parsons (1937, p. 5), I must say that the underlying causes of change in theories are to be found in large-scale changes in society that become embedded and transformed in men's minds. And again with Parsons, I must confess that such an investigation goes beyond the scope of this essay and transcends my own abilities. It can only be suggested here that just as utilitarianism arose in an age of belief in reason, in progress, and in the perfectability of the mind, so also did functionalism arise in a time of relative stability, order, and complacency.

Functionalism, as a viable unifying theory in the social sciences, is a casualty of the profound disturbances in the Western world that had their beginnings in World War I and that may possibly find their climax in the near future. In its place there is a growing tendency toward a dialectical mode of analysis that is radically opposed to the positivism of functionalism, although it sometimes speaks in the language of the latter. It is not the dialectics of Marx, for it combines elements of phenomenology and an increased concern for subjective states. It takes off from the base laid by structural-functionalism, but goes beyond the empirical structures derived from actual observation to infrastructures that are logical products of the investigator's mind and transformations and negations of the apparent reality. It is a philosophy for a period of dissolution in which firm verities are replaced by shifting mirages, in which predictability from the perspective of past expectations has been lost, and in which skepticism has become a mode of perception and not just of evaluation.

We commence by considering the nature and intellectual ramifications of functional anthropology. The discussion hews fairly closely to disciplinary lines, although occasional excursions into the sociological literature are taken, because the revolution has affected anthropology first and most deeply.

Considerations of sheer economy, however, also dictate this restriction. Much of the material covered can, nonetheless, apply
equally to both disciplines. The analysis then continues to a
consideration of the principal assumptions, both explicit and
implicit, of functional analysis in anthropology. In a much
broader sense, we review the positivistic bases of modern social
theory. Following this, the book turns to the tradition of dialectical thought, encompassing a brief summation of its epistemological premises and its uses in the social and psychological
theories of Simmel and Freud. Having posed a counterpoint between the positive and negative views of social life, we close
upon their mediation in modern structural theory. Much of the
discussion thus turns on the work of Claude Lévi-Strauss, but
it must be stressed that this book is not at all an exegesis on his
theories. Although my admiration for the man is unstinted, my
acceptance of his ideas is not. His work is subjected to quite
critical scrutiny and is placed in the over-all context of modern
social theory, which is our proper subject matter. More significant, our review of certain theorists provides a base line from
which to reconsider the nature of the dialogue that goes on
between man's thoughts and his actions, for within this strange
domain lie all of the principal problems of the social sciences.

Sociology, Pure and Popular

The social sciences labor under the impediment of being
investigations of the mundane and the ordinary, fields in which
all men claim a degree of expertise. The anthropologist Leslie
White once said that the study of human behavior was the last
of the sciences to develop because it had the most immediate
bearing upon, and therefore constituted the greatest threat to,
established political and religious interests. In view of the many
short-term accommodations of the human disciplines to the
moods of the times, this position appears dubious on its face.
Rather it is probably more accurate to state that the social

sciences were latecomers because they had been there all along. They were not invented but merely professionalized; the revolution in the study of man came when people began to make a living from what their ancestors had always been doing in a crude and subjective way.

One of the most useful lessons in the study of society is that Everyman is an anthropologist or sociologist of sorts, equipped with certain bodies of knowledge about established customs, fixed expectations regarding persons and situations, and an operating notion of what his society is like. This is the cultural apparatus of coping and survival. For social activity, to be possible, it must be predictable and made intelligible to others through the bestowal of meaning upon it. There is no truth value to social activity and its mediating symbols. They need only be somewhat coherent with other forms of activity and other symbols, and the folk sociology of the actor need only be appropriate to his position in life. Nonetheless, he is a student of society, however untalented or limited in perspective, and not merely a victim of custom.

Everyman as sociologist is concerned only with his own society and his own segment of it, and not with a general science of man or with an understanding of the exotic forms of social life. The two types of inquiry overlap, however, in that both are concerned with an observation of the chaos of the human condition and a reduction of its seeming randomness to modality and order: the folk sociologist requires the order as a condition for getting along in society and the professional requires it because it is the only way he can handle his material. Both the folk and the professional sociologist generalize as a means of understanding the particular. It should surprise nobody that their results are frequently similar and that sociology, especially, appears to be the science of the obvious.

It is indeed possible for a sociologist to survey the courting behavior of several hundred students and arrive at the conclusion that there is direct covariation between the number of times that a couple dates and the chance of occurrence of sexual intercourse. The wisdom of the street corner also tells us that if one tries hard enough and long enough he can't go wrong. Or Talcott Parsons may devote hundreds of pages to the thesis that consensus on what is being done and how it should be done makes encounters run more smoothly, a proposition that has long been accepted by most people and that is probably untrue. Neither statement, of course, is put so bluntly, even vulgarly, but is couched instead in the language of the discipline. This jargon has the manifest purpose of conveying ideas precisely and unambiguously. The very fact that people have always speculated on these matters requires that scientific study be couched in terms unsullied by past usages and unclouded by the multiplicity of meanings that characterize vernacular speech. But the latent function of social science terminology, as has long been understood, is a bit different. The true professional derives order, to be sure, but he then renders it unintelligible to all but the initiated. Language functions to provide communication, but the existence of thousands of mutually incomprehensible languages suggests that it serves also to block communication —a form of anticommunication, one might say. So also do professional sublanguages provide a means to establish the limits of the discipline and a measure of professional competence.

Anthropology, however, has been somewhat less obscured by words than has sociology because of the nature of its subject matter. There is less of a need for a house Latin to describe the already unfamiliar and bizarre, which have traditionally and properly formed our stock in trade. Nonetheless, the increasing involvement of anthropologists in research on Western culture and the cities of the West, the former preserves of the sociologist, has inevitably resulted in a proliferation of language. It is probably not at all an accident that anthropologists, who have been capable of giving quite straightforward accounts of the kinship nomenclatures of primitive peoples become rather incomprehensible when discussing that of the United States (cf. Goodenough 1965). In part, jargon grows apace with the refinement of methodology, leading one to believe that the latter is a highly specialized subspecies of the former, a suspicion that gains some confirmation in the rise of computer terminology. As anthropology becomes more sophisticated in its procedures, its results become more opaque, and even its research goals become unclear.

The social sciences have literally exploded in their scope and activity, but many of their practitioners are left with the feeling that they have not progressed much. Rather, there has been a considerable process of "involution," to use Goldenweiser's (1936) term so happily resurrected by Geertz (1963); the disciplines have grown and become more complex and differentiated, but they have not broken out of their original mold nor shaken off some of their rudimentary premises. Our unspoken axioms lie in our seldom revisited intellectual history, but they are ultimately derived from the fact that the study of man is emergent from man's activity as a sociologist despite himself. Social scientists may have indeed succeeded in making themselves unintelligible to the lay public, but their basic units of observation and mode of analysis of the human scene remain the same as those of the people under their scrutiny. This should not be cause for too much surprise, for we were trained as observers and manipulators of our social milieu long before we were trained as sociologists or anthropologists. We have long known of the margin of error that is inherent in the fact that the observer frequently has values in common with the objects of his study, but not enough attention has been given to their sharing of a common cognitive framework. The very perception of social reality, and not just its evaluation, is thereby skewed.

Social science has, however, departed from the popular and persistent belief that some of our most cherished values and entrenched patterns of behavior are part of a "human nature." This nature has been thought to be somehow or other inborn and instinctive and to be distinctive and specific in content. It is a sort of agglomeration of quite discrete things, most of which bear little relationship to each other, making it all the more easy to invoke them selectively as justifications of that which we are constrained to accept without question. The social sciences, especially anthropology, have effectively refuted this folklore, and sometimes scientism, of immalleable human nature and instinct, but they have provided no substitute view, except by omission, of an irreducible and common humanity. It is as if, having rejected the biological specificity of panhuman instincts, we were left with neither a view of existential problems universal in mankind nor a curiosity about the general propensities and structures of the mind.

The abandonment of interest in human nature has had salutary results, but it has left a vacuum into which has recently rushed a plethora of speculation that seeks to explain certain seeming constants in the human situation by tying them to man's biological evolution. Thus, the ethnologist Konrad Lorenz postulates aggression as part of our instinctive equipment, and a playwright, Robert Ardrey, has captivated an American audience with the idea that the territoriality of certain animal species is preserved in nationalism and private property among modern men. The most interesting thing about Ardrey specifically is not his theories but the success of his books. They have the merit of being intellectually simple, even simplistic, and they lend credence to the inevitability of our most cherished institutions: war, capitalism, and patriotism. His ideas are negations of man's hope for transcending himself and are appropriate to an era of pessimism and fearful retrenchment. Happily, the new biological theories have been widely rejected by the social sciences, which have maintained the position that to reach the unknown we must proceed from what is already known and not vice versa. Dependence upon a genetics that has not yet been developed is biological mysticism and an abdication of the scientific attitude.

Another premise in our Western tradition that merits close

examination and forms part of the subject matter of this book is our reliance upon "common sense" as the screen of experience and the ultimate determinant of what we perceive as reality. Human reason, as opposed to plain common sense, is generally viewed as a process that works upon experience but that follows after it. The actual reception of data from the environment is treated as a mechanical, sensory matter; we trust such evidence. We may have lost our faith in inductivism, but all social scientists are empiricists, in the same way that most ordinary people are. On the other hand, these same social scientists well know that perceived reality is conditioned by a variety of factors. It is not just "out there" to be picked up, but is part of a total situation, the most important elements of which are probably the social, including language. I am not suggesting that reality does not exist, that the world goes away when we close our eyes, but it is certain that the immediate images that we receive of the world are not to be trusted. Yet, common sense tells us what is obvious, and we can usually find good consensus among a number of observers confirming our impressions. Common sense and the data of immediate experience, unencumbered by thought, however, tell only half-truths; by their nature they are incomplete. Some of the most profound insights into man's condition have come about through a simple inversion of the obvious or a reversal of a basic premise. Freud was a master of the art. He horrified all of Europe by challenging the notion of childhood innocence, and evoked what everybody unconsciously knew when he pronounced the doctrine of ambivalence. And in an androcentric society in which all males believed in their sexual mastery, he told them that they were being eaten.

Anthropology is emergent from man's necessary preoccupation with social life and suffers from some of the same defects of perception and evaluation that encumber the social actor. Whereas the ordinary man's misperceptions and misevaluations are part of the way that he exists in society, these failings are a liability to the professional student of society, who is in a classic type of double bind in finding it difficult to transcend his subject matter. In the final analysis, one who studies society can do this only by transcending himself. Thus we speak of the need for "objectivity," which means, in part, that we should not be led astray by our subjective states regarding the people under study. At the same time, however, we strive for "empathy" with our subjects, which can be downright perilous for the maintenance of objectivity. We want to be inside our informant's head and emotions, but we wish also to stand aside and be aloof from them. This is what Claude Lévi-Strauss has called being *engagé* and *dégagé* at the same time. It is the dialectics of reducing people to objects while trying to achieve understanding of them and of converting ourselves into instruments while struggling to maintain our identities. The yield of the agonizing process of ethnography is always incomplete; we skim off the top and come away, if we have done our jobs properly, with a sense of loss and unfulfillment.

The Functionalists

Anthropology has produced some surprisingly good works of description and analysis, despite the contradictions inherent in its methods. The very best work has been done under the auspices of those who are generally identified as structural-functionalists, or just plain functionalists, although it would be an error to consider this a distinctive school. The defining characteristic of functionalism is here taken as the premise that societies are structured—which comes close to being a tautology—and that their component institutions and regularized activities are adjusted to each other in such a way that they maintain the system in its entirety. It assumes a whole structure that is more than the mere sum of its components. Moreover, the tendency of the structure to maintain itself in a rough approximation of equilibrium is effected by the shaping of the components in such a way that they function toward that end. Structures can be described in terms of the interrelated aggregate of groupings and offices, or roles, into which a populace is ordered and assigned, and the activities appropriate to these groups and offices may be seen as the life process, the functioning, of that structure. The task of the social anthropologist, then, is to analyze the rationality and internal coherence of the structure both through a consideration of the logical fit of the parts to each other and by a study of the means by which social action activates the elements of the structure and brings them into a working relationship with each other. There are as many variations on this general theme as there are structural-functionalists, but this is the core of the enterprise.

The term "structural-functionalism" in sociology has become almost synonymous with the theories of Talcott Parsons, whose great contribution to the discipline was the synthesis of the works of a number of turn-of-the-century behavioral scientists into what he called a "voluntaristic theory of social action" (Parsons 1937). Parsons saw in these men, especially in the German theorist Max Weber and the French sociologist Emile Durkheim, the overthrow of the nineteenth-century rationalistic and utilitarian tradition in social thought and a conversion toward a theory that related means and ends through an analysis of the psychological, social, and cultural elements influencing choice and that further related the ends themselves to each other to form a coherent institutional system. The basic unit of study, the empirical data upon which theory is built and to the understanding and illumination of which theory must return, is seen by Parsons to be "social action." This Weberian concept, an old and common-sense notion according to Parsons, refers to discrete units of ordinary social life, to any activity that limits or determines the activity of another person. The theory, which is thus built upon the data of social behavior, attempts to see this behavior within a larger context, in terms of and as part of an over-all system of social action. The scheme combined Durkheim's organicism and concern with the problem of order with Weber's methods and systematic idealism. *The Structure of Social Action* (1937) and, later, *The Social System* (1951) were tours de force that served to focus sociological attention on its roots and to crystallize some of the main elements in contemporary sociology.

Parsons was hardly the only interpreter of Durkheim, Weber, Pareto, and Marshall, but he deserves mention in an anthropological context because his impact upon the profession has been greater than that of any contemporary sociologist. Parsons' influence has also been of an immediate and personal nature because of his past leadership of the Department of Social Relations at Harvard, in whose framework many prominent American anthropologists were trained, and this influence has extended to Britain. Despite Parsons' significance, the main outlines of his approach are far from unique. Kingsley Davis has cautioned that all the social sciences are concerned with structure (or system, organization) and with function, and that it is hardly the exclusive possession of those who use Parsons' special language and syntax (Davis 1959). This is true, but only serves to corroborate Parsons' main premise stated in *The Structure of Social Action:* that structural-functionalism is synonymous with contemporary social theory.

Within anthropology, the "school" of structural-functionalism has tended to be confounded with the followers of A. R. Radcliffe-Brown and, to a lesser extent, Bronislaw Malinowski. Their influence was especially great in England but extended well beyond the confines of English scholarship. Radcliffe-Brown was indeed British and his last teaching post was at Oxford, but he also taught in Australia, Egypt, and South Africa, and left his mark upon the University of São Paulo. His years as a visitor here at the University of Chicago made an indelible imprint upon its Department of Anthropology, giving the impression that, like New Zealand and many other colonial outposts, it is more British than London. Malinowski, an expatriate Pole, found his most enthusiastic audiences at the University of London, migrating to the United States too soon before his death to have had wide personal influence here. His books, however, have probably had a greater audience in this country than have those of Radcliffe-Brown. Far superior in ethnographic richness and sensitivity, they have been used for years as exemplars of the anthropological method. Never a great theoretician, Malinowski was a meticulous empiricist. In this sense, he was exactly complemented by Radcliffe-Brown, who was not greatly gifted in ethnography but whose theories were positivistic in the strictest sense and whose methods called for the kind of factual richness that Malinowski's work exemplified.

Radcliffe-Brown is often credited with the introduction of Durkheim's functionalism into anthropology. It is quite correct to say that he did much to make Durkheim respectable, for the latter's most important contribution to the sociology of primitive peoples, *The Elementary Forms of the Religious Life,* received a poor reception in the field, undoubtedly to the detriment of Durkheim's total impact upon anthropological thought. But it would be misleading to deduce from this that Radcliffe-Brown can be understood simply as a Durkheimian. He showed none of Durkheim's deep interest in systems of thought, nor were his generalizations of such wide scope. By the time of his death, Durkheim had become a *philosophe,* but Radcliffe-Brown always remained within the tradition of English empiricism. We can see a reflection of Durkheim's *Rules of the Sociological Method* in Radcliffe-Brown's essays on function and social structure (1952), but we can find a far more striking parallel in an 1827 work of Dugald Stewart:

To understand the structure of an animal body, it is necessary not only to examine the *conformation* of the parts but to consider their *functions,* or in other words, to consider their *ends* and *uses;* nor indeed does the most accurate knowledge of the former, till perfected by the discovery of the latter, afford satisfaction to an inquisitive and scientific mind. Every anatomist accordingly, whatever his metaphysical creed may be, proceeds in his researches upon the maxim that no organ exists without its appropriate destination; and although he may often fail in his attempts to ascertain what this destination is, he never carries his skepticism so far as for a moment to doubt of the general principle. [in Schneider, L. 1967, p. 149]

The Scottish moralists and the later students of comparative jurisprudence were, of course, fully cognizant of parallel developments in England and on the Continent, for positive science had manifold roots. Diverse even in its seventeenth- and eighteenth-century origins, the main ideas of "structural-functionalism" had spread throughout Europe by the late nineteenth century and were completely disseminated and solidly grounded in the Western intellectual tradition before the professionalization of the social sciences.

Paradoxically, then, it is both fitting and a distortion that the anthropological variant of the functional tradition in sociology is so often referred to as "British social anthropology." It is distorted in that no nation has a monopoly on the simple idea that society is an organization, has a structure, and that its institutions and activities are compatible with, and even contributive to, the working of that organization. What is distinctive about the British branch of the tradition, however, is its empirical rigor, a caution that approaches timidity, the low level of its abstractions, and a restrictiveness in its scope that is congruent with these methodological orientations. Substantively, an obsession with the problem of order stands out as an abiding characteristic of the English group.

These remarks are not intended to be as critical as they may appear, for the quantity, reliability, and detail of data in any science are a key to its qualitative standards; British anthropology is superb on all these counts. It has carved out a small domain and has excelled in it, but these are also the preconditions of the involution to which I referred earlier. The differences between British social anthropology and American cultural anthropology are otherwise not of great magnitude, though they may overwhelm the specialists who are immersed within them. The British penchant for the word "social" and the centrality of the concept of "culture" in American anthropology are not significant differentiators when one considers how diversely each is used in actual analyses. Even more important is the fact that in most monographs the words could be totally omitted without changing the perspective or results. Culture and social structure are often used in exactly the same way and to refer to the same things by their respective champions. This has been recognized by Fortes (1953, p. 21), who said that social anthropologists study what others call "culture," but from the perspective of social structure. What are called "structural principles" by one may be called "values" by the other, just as one may prefer the word "agnatic" to another's "patrilineal." In most cases the choice of words makes little difference to the analysis, but they are significant because differential loyalty to these fuzzily defined and even more fuzzily used words has been thought to have sectarian, and even national, importance. The sects are prior to the words, however, and the words are symbolic of these differences and not their substance.

Many social scientists draw a strict distinction between society and culture, reserving culture to describe fairly fixed systems of norms and standards, values and expressions, which mediate social activity but are to be differentiated from it. Social structure, from this viewpoint, consists of the organization of ongoing social activity, related to culture but not homologous with it. There are of course, endless variations on this theme. Most anthropologists, however, have been singularly sloppy in their use of the terms "culture" and "social structure." It is quite common for American anthropologists to use culture to refer to behavior itself in addition to norms, and for British social anthropologists to refer indifferently to both standards and actions as components of social systems. What each has done has been to practice an imperialism of words, placing the total subject matter of their study under one rubric or another, and thereby destroying the differentiating and analytic functions of terminology. Not all are guilty of this by any means, but usages are sufficiently variable to make the distinction of "cultural" anthropology from "social" anthropology meaningless. What perhaps had some relevance four decades ago, when it was argued that the study of ongoing social life should take primacy over cultural history, is of little significance today. Indeed, the proponents of the sociological view have won the day so thoroughly in both Britain and the United States that one could well present a strong case for the need to engage once again in cultural historical studies.

The Academies

American social anthropology has shown greater eclecticism and wider breadth of subject matter than is prevalent in Britain, but the essential approaches are almost identical. The breadth and diversity of American anthropology, as opposed to British and Continental anthropology, are not so much a matter of intellectual influences as a function of the prevailing rules of tenure and modes of academic organization. A "hundred flowers" have bloomed in the United States, because hundreds of professorships have bloomed. Our heterogeneity is in part a function of sheer size; as our numbers grew, a natural process of differentiation took place much according to the mechanics of evolution. Anthropologists now fill almost every niche in intellectual life, spilling over into allied disciplines and even into the writing of children's books and science fiction. The range of interests of American anthropology is so vast that the discipline has almost lost itself. By becoming everything, it threatens to become nothing—this is not a paradox but a true contradiction.

Even more important for an understanding of anthropological eclecticism in this country is the fact that there is no such thing as *The* Professor who holds *The* Chair, as is true in England and Europe. Indeed, many of our academic departments are modeled along European lines only turned upside down—pyramids resting on their apexes. As departments of anthropology become stabilized in composition and size—which they are at last doing—normal advancement brings a greater proportion of their personnel up to tenure rank and to full professorship. Departmental chairmanships bring no distinction and are generally considered to be bureaucratic nightmares that must be rotated every few years to new victims. There are no dominant figures in such a system, no respected arbiters or final authorities on standards. Each person acts to protect his niche, producing a tendency for departments to diversify rather than reduplicate their talents. The expert on Bongo-Bongo scatological reference terminology becomes a prize because he contributes to academic ecumenism and does not step on anybody else's professional toes. The employment of such an arcane talent raises no problems because his fate is really to teach two sections of introductory anthropology and a graduate seminar on "whatever in hell is on his mind." Not even the pioneering anthropologist Franz Boas could become a Boas in today's ambience. This may be all to the good.

The structure of grant-giving is homologous with academic organization and has the same proliferating effect. Research grants are made to institutions for fiscal purposes, but for all practical intents they are individual endowments. A scholar's nominal academic superiors generally have no more to do with his projects than to certify that the institution will release the applicant from other duties so that he may pursue his program and to vouch that certain facilities will be made available to him. On the Continent, research funds are usually given to, or channeled through, heads of institutes, professorial notables, or the research establishments themselves; they may trickle down to underlings but only at the price of scholarly compliance. In contrast, individual American scholars of all ranks are generally encouraged by their institutions to seek research funds. First, they add luster to the recipient and thus to his university and, second, they may serve to buy equipment and personnel that can ultimately be used to strengthen the department. Many academic departments find such "soft money" to be an essential part of their budgets, and administrators have been known to consider the ratio between governmental grants and the university's fixed commitment to the department as a criterion of scholarly strength. This may seem rather crass to the outsider, but the precarious situation of university financing makes it necessary. Whatever the justification, each scholar becomes an independent entrepreneur. To the extent that he depends upon outside sources of financing, he is thereby separated from dependence upon his university and the community of his colleagues. In extreme cases, the scholar is almost completely attached to his independently funded project, and his identification with the institution is merely nominal and formal.

Research grants are awarded by governmental and foundation agencies, usually in consultation with panels of scholars who serve for limited terms and who are not employees of the agency. There are several criteria upon which applications are judged, but the one that is most important for the moment is that the research be oriented to a problem having theoretical significance and that it be fairly original in design and conception. This encourages a high degree of innovativeness on the part of the recipient of the grant, often to the extent of producing research that is forced and artificial. It is not enough to say that the applicant will pursue the promising research of Dr. X, for he must add that he is going to do it somewhat differently, or he is going to correct one of X's conclusions, or he will use X as a starting point for a theoretical venture. This too encourages diversity, however slight each differentiating step may be. The premium placed upon originality and innovation is one of the healthier aspects of American scholarship, although one suspects that it stems from the progressive nursery school. Perhaps this is the payoff of liberal education, just as nasty and disorderly kindergartens are its price.

American anthropology is large in membership, eclectic in content, and amorphous in orientation. These traits, which derive from organizational factors rather than from an American zeitgeist, are at once the sources of the strength and weakness of the discipline in this country. In contrast, European scholarship is personalistic and restrained, rigid and closed. The academic community is small because higher education is still largely an elite process. Indicative of the clublike nature of the discipline abroad, practically all members of the Commonwealth Association of Social Anthropologists know one another personally. Even more surprising to an American is the fact that every English anthropologist knows of every new Ph.D. in his country and probably even knows him personally. In the United States, it is quite possible for a student to complete his doctorate and to be only marginally acquainted with some members of his department; there are, indeed, some cases in which the new Ph.D. is unknown to several department members, usually by mutual intent. A face-to-face scholarly community inevitably imposes constraints on the originality and intellectual mobility of its members. Individuals may engage in microheterodoxy, but they must be careful to conform to the standards that define membership and guarantee professional status. This is not entirely a negative process. Students in such a setting reflect immediately upon their mentors, and training and supervision are generally far more rigorous in English universities than in the United States. British seminars develop the critical faculty to a morbid degree, for mutual criticism, while parading as the forge of discipline, is also a well-known means for maintaining orthodoxy. Its products think well, but they don't think much.

That one's writings, lectures, and verbally expressed opinions become immediately and totally known throughout a professional community is a source of caution to any scholar. His performance of his role is highly visible and subject to censure, his speculatory excursions prone to dampening by the critical activity of his peers. Anthropologists will recognize this as a characteristic of any small and undifferentiated society. Another governing principle within European scholarship is that of rigidity of hierarchy. American men of letters are legion and there are more "chiefs than Indians," but university systems that have only one professorship per subject and deliberately underpay all ranks produce an entirely different structure. Under these circumstances, it is possible for a single man to determine the limits of debate within a department and for a small group of scholars to accomplish a similar circumscription within an entire nation. This does not require a gerontocracy in which tyrannical old professors terrorize their juniors and coerce their thoughts under a threat of expulsion. The "despots" are, in fact, usually more tolerant and permissive of originality than are the younger scholars. Rather, conformity is exercised within broad limits and defined not so much by the center of orthodoxy as by its limits, the point beyond which one becomes *outré* and "unprofessional." The very uncertainty of these limits provides the push toward the center.

The elders in the British academic system are also in a vital position to enforce disciplinary regularity. Desirable posts are almost intentionally kept scarce, and each year many anthropologists are forced to accept teaching positions in Commonwealth countries outside the United Kingdom or to migrate to American universities—the so-called brain drain is not so much a result of pirating as of deportation. Within the Commonwealth, salaries are generally comparable, and the attractiveness of a position depends very largely upon the seniority and luster of the university itself. One receives a "call" to join this or that venerable institution, an archaism that used to be employed in this country but now elicits little more than a cynical grin among younger American scholars. Competition appears open to all, and even vacancies in distinguished professorships are publicly advertised. The reality, of course, is that major appointments involve wonderful scheming and Byzantine political maneuvering, and much scholarly activity and deportment is anticipatory of an eventual "call." Critical to all choices are the evaluations of a candidate by his peers, and favorable reviews are not given to those who stand too far apart either theoretically or in personal demeanor. One can be damned by faint praise, by omission, or by allusion. Persons of indisputable excellence are chosen, but they are always close to the center of their discipline.

It should be emphasized that the restrictiveness of British anthropology does not mean that its practitioners are servile and unoriginal. Both the *amour propre* of the scholar and professional competition require that each differentiate his intellectual products from those of his peers, and debate is often caustic and splenetic. In a small scholarly domain, each person is ranked and compared with everybody else, and argument over issues raises and lowers reputations in a direct and immediate way. There are elements of the potlatch in this kind of relative-ranking validation, and to the outsider the issues appear just as ephemeral. Americans frequently comment upon the homogeneity of the British "school," much to the latter's honest puzzlement. This is not simply a case of everything looking the same to the outsider—as all Orientals are said to look alike by Europeans—for the area of agreement in British anthropology is indeed much greater than it is in America, despite the fact that disagreements are often freely and strongly expressed. One is reminded of the narrowness and ferocity of differences in ideologically defined groups with a cellular organization. Just as one suspects that in the latter small doctrinary disputes are the facade of more basic struggles, so also can one see that careers are at stake in many of the disputes between scholars. This should not be seen to discount the significance of such debate for the progress of the discipline, however, because the general interest always enlists personal ones.

One by-product that is not generally understood to emerge from the minor dialectics of the life of the mind is their function in developing competence. The kinds of argument that hone the mind and inculcate skills are those that revolve around fine detail and meticulous interpretation. A truly educational debate requires that the contestants share a common ground of assumptions and method, but it also follows that major syntheses cannot result from minor oppositions. Disputation in British anthropology thus tends to be incisive, expert, empirically detailed, and finely stated. British scholars do not argue in this way because they are "social anthropologists"—they become social anthropologists because they argue in this way.

Research Scenes

Continuing our theme that the differences between British and American anthropology are primarily ones of style and are attributable to their respective numbers and activities rather than to nebulous intellectual influences, we move from the places where scholars make their living to the kinds of work they do. Both American and British anthropology were direct products of their respective ethnographic experiences during the late nineteenth and early twentieth centuries. Each group worked among primitives in areas within their governments' spheres of influence for reasons of convenience and because financial support was more readily available for work that would seem to have some political or social utility. This brought the Americans to study the North American Indian and the British to work in Africa, Australia, and the Pacific. American Indian societies had long since lost their autonomy when the first professional anthropologists studied them. Those in the East had either been exterminated or driven westward, and the remaining Indians of the Plains, the Southwest, and the Far West had been cut off from their subsistence and herded into the semi-imprisonment of the reservation. The observation of traditional social activity that is so central to structural-functional analysis was hardly possible under the prevalent conditions of the reservation, for this activity now consisted merely of desultory farming, wage labor, or just sitting. The disaster of the American Indian had been complete and final, and all that was left of most native social and political systems were the cultural residues of the mind. The American students turned to this surviving source, wringing out the last bit of memory from the oldest Indians they could find before even this information was completely lost. The few extant social systems available for analysis were, however, documented with excellent attention to the details of social behavior and the organizational requirements of a society. Kroeber's *Zuni Kin and Clan* (1917) was superior in this regard to most ethnographies of the time.

The circumstances of fieldwork commonly produced monographs that resembled laundry lists of culture elements. The customary behavior remembered by informants was combined with that still observable and was described in an order that obeyed the classificatory tidiness of the writer rather than the mode of operation of the society. When attention finally turned to the actual conditions of reservation life, it was cast against the background of the aboriginal culture, or at least what was believed to be its pristine state. How indeed does one reconcile the proud warrior of the Plains with the drunken Indian lying in a pool of his own vomit in a backstreet gutter in Billings, Montana? This, after all, was the most meaningful question that one could ask of the American Indian material, and it resulted in the spate of literature on "acculturation" that began in the 1930s. While most British scholars were asking how societies stay together the Americans were asking how they change, although both are really the same question. Historicism figured heavily in the reaction to the theories of cultural evolution once prevalent in both Britain and the United States, and the analysis of social change among the American Indians seemingly continued this tradition. In actuality, acculturation studies represented a radical departure from the older culture-historical studies of diffusion and were just as firm a rejection of "conjectural history" as was functionalism in Britain. We will return to this thought later.

American Indianist ethnography has become transformed in recent years into reservation sociology, or the analysis of Indian society as it is alleged to operate. One reason for this shift has been the growth of what is often called Pan-Indianism, which refers to the demonstrable fact that, as the particular cultures of Indian groups come to have increasingly less relevance to behavior and then finally largely disappear from memory, the reservation peoples become more and more alike. In part this results from an approximation toward American norms, but a distinctively American Indian pattern has also arisen that is best explainable by the similarity of social circumstance on the many reservations. The pattern is a mélange of dependency, discrimination, despair, and poverty—dependency and a sense of paradise lost being the definitive elements (cf. Eggan 1966, p. 8). A series of studies have focused upon the peyote religion, Indian alcoholism, employment, and residence, and have sought explanations in the realities of contemporary reservation life. The social system of a reservation, and not a culture, becomes the unit of study, and comparative controls are exercised by evaluating the results against other reservations or other people living under similarly deprived conditions.

This shift to a more functionalist approach was not merely a response to changes in American Indian society, for after World War II most American anthropologists had stopped working with North American Indians. By the late 1930s, Ruth Benedict had sent Columbia University's first group of students to Brazil, and Melville Herskovits' interest in the American Negro had brought him to Africa. Various parts of the Pacific were also being investigated by such scholars as Edward Gifford, Margaret Mead, W. Lloyd Warner, Ralph Linton, and Fred Eggan. The war's end brought a large number of well-traveled students into the graduate schools, and many of them went far afield to do their research. This process snowballed, and the American anthropologist is now almost as omnipresent as the Peace Corpsman. The extension of our interests into areas of the world where native peoples had not become completely engulfed resulted in studies of societies that still enjoyed a high degree of political autonomy and in which social institutions seemed to be still embodied in social interaction. Their social systems functioned, and a structural-functional mode of analysis was applied to them pragmatically and not because of the persuasiveness of elegant theories.

It has been noted that when British scholars work among American Indians, their results and mode of operation are much like those of American scholars. It has also been noted that when British scholars move into American university settings, their interests become just as diffuse and vagrant as those of Americans. The converse is also true, for when American scholars studied African or Oceanian societies, they generally expressed themselves in the language of their British colleagues, although rarely with that empirical rigor and methodological purity so characteristic of the latter and only obtainable in their seminars. The Americans who worked in the colonies also inherited the theoretical legacy of indirect rule, that remarkable system of government that, by perpetuating local political institutions, preserved for native societies a far greater amount of autonomy and stability than they ever enjoyed before the coming of the British. It was, alas, mistaken for the state of nature.

American and British social anthropology thus share a common orientation and operate within a theoretical framework that revolves around minor variations on the structural-functional theme. I have stated that past differences were primarily ones of style and detail. British anthropology is restrictive in scope in that it tends to the study of tightly delimited units within a strictly social frame of reference; American anthropology is diffuse and continually pushes at and across disciplinary boundaries. British anthropologists tend to be more cautious than their American colleagues in making generalizations; abstractions among the former generally are in the form of statements about the operation of a single system and tend toward a closure of analysis. American ethnography also tends to be empirically impoverished in comparison to the British products; this is only in part a result of the somewhat longer period of ethnographic fieldwork common among the latter.

Having exercised this American penchant for sweeping generalizations, I hasten to add that these strictures do not by any means apply to all British and American ethnologists: some of theirs are remarkably loose-jointed and some of ours are as tight as a tick. Moreover, these distinctions were more true for the period from 1920 to 1950 than they are today, as I have already argued. Similar field situations and the growth of the British anthropological community are today producing convergence. We might all just be reading each other's books more, of course, but I suspect that the rise of the English "red-brick" university is more decisive in producing this convergence than any intellectual cross-pollination. What is important is that the differences are not great, nor are they the reflection of radically divergent epistemological assumptions. Rather, they are much more easily understood with reference to where scholars are employed and what they work on.

American Anthropology

Three schools that have been regarded as distinctive of American anthropology are those of "acculturation," "cultural ecology," and "cultural evolution," the latter to be understood as referring to the "neo-evolutionism" of the 1940s and thereafter, and not to the older variety. Acculturation studies in the United States, it will be recalled, grew out of studies of reservation Indians and became enlarged into a general inquiry into the impact of Western civilization on native peoples. In England, a parallel inquiry into "cultural contact" was articulated by Malinowski and his students as a response to the requirements of colonial rule. Both the English and the American schools of culture change had their empirical roots in the late 1920s and moved into a theoretical formulation of their research in the mid-1930s. But British interest in the subject remained theoretically marginal, whereas it achieved a central position in the United States. Unlike the conjectural history of the evolutionists, who used surviving culture traits as a means of uncovering past stages of development, or the nominalistic and equally undocumented historicism of the diffusionists, acculturation studies relied heavily upon documentary and oral records of the recent past, and the present, for data. They were not, however, merely histories of peoples, for the aim from the beginning was to reveal the mechanisms or processes by which interchange of culture took place between societies in contact and to ascertain whether the order of change followed certain regularities. The defining feature of the acculturation situation was that the societies in question must "come into continuous firsthand contact," as stated by the original Social Science Research Council symposium on acculturation (Redfield, Linton, and Herskovits 1936, p. 149), or have "conjunctive relations" with each other, as a 1953 symposium chose to state the matter (SSRC 1954, p. 974). Acculturation was seen, then, to take place in an interaction setting and to concern, as well, the development of contemporary societies.

The entire thrust of acculturation studies was just as much toward documenting continuity as in seeing change, for one of their abiding preoccupations was the transformation of borrowed material to fit into a pre-existent set of meanings. It was in this spirit that F. E. Williams' study of the Vailala Madness (1923) drew attention to the reinterpretation of many elements of European culture and that Melville and Frances Herskovits attempted to show the tenacity of Africanisms among New World Negroes (cf. 1934, 1947). What was seen to emerge was a new kind of integration, a mélange of the aboriginal and the foreign, that provided an altered but internally coherent cultural system. The origins of cultural items are diverse, and it was in this sense, and this sense only, that Robert Lowie considered civilizations to be things of shreds and patches (Lowie 1920, p. 441). What intrigued the students of acculturation was that cultures were nonetheless "complex wholes" showing continuity between their component parts as well as with their pasts. They saw societies as absorbing vast amounts of the culture of other societies, reworking these borrowings to produce consistency with traditional patterns, but becoming transformed in the process into something different from either the impinging society or their own past.

The concern with reintegration and pattern consistency was nothing more than another variant of a structural approach. Indeed, something very close to the equilibrium model of society was employed in many of the studies. Granted that one does not learn much from the assumption of homeostasis when writing about an Indian reservation in the United States, Charles Wagley, Sol Tax, Ruth Bunzel, and other students of Middle America did find stability in societies of mixed Spanish and Indian roots. Acculturation studies often give the impression that the process of change had stopped at the time of the fieldwork, for one can find within the descriptions of the present situation tidy functional analyses of how the society operates. This is not surprising, for an acculturation study is little more than an ethnography supplemented by documentary research and some knowledge of the culture of the society at the time of contact. The chief assumption of the school and the scientific rationale of the research is that change is not random and chaotic but is determined and productive of new kinds of order. The analysis of the ethnography is an attempt to derive this new order. Acculturation fieldwork has little time dimension and is fundamentally synchronic, like most ethnography; the data derive their intelligibility from their relationship to other data obtained at the time of the study. The results are comparable to those of structural-functional analysis because the work is done under the same kinds of limitations. Both are descriptive, atemporal, and functional.

The student of acculturation, however, sees the present against the background of the past and attempts to trace the transition from one to the other through documents and some recourse to the memories of informants. The handling of the aboriginal state is illuminating. In most studies, an attempt is made to draw a "base line" from which to trace historic change. This base line is derived from chronicles of early explorers, from administrative documents dating from the contact period, from the recollections of aged informants, or from a mixture of all of these sources. It is generally assumed to represent a pristine state and, even more critical, it is further assumed implicitly that the society in question was in a condition of stability, if not isolation.

The resultant model of acculturation posits a state of equilibrium that is disturbed by outside contact. The contact induces a series of economic changes, disturbances in adjustment to the environment, the establishment of social linkages with the intruding group, and a flow of culture, all of which set in motion large-scale institutional changes. These changes are understood with reference to the structure of the aboriginal society and of contact relationships as well as with reference to the content of the cultural exchange. Acceptance and accommodation are conceived of as processes that strive toward a new equilibrium, usually reached at the time of the research, although this varies with locale and circumstance. If the historical materials are particularly rich, the contact period is often broken down into stages, each of which is described as a structure. The aboriginal social system and the organization of intermediate stages are commonly analyzed in what purports to be a functional mode, but the paucity of behavioral material generally allows little more than statements of institutional congruence and logical fit.

Another problem arises from the fact that we usually lack continuous historical records. The data may consist of slices of time, representing the occasional visits of a chronicler or ethnographer and giving a picture of quantum jumps in cultural change without sufficient information on what happened in the long intervening and unrecorded gaps between records. This kind of sporadic data, just as much as a richness of documentation, makes the breakdown into stages a tempting procedure, but we are often left with little information on how one stage became transformed into another. But it is not just the nature of the data that elicits this procedure. More important is the fact that thinking in structural terms is so thoroughly embedded in the social science tradition that even when we study change we tend to work with stable systems. The study of "process" and "dynamics" is thus not as processual and dynamic as we would like to believe, for it commonly approximates a seriation of structures through time. The chief fault of acculturation studies is not that they depart from functional analysis but that they have hewn too closely to it.

It was only after documentary historical investigations had become well advanced that anthropologists came to realize that the "steady state" of native societies—these allegedly "cold" societies lacking historical movement—was a product of paucity of data and their own preconceptions about primitive life. North American Indian societies had been in flux and turmoil long before our records began. The classic culture of the Plains Indians, for example, had a lifespan of perhaps a half-century. Population movements and political upheaval were equally characteristic of African society at the time of European exploration and before, and the same can be said for South and Middle America. Much of this dynamism was a function of the impact of native societies on one another—acculturation if you will—suggesting that unstable intersocietal relations are a constant condition of social life rather than an interruption of it. It would follow, then, that this is also true of social change.

Cultural evolutionism had its great revival in the United States after World War II. To be sure, Radcliffe-Brown had discussed evolution as progressive differentiation and increase in scope of social units, but this hardly got us beyond Herbert Spencer and

Emile Durkheim. They at least also tried to explain how it occurred and what forms it took, which are the real problems. The least functionalist of the new evolutionists was Leslie White, who was so preoccupied with demonstrating a single-minded theory that attributed ultimate social causality to control over energy that his theoretical writing seldom got down to the bedrock of detailed social analysis. Students, however, do not ordinarily enjoy the privileges of the master in dealing with the abstract, and their attempts to bring White's theories to bear upon bodies of interrelated data and to communicate the theories to an empirically oriented audience resulted in shifts in emphasis. Ethnographic analyses from the White school stressed the material factors, especially technology and environment, as underlying social structure and seen as determinative of it. This, of course, was neither new nor especially evolutionary, and the studies bore strong resemblances to those of the structural-functional persuasion, a point that is pursued in the discussion of cultural ecology.

Two of White's former students, Elman Service and Marshall Sahlins, have attempted to rescue evolutionism from becoming an interesting but not very useful abstraction by dividing it into two varieties, general evolution and specific evolution. (Sahlins and Service 1960). Both are concerned with the unfolding of new kinds of order from old, but general evolution deals with a universal taxonomy of cultures whereas specific evolution refers to genetically connected historical sequences. Specific evolution is known in less wordy circles as "history," although it is a history that deals with the emergence of forms rather than with events. This concept provides a niche for the theories of Julian H. Steward, who also influenced both men and who has referred to his own work as "multilinear evolutionism." Marvin Harris has aptly pointed out that Steward's contribution is not to evolutionism but to methodology (1968, pp. 655–656), for he is fundamentally in search of social laws that will state with some degree of surety that "given A and B, then C." His theory takes as an operational assumption the causal, and structural, importance of that nexus of social activity surrounding man's work within a certain environment. Hypotheses that state the connection between that nexus and corresponding institutional forms are derived from the study of specific cases. These hypotheses are then tested against all other cases in which the same production-environment situation—the cultural ecological equation—exists to ascertain whether like indeed begets like. A further control is found in the temporal or diachronic dimension, for if like does produce like, then this process will be found in the form of historical parallelisms. These parallel developments are called "lines," and since there are obviously as many lines as there are types of cultural ecological relationships, the scheme is "multilinear." That it is concerned with the orderly appearance of forms makes it a kind of evolutionism, but this is a small matter; designation as such has only served to obscure the significance of Steward's strategy.

Steward's best-known application of his method was an analysis of the institutional and developmental correlates of irrigation agriculture in the Old and New World focuses of early civilizations. He found that in each center the development went through phases, or stages, to which he attached the labels of hunting and gathering, incipient agriculture, formative, regional florescent, initial empire, dark ages, and cyclical conquest (1955, p. 189). Each stage was characterized by the independent recurrence of highly similar institutions in all the societies in his group, and he explained this recurrence as a result of structural congruence with common cultural ecological factors. The method was essentially structural and functional despite the time dimension, for, as in the acculturation studies, evidence was incomplete and often highly inferential on exactly how the society got from one stage to another.

That Steward is essentially oriented toward a structural kind of functionalism could be amply documented by his own explicit statements on the subject. His theory of "cultural ecology," however, serves to provide a substantive illustration of this commitment. Much has been made about this being simply a more sophisticated economic or environmental determinism, but the criticism goes entirely astray. As I have tried to demonstrate elsewhere (Murphy 1970), Steward's main concern is with the sociology of work—its tools, its organization, and its cycles—and in primitive societies, work cannot be understood without reference to the natural resources upon which human effort is exerted. Work, of course, is a preeminent form of social activity. Like other forms of social activity it must be analyzed in terms of its mesh with other social actions. It is also institutionalized, embedded with values, and integrated with the rest of the institutional system of the society. Cultural ecological analysis follows the same methods as all sociological (i.e., structural-functional) analysis, except that it takes work within a specific environment as a starting point. This may not be immediately evident to the reader of Steward's summary and programmatic statements on cultural ecology, but it is manifest in his empirical writings. His classic work on the Western Shoshone (1938) is less concerned with "culture" than with social activity. It describes the cyclical nature of the environment, the modalities of work and their relation to the fruition of resources, and the concrete activities and movements of people. From this he generates the structure of Shoshone society, but unlike the pure functionalist he not only tells *how* the society operates but why it *has to* operate in this manner. Basic to the procedure are the premises that societies are indeed organizations and that social activity is contributive to their persistence. The prime difference between his method and that of the British school is not only in the ecological emphasis but in the fact that he derives structures from certain key forms of activity, whereas the British tend to derive the activity from the structure. It is this neat little inversion that allows Steward to stress "cause" whereas the functionalists seek "maintenance." Their efforts are not contradictory, however, for at the root of most modern social theory are twin theorems: action generates structures and norms, and structures and norms stabilize action and convert it into expectation.

Sloppy, uneven, freewheeling, factually loose, and undisciplined although it may be relative to British practice, American anthropology is nonetheless structural in its model of society and culture and functional in its view of social process. It has its own distinctive style, but its intellectual roots are the same as those of British social anthropology. Both sides will undoubtedly be offended by this comparison, but we are all so immersed in the implicit assumptions of contemporary social theory that the differences within each camp seem highly significant and those that lie between them appear unbridgeable. There has, of course, been a continuing, and now burgeoning, underground of non-functionalist, even nonpositivistic, thought within the social sciences, but they have remained quite unitary in their principal assumptions and unspoken premises. We do not just fail to return to the basic questions—we have forgotten what they were.

2

First
Principles

Social anthropologists have been notoriously lax in self-examination, a failure that has had its good aspects as well as its bad. On the good side, we can say that such soul-searching is an introspective and moody business (making this an introspective and moody book) that can paralyze productive research. The investigator who continually asks himself "What am I looking at and how am I seeing it?" will very likely stop looking and seeing, experiencing a kind of reality alienation that is worth clinical classification. Or, if his approach is rigidly scientific, he may well decide that certitude and procedural correctness can only be attained by concentrating upon problems that are not worth investigating in the first place. He may even set standards of such rigor that a study of aggregates of individuals becomes impossible. Anthropologists have chosen instead to be blithe spirits who stifle their doubts, externalize their data, and keep their bags half-packed. When thought intrudes upon their work, they suppress the malady by taking a quick trip to Africa. Other scholars profess wonder at the field orientation of their anthropological colleagues and admiration for a research enthusiasm that persists into old age. Few query whether this is done at the expense of a consideration of what exactly we have been doing. This is the bad side of our empiricism.

Most theoretical and critical writings in anthropology have been aimed at its most abstract ideas. Our greatest battles have raged over synthetic schemes, such as evolutionism and equilibrium models, whereas the nature and reality of our data have been assumed. Epistemology is certainly alien to the anthropological world view, despite the fact that Emile Durkheim's most important contributions lay in that field. The work of Edmund Leach, Claude Lévi-Strauss, and the American analysts of cognitive systems have come close to epistemological concerns, although they are directed more toward problems of knowledge among primitive peoples than among anthropologists. The most complete, perhaps the only, systematic critique of the nature of anthropological data since Durkheim's *Rules* has been Marvin Harris's book *The Nature of Cultural Things* (1964), which was received by the profession as a curiosity. Its chief virtue was as a critical essay, but it foundered on its introduction of a methodology that was so laborious that if pursued it would instantly end research. But Harris's argument that there are great gaps between ideas and actions was ignored, making it clear that the discipline was not yet ready for so fundamental a challenge. Anthropology not only refrains from questioning its first premises, it also actively resists efforts to do so. In this, social scientists are again much like the objects of their study: they cling tenaciously to systems of meanings that allow them to function, and they are far more conservative in their elementary perceptions than in the elaborate ideas with which they play.

Things

Emile Durkheim, the founder of professional sociology, once wrote: "The first and most fundamental rule is: *Consider social facts as things.*" (Durkheim 1964, p. 14) This quotation is systematically overlooked by social science by virtue of its unquestioning acceptance as a cardinal and axiomatic truth. It is built into our very perception of society and human behavior, for it involves the kind of objectification and fixation of reality that underlies the contemporary study of behavior. The treatment of social facts as "things" has generally been considered to be a matter of provenience and function. Talcott Parsons states that "exteriority to and constraint of the actor" are the major implications of Durkheim's axiom, thus placing the emphasis on the autonomy of the sociological as opposed to the individual (Parsons 1951, p. 352). Social facts, according to this well-known view, are embodied within the individual but emanate from the domain of the social. Durkheim wrote, "Indeed, the most important characteristic of a 'thing' is the impossibility of its modification by a simple effort of the will" (Durkheim 1964, p. 28). And he continues, "Far from being a product of the will, they [social facts] determine it from without; they are like molds in which our actions are inevitably shaped" (ibid., p. 29). These "things" are both external and coercive. The facts of society are not the expressions of wills but rather the converse. This, of course, is a famous part of Durkheim's critique of utilitarian idealism, as well as a necessary step in his argument for a sociological level of analysis. But a great deal more than this is implied in his rules for the observation of social facts.

Durkheim knew that to think about anything is to transform it, and he thus attempted to maintain a scrupulously empiricist stance. "Since objects are perceived only through sense perception, we can conclude: Science, to be objective, ought to start, not with concepts formed independent to them, but with these same perceptions" (ibid., p. 34). This dictum is in strict accord with the best of David Hume, but it introduces some necessary steps between crude observation and the elicitation of a social fact, for social facts are not at all observable as such. Their tangibility is elusive and their nature is dual. As constraints, they are very real indeed, but as data they are not immediately immanent or discernible in ongoing social life. And it is their status as data that now concerns us.

Social anthropology is beset by a basic contradiction that

perhaps will never be surmounted. This contradiction arises from the fact that, although we search for order, social life is visibly chaotic. Its basic characteristic is flow and flux; its concrete ingredients are people, numbering into the millions and hundreds of millions; the substance of our observations is events, each of them unique, just as each human is unique. As strict empiricists, we must confront the truth that we work with *apparent* (i.e., sensate) disorder, nonreplicable people, and non-repetitive events. The sociologist working in urban and industrial society is well aware of this, and his model of society and of social action is probabilistic. Not being able to say anything for certain, he has devised mathematical means for stating tendency. It would be a mistake to think that primitive life enjoys greater regularity of action, despite the structural simplicity of such societies, and anybody who has ever done ethnographic fieldwork knows that his subjects appear to do quite mundane acts in a random fashion. What greets the investigator's senses, then, is not a social structure or even "social facts," but a mass of confusing impressions.

The confusion is worse for the alien observer than for the resident actor; the latter has been socialized to his milieu, and part of his socialization is the impress of a model of order. The actor is looking at the same chaos as the observer, but he thinks that he is seeing something else. The newly arrived anthropologist, on the other hand, sees randomness, but he assumes that this is a result of his ignorance of the system and the insufficiency of his observations. The signal-to-noise ratio is very low in social life—it can be argued that noise is stronger than signal—but the anthropologist has certain items in his intellectual equipment that are noise dampening. Among these tools is the notion of norm, which allows the social scientist to shift his focus from actual behavior to rule and expectation. Another of these behavior-muting devices is the concept of "role," which is roughly the same thing as norm but with specific reference to the actor. The latter term—"actor"—is a means of submerging people, or of seeing people only from the standpoint of norms. Moreover, actors are classifiable into types, and we call these types "statuses." On higher levels of analysis, we deal in loftier and more remote categories, such as "culture" and "social system." These are elements by which we construct our descriptions of societies, but, looked at in the negative way I have outlined, they are also techniques for suppressing observations and ridding ourselves of people and their petty activities. This is why most anthropologists find that their most productive analyses require an absence from the field of at least two years. It is not so much a matter of analyzing all that data as forgetting all those people and happenings. The most important procedure in ethnography is the elimination of the sensate data—we may dignify the process by calling it "selectivity," but that does not change anything at all. And contrary to the view held by almost all anthropologists, the essence of what they call "culture shock" may be that they are seeing behavior with a clarity, objectivity, and completeness that they were never able to bring to bear upon our own society and that passes after a few weeks of residence in the society under study.

It might be said at this point that my strictures on seeming randomness may be applied to any science. Marion Levy, a sociologist, defends the contradiction between reality and theory in the social sciences by asserting that this is common to all sciences:

It is also important that one realize that there is no genuine alternative in scientific procedure in this respect. The problems raised by the abstraction element inherent in scientific analysis no longer seem to disturb the workers in the more advanced sciences. [Levy 1952, p. 47]

Nature is certainly chaotic and noisy, yet science has devised ways of studying the natural order underlying the surface reality. The natural sciences have achieved their great success by falsifying nature through studying it under the tight controls of the experimental situation. One may indeed be studing nature in a test tube from which certain variables are excluded while others are introduced, but the investigator is certainly not studying *the state of nature*. He creates a bit of nature for study, from which he derives general principles; these results are then extrapolated back into the state of nature. Experimentation is not strange to the social sciences, of course, but thus far the results of these experiments have shed little light on societies in their natural settings. The social dimension is more complex than the organic and the inorganic, its variables being excessive for effective control. We have been able to make excellent predictions about what will happen in the experiment if it is done in a prescribed manner, but we have not had the same success as have the natural sciences in applying these findings to everyday life. Furthermore, we can study starfish better than people, and pond ecology better than society, because we are not starfish and we do not live in ponds. If starfish were able to convince us of the validity of their own perceptions and if pond biota had ideas about pond ecology, we might then find ourselves in a familiar dilemma. But this is the subject of another chapter.

Social anthropology has thus partially accomplished its own falsification of objective reality, through the distillation of people into actors and behavior into conduct. To the extent that we treat actors, conduct, and the like as entities, we depart from pure, observer-oriented empiricism. We have *thought* about what we have observed, which is sensible enough, but we err when we assume that we have exhausted the possibilities of thought about these sensory perceptions. Durkheim departs from his strict empiricism almost immediately after avowing it. One of his rules for observing social things—or, more accurately, for reducing the social to things—is given as follows: "When, then, the sociologist undertakes the investigation of some order of social facts, he must endeavor to consider them from an aspect that is independent of their individual manifestations" (1964, p. 45). In thus announcing the transcendent nature of social reality, Durkheim sought to escape the restlessness of events and appearances and to get to the level at which he thought events were understandable—as manifestations of collectively held ideas that exercise coercive power over individuals. That Durkheim dealt with classes of phenomena, rather than the phenomena themselves, is shown by another of his rules: "The subject matter of every sociological study should comprise a group of phenomena defined in advance by certain common external characteristics, and all phenomena so defined should be included in this group" (ibid., p. 35). He later makes clear what he has in mind by suggesting that the endless variation in family form may be properly broken down into types by choosing "the legal structure of the family, and more specifically, the right of succession" as principal criteria (ibid, p. 46). This was not so much an inspiration as a logical precursor of some twenty years of research on descent by British anthropologists. Durkheim founded a science which took social norms as its subject and typology as its method.

Durkheim, nonetheless, put his finger directly on the major problem of social science. This, again, is the fleeting nature of events and the paradox of preserving reality while formulating it so that it may be studied. He wrote; "Social life consists, then, of free currents perpetually in the process of transformation and incapable of being mentally fixed by the observer, and the scholar cannot approach the study of social reality from this angle" (ibid., p. 45). The emphasis in this statement is less on the locus of social reality, the determinants of action, and the problem of classification than on the dilemma of *how we are able to think* about society. The entire thrust of social anthropology has been to reduce events and people to things as one way out of an extreme nominalism that would defeat all attempts at understanding. In this, we have proceeded in the spirit of positivism and have sought *substances* that can be located, described, and measured in much the same way that the physicist handles matter and energy.

Sociological thought, to repeat the caution of Chapter 1, is not very different in its basic operations than folk sociology, despite somewhat better objectivity and far greater exactitude. Our quest for the endurable and substantial has produced units of data that are distinctive by external, positive attributes. We ask of the various "things" of social life such questions as "What *is* it?" and "What are its *essential* qualities?"

The very nature of this intellectual operation produces one-dimensional categories, despite frequent caution that every social institution and every social fact is multifaceted. We objectify, we reify, in order to think about social life in terms of the ordinary categories and processes of thought, but we do this also so that we can handle and manipulate our facts. Thinking about facts requires that they be clearly labeled, designated, and differentiated from each other, and we do this by characterizing them by what is to us a salient feature as well as a stable and recurrent feature. This introduces a problem of subjectivity that has long plagued anthropologists and historians, but that will have to await further discussion. For the present, it is important only to note that thinking of social facts as things not only limits them to a certain time but also catches only a partial aspect of empirical phenomena. The facts are very much like still photographs, and the human mind is like a machine that breaks continuity into bits and pieces. Beyond this, the objects of the enterprise must be fitted together, for one of the main purposes of the objectification process is to create units that can be juxtaposed to others of a like order. Anthropology has become so accustomed to and unquestioning of its nineteenth-century mechanical and/or organic models that it endows the social with properties that approach the spatial-physical. The division of labor in a society becomes transformed from a mass of quite varied activities into a neatly delimited type and, in turn, this is fitted into a residence type, based on certain statistical tendencies of choice of household location after marriage. These wheels grind against each other according to the principles of old-fashioned mechanics, with an occasional modernism such as "feedback'" thrown in.

Paradoxically, it is often those features furthest removed from behavioral reality that become most substantive, or "thingy." My example of the relation between the division of labor and postmarital residence, given previously, is probably most descriptive of the way American anthropologists analyze covariation, an approach that has been roundly criticized by Edmund Leach and others. British anthropologists are more prone, however, to adduce general structural principles from their material and then to analyze the influence of these principles on the empirical data. Thus, one may find a general principle of patrifiliation, as exemplified in patrisuccession, virilocality, and a series of other derivative institutions. It may often be suspected that the principle is employed to explain exactly and only those phenomena from which the principle was derived, but this is not our immediate concern. Rather, it is that the abstract achieves a determinate role and empirical being that is in inverse relationship to the immediacy of its behavioral exemplification. This is all good Durkheim, but any high level principle applicable to a wide range of empirical phenomena must be stated with absolute parsimony: that is, there must be an inverse relationship between the range of cases to which the principle is applicable, on the one hand, and the number of limiting provisos of the principle, on the other. This means, of course, that the principle must approach the unidimensionality and single-faceted quality to which reference has already been made. This dilemma is familiar to anybody who has indulged in typology: the type may be so specifically defined as to apply to only one case, or it may be so broadly defined that it applies to all, or almost all, cases. In either case it is operationally useless. It is not generally understood that the same commentary may be made on what passes for empirical description.

Durkheim said that we should *think* of social facts as things, although most of his successors have treated the facts as if this were indeed the nature of their existence. But he really only told us to do what people had been doing all along. The human brain and human language function to classify and reduce reality; we may only hope that the reality that we study has an order that corresponds to that encoded by the mind. This gets us perilously close to the classic debates between the realists and the nominalists, but it is not necessary to plunge our entire argument into metaphysics. The important lesson is that it is just as human to simplify as it is to err. Moreover, none of Durkheim's rules, or anyone else's for that matter, has taught us how to avoid accepting as an ultimate reality the popular categories that we are supposed to be studying or, conversely, imposing our own categories upon our subject matter.

Positivism has encouraged us to look upon social life as having a natural order, but this need not mean that it is physical and amenable to the same techniques of investigation as matter. Many things are happening together in social transactions, and the artifice that reduces the events to units must necessarily distort them. The distortion is almost invariably in a simplistic direction, and the aspect of reality that we sort out as distinctive and substantive may only be the one that is most evident to the senses or, more probably, the one that has been predetermined for us by convention, either our own or that of the subjects of our study. This is the essence of "common sense."

Idea and Act

Culture has been defined in as many different ways as there have been writers on the subject, for it is a mark of pride that one should coin a more "elegant" formulation of the concept than his predecessors. All definitions of culture, however, can be divided into two general types: the behavioral and the normative. The behavioral definition of culture states in various ways that culture is learned and shared behavior. Stated as a residual category, which it often is, culture then becomes behavior that is neither idiosyncratic nor wholly genetically inherited. But the test of idiosyncrasy versus collectivity is highly unsatisfactory for delineating the cultural from the noncultural, if one is to indeed view culture as *behavior*. First, all behavior is idiosyncratic to the extent that it consists of action sequences that are never exactly repeated down to the finest detail. If, however, we assume that the basic criterion is whether others in the same society regard the actor's behavior as idiosyncratic, we are saying that culture exists in the minds of the beholders and have thereby departed from a behavioral definition and taken the normative position.

The behavioral definition of culture—stressing learned and shared behavior—contains a redundancy. For behavior to be learned, there generally must be models for instruction and emulation, and this automatically implies that the behavior is shared. One may think of many instances in which this is not true, but for most of social life shared behavior is reducible to learned behavior and vice-versa. Given the natural endowments of the human species, it is impossible to catalogue learned behavior, and most writers approach the subject from the negative aspect of the nonlearned. Again, just as we find it difficult to sort out the unique from the shared, so also do we find it nearly impossible to distinguish the purely learned from behavior that is biologically inherited. This is an old problem, of course, that has been argued for decades in terms of heredity and environment without substantial enlightenment. Suffice it to say that nearly all of our hereditary predispositions are to varying degrees influenced by society, just as much of our learning is contingent upon, although not determined by, our biology.

The residue of human behavior that is purely instinctual in roots as well as in manifestation is inconsequential, a remark that is equally applicable to behavior that has no counterpart or parallel, however approximate, in the behavioral inventory of others. The behavioral view of culture, then, categorizes almost everything that people do as culture. Logically, any category that includes everything is therefore nothing; that is, it ceases to be a category. Moreover, it defeats any utility it may have for analysis, as the latter term denotes dissection, and one cannot use an all-inclusive class for purposes of differentiation. The behavioral concept of culture is thus of little use in studies that restrict their scope to human societies, and we find that it is currently most employed by scholars concerned with the evolution of man and culture.

The strongest adherents of the behavioral definition of culture are those physical anthropologists who study primates in the belief that the results of their work will cast light on human social evolution. Most have simply assumed that the "learned and shared" criteria are universally accepted as the definition of culture, and they proceed to treat it as a concrete entity rather than as an analytic rubric. Proceeding from this axiom, they show, for example, that a chimpanzee can learn to use a stick to obtain food that is out of his reach and that this technique is communicated to other residents of the cage, becoming a part of cage tradition, so to speak. This certainly is "culture" from their point of view, a conclusion that is triumphantly confirmed by classifying the stick as a tool. The chimp may even elevate himself to a parity with man as a "toolmaker" by joining two sticks (as chimps indeed have) to make a longer instrument. The higher primates obviously have a considerable capacity for learning and it follows that they will also learn from each other, and therefore come to share behavior that will be socially transmitted to the younger generations. It also follows, if one accepts the basic definitional premise, that the primates have culture and that the different capacities of man and the primates for culture are a purely quantitative matter. Therefore, one can study the origins of human culture and society by studying apes.

This position offers nothing new, for experimental psychology has long assumed that the learning experience of white rats is directly applicable to the human condition on the premise that humans and animals differ in degree and not in kind. In fact, behaviorists consider their field to be the study of the behavior of organisms—not merely white rats or people. The justification for the extrapolation of rat learning to human learning rests, however, entirely on the rigidly controlled experimental procedures of the psychologist. He studies the mechanics of the conditioned response, relating his findings to humans only insofar as human and rat neurophysiology are the same. He understands that rats and humans in the free-ranging state are utterly different in the organization of their respective behavior and that they respond to grossly different orders of stimuli. A good experimental psychologist would never study a colony of wild rats to learn something about humans, although this is exactly what some ethnologists and physical anthropologists do with primates.

I do not wish to appear ungenerous to certain of my colleagues and hasten to add that primatological research, while not telling anthropology much about humans, has corrected some misconceptions that we have had about animals. Under the influence of the behavioral view of culture, anthropologists have tended to grossly understate the amount of learning of which nonhumans are capable, a perhaps forgivable anthropocentrism. Whether this error arose because anthropologists tend not to keep animals I will not venture to say, but anybody who has kept hound dogs knows that they can only be trained to hunt in a pack, preferably one led by a wise and experienced bitch. Hound dogs have all the necessary instincts for hunting, but this native endowment remains diffuse and ineffective until it is properly guided. The untrained dog will hunt avidly, for it has the proper olfactory equipment to scent game, but it will crisscross a spoor endlessly without picking up the track. Under the tutelage of an older dog, the pup soon learns how to follow a spoor and how to pick up the track again when it is lost. It also learns a number of collective hunting patterns, which are not identical from one pack to another. Do hound dogs have culture? If the answer is yes, then we have reduced the concept to the absurd, as any hound dog raiser knows.

An enormous range of animals, and not just primates, have learned and socially transmitted behavior, and only a nit-picker would speculate about what ratio of learned to instinctive behavior is necessary before we have "culture." It is much more productive to dismiss the behavioral definition of culture as being useless at best and highly misleading at its worst. If cultures are regarded as statistically significant recurrences of behavior not specifically attributable to biological inheritance, then we have coined an empty word that at once ignores the symbolic and moral component of human behavior and is oblivious to the behavioral requirements of systems of social action.

One of the most serious drawbacks of the behavioral definition of culture, and the one that motivated my introduction of this problem, is its failure to distinguish between behavior and expectations of behavior, between action and ideas about action. This has long been recognized by proponents of the behavioral view of culture, who have spoken of "real" and "ideal" culture as a way of circumventing the question. Real culture is generally seen as being in the nature of expected individual variation around the ideal, although a certain amount of this variation is classified as deviant or innovative. Despite such refinements in the direction of a normative definition of culture, the behavioral one is a purely statistical concept. If culture is behavior and therefore highly variable, yet sufficiently regular and expectable to be both learnable and transmissable, then when we speak of a culture element or trait, we must be speaking of a statistical norm, that is, an averaging of differences. Therefore, there can be no problem of congruity or incongruity between the real and the ideal, for the ideal is a construct from the real. Many anthropologists circumvent this logical impasse by treating culture as a hodge-podge of both behavior and expectations. This dodges one of the thorniest problems in social science: What do people really do, and how does this correspond to what they think they are doing and what they think they should be doing?

The normative definition of culture differentiates it from behavior, per se, stating generally that it consists of stylistic and ideational models for and of behavior, as well as a system for viewing and interpreting the world. This, essentially, is Durkheim's position, although cast within the phraseology of "social facts" and "collective consciousness." Durkheim quite specifically stated that social facts are external to the individual and his activities and are not statistical summations of what collectivities of individuals do. The notion of a collective consciousness did not necessarily imply an awareness of the component facts, and, in this respect, the elusive French word *conscience* may perhaps be also translatable as the English "conscience." The social elements underlying suicide, for example, are generally not understood by members of the society, although they meet Durkheim's criteria of externality and constraint. In such instances, he saw statistical procedures as necessary to *discover* the facts rather than to establish their authenticity as social facts. The classification of a phenomenon as a social fact does not depend upon its prevalence within the group, *but rather* the constraint exercised by a social fact commonly results in making it prevalent (ibid., p. 10). To paraphrase Durkheim, generality proceeds from constraint and not vice versa. He recognized that practice and norm were often at variance, but he assumed that there was a strain toward consistency. Durkheim's *conscience collective* was a universe of morals and like any good middle-class Frenchman of his day, he believed that people, by and large, were governed by the moral order. This adumbration of act to idea fitted well with his principal aim, which was to demonstrate the autonomy of the social, and the primacy of the ideal over the material.

Durkheim's writings are shot through with unresolved problems raised by his failure to reconcile action and norm. For years it was fashionable to criticize Durkheim on the grounds that he paid no heed to the individual, that his theories were tantamount to a cult of society. "For Freud God is the father, for Durkheim God is society," wrote E. E. Evans-Pritchard in one of the grosser characterizations of Durkheim's well known theory of the social roots of religion (Evans-Pritchard 1965, p. 63). This critique ignored Durkheim's remarks on the "personal sacred," a concept that was brilliantly developed by Erving Goffman (1956) after being completely overlooked for a half-century. Or consider Leslie White's use of Durkheim to downgrade the relevance of psychology to the study of culture, despite the unmistakable psychology of Durkheim's works. Actually, Durkheim was primarily opposed to the instinct and utilitarian psychologies of his time, which were prebehavioristic and pre-Freudian. His major concern—in common with most other eminent social thinkers, such as Marx, Simmel, and Weber —was the relationship of man to society, and this is what his sometimes confused and always confusing thoughts on collective versus individual representations are all about. To be sure, it was Durkheim who said that "every time that a social phenomenon is *directly* explained by a psychological phenomenon, we may be sure that the explanation is false" (1964, p. 104, italics mine). But it was the very same Durkheim, only seven pages later in the same chapter of the same book, who wrote, "If collective life is not derived from individual life, the two are nevertheless closely related; if the latter cannot explain the former, it can at least facilitate its explanation. First, as we have shown, it is indisputable that social facts are produced by action on psychological factors" (ibid., p. 111).

Durkheim was not monolithic in his sociological determinism, but, given the battle that he had to fight, it was more urgent that he stress the sociological. If we depart from the text for the moment to consider the totality of Durkheim's work, it is evident that he saw some interplay between social and psychological factors. The total impact of his work, however, was to establish sociology, and social anthropology, as the study of the normative. Durkheim contrasted this social dimension to the biological individual, whom he saw as a small society (ibid., p. 111), as the two *entities* in his tidy, positivistic world. Durkheim's greatest influence upon us was in reducing everything to boundable, tangible substances and excluding the world of flux and movement that he said could not be conceptualized, let alone studied.

I would submit that Durkheim's assumption—that activity follows from norms because of the factor of external constraint —has become one of the great axioms of social anthropology and sociology. It is inherent in the behavioral view of culture and implicit in most normative definitions. I do not thereby imply that a simple one-to-one relationship has been posited between standard and action. Everybody understands, of course, that the norms are complex; they overlap each other; they are sometimes mutually contradictory; they pertain to differing segments of society; they do not at all elicit uniform response and acquiescence from all its members. The acceptance of congruity between norm and behavior does not necessarily entail the notion that man is a totally passive victim of tradition—despite the fact that many sociologists still think this to be true of primitives. Each behavioral situation is understood to be unique, and each standard of conduct therefore applies to a multitude of possible interactions. There can be no exact conformity to norm because this is antithetical to the very nature of norms. But, nonetheless, there is assumed to be a strain toward consistency, especially if one accepts the widespread position that norms are crystallizations of activity just as much as its governors.

Sociologists probably rely on this assumption more than anthropologists because of the complexity of their units of study. The anthropologist can check normative material against behavior in concrete situations, ideal configurations against the on-the-ground juxtaposition of actors. If he is sufficiently rigorous in his fieldwork, he will be able to develop a coherent description of the normative system, which will yield something that he can call the social structure. This can be cast against a statistical summary of the interaction system that is derived from minute behavioral observations. This is what Claude Lévi-Strauss tells us to do, but the difficulty of the task is attested to by the rarity of its performance, even in primitive ethnography. The sociologist, however, most often uses statistical analysis just to ascertain the norms; in effect, he derives the norms statistically, but rarely produces statistical descriptions of action systems. Little survey research is done on interaction itself, but rather on attitudes toward interaction and verbal reports on what the respondents perceive to have occurred. Sociologists are well aware that individual respondents may be highly unreliable, but they operate on the premise that error, deceit, and ignorance are randomized if there is a sufficiently large sample of responses. Thus, it is hoped that bias will not be systematic and unidirectional and that the norm will approximate the statistical mean. The very size of the sample necessary for normative reliability, however, makes it impossible to check these norms against conduct. Whereas we assume that the massiveness of survey research data will iron out the various deviant factors and tell us what is really happening in society—what people are thinking and, therefore, are presumably doing—this very massiveness negates the possibility of verifying the initial assumption. This can be stated as a rule: there is an inverse relationship between the empirical validity of any normative mechanical model and its testability against actual behavior. Phrased more concisely, the more survey data you gather, the less you know about what is going on.

Talcott Parsons' massive attempt at sociological synthesis addressed itself to the central problem of how the requirements of society become translated into the behavior of the individual. As a first step, he sorted out from the real world of interacting individuals, or the concrete system of social action, three domains that he found to have analytic and instructive significance. The first of these, the cultural system, includes the symbolic and ideational realm of value, concept, and style: this is a normative definition of culture as a system of meanings and morals. The second of Parsons' three levels of system is the social, which encompasses the theater and dramatis personae of interaction. Whereas culture is integrated by logical and aesthetic consistency, the social system is held together by mutual adjustment of the activities of people. The last of the trilogy is the personality system, which is defined by Parsons and his associates as "the organized system of the orientation and motivation of action of one individual actor" (Parsons and Shils 1951, p. 7).

All of this seems to make good sense, for it removes behavior from the concept of culture and returns it to its original meaning of tradition and custom. Parsons specifically states that the cultural system is not an *action* system but that those of society and personality indeed are. Moreover, this very difference of content and organization precludes the possibility of over-all, complete integration of the entire system of action.

In action terms this problem may be summed up as that of whether a completely pattern-consistent cultural system can be related to the exigencies both of personalities and of the social system in such a way that complete "conformity" with its standards may be adequately motivated among all the individual actors in the social system. Here it may be merely asserted without any attempt to demonstrate, that such a limiting case is incompatible with the fundamental functional imperatives both of personalities and of social systems. The integration of the total action system, partial and incomplete as it is, is a kind of "compromise" between the "strains to consistency" of its personality, social and cultural components respectively, in such a way that no one of them approaches perfect integration. [Parsons 1951, p. 16]

That the total system and its parts are never integrated should make the Parsonian theory a dynamic one, but the "strain to consistency" is even more powerful in his sociological practice than in his theoretical model. The reader learns that the system does have a remarkable tendency toward an equilibrium and that this is chiefly because the major determinants of interaction lie in the inactive and ideational cultural system. We learn little of how activity becomes enshrined in norms but much about how norms become embedded in activity.

One of the reasons for this normative determinism lies in the unsatisfactory way in which Parsons distinguishes his three systems from each other. He is very concise in what he means by the personality system, fairly consistent with general usage in his view of culture, but questionable in his handling of the social system. Parsons' basic definition of a "social system" is less than illuminating:

Reduced to the simplest possible terms, then, a social system consists in a plurality of individual actors interacting with each other in a situation which has at least a physical or environmental aspect, actors who are motivated in terms of a tendency to the "optimization of gratification" and whose relation to their situations, including each other, is defined and mediated in terms of a system of culturally structured and shared symbols. [Ibid., pp. 5–6]

This definition differs little from that of the entire "system of social action," of which the social system is purported to be but an analytic part. Parsons, however, reduces the definition to even more simple terms than those mentioned in writing that, "For most purposes *the conceptual unit of the social system is the role*" (Parsons and Shils 1951, p. 190, italics theirs). This comes as a great disappointment to those who feel that there are certain requirements in interaction, per se, that are not simply caused by the conjunction of traditional norms and certain kinds of personalities but may be attributed to such factors as space, proximity, numbers, hierarchy, opposition, visibility, distance, and others, which are only loosely connected to culture. But roles strike one immediately as cultural phenomena, for they are symbolically designated, they are external to the individual and coercive upon him (to use Durkheim's criteria), and they are traditional. Clyde Kluckhohn, one of the participants in the symposium that produced the book *Toward a General Theory of Action* (Parsons and Shils 1951), entered a demurrer from the introduction to the volume:

Many anthropologists (and certainly the undersigned) will agree today that there is an element in the social (i.e., interactive) process which is not culturally patterned, which is in some sense autonomous from culture. Nevertheless, one whose training, experiences and prejudices are anthropological tends to feel that the present statement does not give full weight to the extent to which roles are culturally defined, social structure is part of the cultural map, the social system is built upon girders supplied by explicit and implicit culture. [Ibid., p. 27]

Kluckhohn was quite right in pointing out the importance of the cultural factor in social roles, but he was wrong in thinking that Parsons disagreed with him. Although it is true that Parsons did not use "culture" in the all-inclusive sense favored by anthropologists of the early 1950s, it was indeed his guiding concept and the governing element of his social and personality systems.

The Parsonian defense of the distinctiveness of the social would be that it is not what it is that distinguishes the cultural from the social but how it is integrated. Roles are thus cultural only to the extent that they become value-embedded, or institutionalized. He gives ample illustration of this, but he sheds no light on roles that are un- or noninstitutionalized. In short, we are back to Kluckhohn's position: roles may not be culture, but most are quite cultural. The social system in Parsons' hands is little more than a residual category containing practically nothing. It is ironic that many anthropologists saw Parsons' division of the social and the cultural as a threat to the primacy of their bread-and-butter concept, culture. In actuality, this is a cultural theory, pure and simple. Culture is distinctive in the scheme in that it alone interpenetrates the two other levels of system; it institutionalizes the role system, and it becomes internalized within the personality. Culture is also the principal source of change in the social system. In theory, the social system is a level of action and the cultural system "just is." In empirical practice, the social system tends toward equilibrium, and the cultural system is subject to the vagaries of the meanings and rules of the ideational realm. It is difficult to state that action follows norms in Parsons' world view, for he allows for very little action there. Instead he allows for predispositions to action; it is a world in which everybody is holding his breath, waiting for something to happen.

In summary, although every social scientist knows full well that ideas about what is or should be done, on one hand, and what is actually done, on the other, are not necessarily congruent, in most theories and in actual practice it is generally assumed that they indeed tend toward homology. Since culture is no more than a statistical summation of action in the behavioral interpretation of culture, the question is completely bypassed. In normative theories, from Durkheim through Parsons, norms are taken to be largely determinative of action. Durkheim's simple distinction of the individual and the collective reduced the problem to the interaction of the person and the moral system—the individual never had a chance against that kind of odds—and he saw personal detachment from norms as the source of anomie. Aside from ritual congregations and the like, there was no intermediate system of interaction that could serve as the social conjunction of individual minds and interests with the moral order. There were actors and lines, but no "scene." Parsons appears to fill this gap, but his "social-system" level of analysis turns out to be a lower order abstraction of his cultural system. There is no system of happenings because nothing happens. And we will see that Parsons' psychological orientation is such that the personality system has as little autonomy as the social.

Schneider's Law

The anthropologist David M. Schneider once observed that the conclusion of all structural-functional analysis is: "If things were any different, they wouldn't be the way they are." It might be objected that this is more a tautology than a law, but it has the beauty of being applicable to each and every statement of a functional nature in social science. Besides, Schneider himself has accounted for this objection by an equally felicitous corollary that states: "All social laws are tautologies, but some tautologies are more instructive than others." Schneider's First Law is another of our axioms, although it is usually phrased in more obscure, and more impressive, terms.

Most structural-functionalists consider their material as being representative of a moment of time, a piece of the continuum of social life sliced with a microtome to such a thinness that no temporal dimension is left. They presumably understand this as a fiction that is convenient for analysis and nothing more. Time and history are recognized as ultimate realities, but they are held constant as a deliberate scientific artifice to enable us to see the system at work. The historical dimension is treated as the subject of another analysis or, providentially, historical data are lacking for the people under study and the issue is beside the point. I would add to these arguments that our epistemology and method allow us no other recourse than the atemporal study—structural-functionalism is not simply a method that by chance and preference has usually been applied to the study of the steady state, but is rather a steady-state framework to which we have adapted our materials.

The most important reason for the static view of structure is the premise that we look upon social life as a series of discrete, isolatable entities—Durkheim's "things." Social life then is not a process of becoming but something that *is*. The basic units into which we divide social life for purposes of analysis are of a fixed nature, and it follows that the relationships of these units with other similarly conceived units will share the same rigidity. This situation is aggravated by the fact that our units are almost always far better bounded and more permanent in our analyses than in empirical reality. Functional analysis can thus come perilously close to replicating the mechanical systems so often used as analogies. The component parts of a machine are certainly fixed, permanent, and material things. And the machine indeed moves, operates, and produces, just like a social system, with the one critical exception that machines do not transform themselves through their operations. On the other hand, computers can transform themselves in this manner but the significant elements of computers are information and impulses rather than gears and cogs.

Variation, the essential fuel of change, also suffers in anthropological works. The very requirements of orderly description expressed in language force us into typology and the leveling of differences. When the effort moves on from the descriptive to the comparative, the limitations of language require an even greater removal from reality, and an even greater fixity of concept. Philosophical realism would seem to grow apace with the alienation from social reality. For example, ethnography impels us to state that a society has lineages, whereas it may only have certain values for lineages and tendencies to approximate what we conceive to be a lineage organization. Nonetheless, analysis proceeds on the assumption that lineages do exist in the society and are fairly uniform within it, and that their existence in the ideal form can then be analyzed relative to ritual, and so forth. The concept is further hardened when this society is compared to other societies that have somewhat different lineage ideologies, but with which they are lumped because of a further reduction of typological criteria and a growing amorphousness of definition. Comparison is made for common institutional correlates and the results rationalized in functional language that often comes close to appearing as a description of a single system of social action. At the very best, the interrelating units in most functional analyses are norms; in comparative analysis, they are models built upon norms. This is an old and familiar problem in anthropology to which we usually doff our hats as we go on doing just this. In any event, the very process of abstraction and reification (which may after all be inescapable in the discipline) impels us from variation to homogeneity and from flux to stability.

The stable and one-dimensional universe is similarly promoted by the previously discussed assumption of the homology between norms and action. This canon, as we have seen, states implicitly that norms govern behavior within certain permissible limits of variation, some of which are quite loose and vague but others of which are stringent in their demand for conformity. As a corollary, the norms themselves are produced by behavior and are emergent from it. Therefore, any marked and unsanctioned behavioral departure from the norm signifies imminent change in the latter, as ideal readjusts itself to reality and once again asserts its constraint upon action.[1] Given the immediacy of juxtaposition of idea and act, their relationship is timeless and almost unitary. Action is assumed to be congruent with structure at any moment—allowing for occasional dysfunctions—and attention can then be turned to the contribution of this behavior to the maintenance of the structure. Or, to be more accurate, we should speak of the contribution to the stability of the system of certain items of behavior selected by the anthropologist.

Time stops in structural-functional analysis because the underlying ways in which we view our data are fixed and timeless. But it is also convenient to the realization of the major enterprise of social anthropology, which is to resolve the question we must ask of each society: "Why doesn't it fall apart?" This is the principal question of social analysis, whether asked

---

[1] This is the basically materialistic viewpoint of social anthropology. The idealistic point of view would see the norms influencing each other without reference to action systems. Curiously, this position has been taken—although most of them would deny it—by some cultural determinists who are prone to style themselves as materialists.

in this way, or as Georg Simmel's query, "How is society possible?", or in its more common positivistic formulation, "What are the roots of the social order?" The opposition of order-disorder is a common polarity in social theory, underlying the concerns of the social-contract philosophers as well as contemporary writers. Much has been written of the closely connected concept of structural equilibrium, or homeostasis, but I will defer discussion of this question. Instead, I would like to turn my attention to the disorder end of the continuum, a point that I will also examine in greater detail in a later chapter.

Marion Levy, a sociological follower of Parsons, considers four possibilities for the termination of a society (Levy 1952, pp. 137–41). These are: the biological extinction or dispersion of the members; apathy of the members; the war of all against all; the absorption of the society into another society. The first considers the possibility that everybody in a society may be killed off or starved out, which is not at all a completely hypothetical situation in view of the fate of many American Indian societies and the potential of modern warfare. The fourth is of the same order as the first in that both imply the destruction of the society by outside forces, whether from the social or natural environments. The second and third contingencies, however, do not necessarily imply such external disturbance but may be caused by structural factors, or the failure of structure. In this sense, they serve as logical opposites to the concept of equilibrium whereas the other two are only empirically connected to this idea. It is consistent with the structural-functional position, however, that in his discussion of the functional prerequisites of societies, Levy makes little use of "apathy" as a consequence of the absence of one or another of his prerequisites but has frequent recourse to the war of all against all. This is the Hobbesian state of nature, which has never released its hold on our imaginations and reappears throughout the history of social thought.

It is well known that real wars of all against all, in which every man's hand is against his brother's, never happen. In Levy, however, the war is against the Parsonian model of society and not against society itself:

> This condition [of war of all against all] is considered present if the members of an aggregate pursue their ends by means selected only on the basis of instrumental efficiency. . . . The choice of means solely on the basis of instrumental efficiency might conceivably result at times in cooperative combinations, but these combinations would, by definition, be subject to immediate dissolution if, for example, exploitation or annihilation of part or all of the combination became (or was thought to become) advantageous for any one member. [Ibid., p. 139]

This is a remarkable passage, for Levy describes as an anomaly an important aspect of the world in which all of us live. One need not deny the importance of morality and values to recognize that instrumental combinations and recombinations are the very stuff of which the social system is built and by which it derives its autonomy from the cultural system. Levy seems also to have innocently discovered game theory, used with considerable success in recent years in the sociological analysis of ordinary encounters as well as of conflict. Equilibrium in Parsonian structural-functionalism is not then a containment of forces but the outcome of a consensus of shared and internalized values. The opposite of Levy's peculiar view of the war of all against all, it would follow, is the legitimation of authority.

A concern with legitimacy as the basis of authority derives from Max Weber but has been strongly promoted in recent years by Parsons and some of his students. It is a valid and important area of inquiry for it poses the question of why people relinquish their autonomy—freedom, if you will—to authorities and give their assent to an unequal allocation of power that sees them on the short end of the distribution. It thus reverses the question of "How do the rulers do it" to read, "Why do the ruled let them?" It is one aspect of the problem of order, phrased for stratified societies. All such societies have a series of myths that legitimate governance, and this is an empirical truth. It does not follow, however, that the converse is true; that is, that the governance of all societies is dependent upon fictions of legitimation. Legitimacy, as C. Wright Mills has told us (Mills 1959, pp. 36–40), is in each case an empirical question, and power is wielded in different polities not only with different kinds of legitimation but to different degrees. Mills makes the case that modern mass society is characterized by a considerable unconcern with legitimacy on the part of the populace; it is as if the very remoteness and unembeddedness of the state gives it sufficient mystique. Perhaps the masses do not really ask "Why?" of the Leviathan but rather "Why not?" One can even argue that "instrumental efficiency," without recourse to force, may serve as legitimation. Despite the Fascist gobbledygook about the reincarnation of the Roman Imperium, believed by very few Italians, the ultimate justification for Mussolini surely was that he made the trains run on time.

Most functionalists have indeed tended to attribute the maintenance of state control to the presence of legitimizing values, and have done so to the corresponding neglect of other factors. This has become sufficiently axiomatic so as to result in a true circularity. Stated baldly, the functionalist view holds that simple, unadulterated power is primarily an abstraction of the academic mind, a residual category that serves as the extreme of a continuum, like the imaginary state of nature. It is essentially unstable and, therefore, cannot be said to characterize the governance of whole polities except in highly disequilibrated situations. What converts power into authority is legitimizing values; it follows, then, that any polity that has a lifespan better than that of the butterfly is legitimate. All states are legitimate and, therefore, the state rests on legitimacy, which is where we started.

The quest for legitimacy has been paramount in the British analyses of African political systems, a preoccupation that derives more from the idea of British sovereignty than it does from Weber. The data range from charter myths on the origin of kingship to the sacred attributes of rulers; rituals are seen in relation to the perpetuation of the realm, whether they appear to be directly supportive or manifestly subversive. The African kingship, and African stratification generally, have been analyzed in all their intricate interrelationship to the domains of kinship and religion—embedded in the society through the former and made transcendental through the latter. Overlordship is part of the African world view, essential to the regulation of nature and even to the fecundity of the women. The analyses are elegant and persuasive. The data have been carefully collected. One does not doubt them for a moment, but one still can wonder why and how the Hutu, almost as soon as the Belgian presence was removed, rose up and massacred their Tutsi masters. One can also wonder why the deposition of the Kabaka of the Baganda elicited so little reaction from his subjects or why the removal of Kwame Nkrumah was accepted apathetically by the populace that was supposedly so heavily under his sway?

In the final analysis, the question of legitimacy is not whether such values exist, but whether they are the critical factor in maintaining stability and authority. To reduce the issue to a simple level, we can show an intimate relationship between the Ten Commandments and the requirements of the social order. Does this mean that if there were no Ten Commandments that people would covet their neighbors' wives (any more than they already do)? Of course not: the only thing they would probably do if the injunctions were removed would be to worship idols, but that gets us into another story. For the present, the point is that the treatment of legitimacy in functional analysis is once again an instance of the assumed homology between idea and act and a further example of normative determinism. Myths and values of legitimacy are most certainly linked to the social order, but how strongly and in what way is an open question. Of greater importance, we may also ask whether legitimation maintains the order or simply derives from it. To cap this heretical train of thought, we may finally ask whether the ultimate targets of myths of legitimacy—the true believers in Divine Right, God-Kings, and ritually produced rain—are the benighted or the anointed. John Calvin's Geneva and the idea of predestination certainly suggest the latter.

Underlying the question of legitimation is the entire problem of institutionalization and its relation to structural stability. This, as we have seen, is a cardinal principle in Parsonian sociology, but it derives directly from the writings of Weber and Durkheim. The idea is really quite simple. The maintenance of a structure depends upon the organization of activities in such a way that they complement each other and are oriented toward the accomplishment of certain tasks necessary to sustain life. Beyond this, the patterned activities and their mutual relations are given stability through being endowed with value; they appear to the actor as good and proper. Values at once motivate action and ratify it. The establishment of a relevant framework of shared values is seen as a prerequisite to any interaction situation; it both legitimizes and gives meaning to the activity and thereby lends it coherence and structure. Moreover, since an important aspect of values is their generality, a single value can permeate several areas of endeavor and thus bind them to one another. This binding is one of the factors promoting equilibrium, for any impulse toward change in a part of an action system would not only disturb other activities but also the value system itself and all the emotional attachments to it.

Values are considered to be one of the factors, albeit an important one, in choice-making, and therefore an element in reasoning, as the term "evaluation" would imply. But values are also viewed as being cathected, that is, emotions are attached to them, and these emotions are commonly seen as reinforcing personal attachments that may have other emotional roots. In short, values serve to guarantee the tendency of the social system toward equilibrium by virtue of the fact that they also serve to promote social solidarity.

Anthropologists have long stopped worrying over whether man is a social animal or a political animal, and have been satisfied to note that he is an animal. This is not as neutral a position as would first seem, of course, and some of the recent interpretations of the antisocial nature of man are based on viewing him as just another animal. But most anthropologists still make the basic assumption that man is at least gregarious, if not social, and a good deal of social analysis centers on the aggregations within which sociability is expressed. Marvin Harris has correctly represented Durkheim's theories in his observation that the French sociologist equated structure with solidarity (Harris 1968, pp. 466–467). It is unfortunate, however, that he chooses to cite *The Division of Labor* in support of this view, for *The Elementary Forms of the Religious Life,* certainly Durkheim's most important book, treats this subject thoroughly. It is well known that Durkheim reached two conclusions in this work: "people who stay together, pray together" and the more commonplace "people who pray together, stay together." Religion stems from the collective life and collective sentiments, but it translates the latter into the world of tangible objects and thereby allows the members of a society to act toward them. The preeminent form of this action is, in turn, a collective one, leading to his dictum that for there to be religion there must be a cult. Religion at once objectifies the diffuse collective sentiments and brings the believers into communion with the sacred and, therefore, each other. It translates the collective life into social solidarity, and there is no doubt that to Durkheim and his followers, solidarity both as sentiment and as cooperative and mutually beneficial activity is the basis of structural stability. The stuff, then, of the social anthropologist is the positive and identifiable ties that bind people and not the shadowy areas that divide and isolate them. And yet how can there be one without the other?

The Psychologist Malgré Lui

Social solidarity has been viewed by Durkheim and his followers as central to the functioning of social systems. On one level, it may be looked upon as structural, insofar as it pertains to patterns of cooperation and interdependency and the organizational potential of a people for common effort. But, on another level, social solidarity deals with the tone of relationships and assumes the existence of emotional ties between people on the basis of their common membership in a group. It bespeaks attachments that are both instrumental and emotional, for it infers that members of a group will suppress their strivings for personal gratification in the interests of promoting harmony and communal endeavor. At the very least, the notion of social solidarity asserts that people will fight less among themselves than with outsiders and that they will present some semblance of a common front to those included in the "they," as opposed to the "we." Social solidarity depends upon a degree of immersal in a collectivity, a sense of oneness with that collectivity and an identification with it that is contrary to the radical individuation of the ego. A prerequisite to this, it would seem, is a process of socialization that will fully enculturate the individual with the values of his society, build into his personality controls that will allow him to defer and channel instinctual and acquired drives, and equip him with a motivational structure that will generate the kind of behavior that is conducive to the maintenance of the social system. The socialization process must, then, produce personalities that are social in the broader sense of being capable of the self-abnegation necessary to group life and given to an altruistic attachment to others. In a more specific sense, it must produce personalities that fit the requirements of particular societies. The entire corpus of structural-functional-ism depends upon the stamp of the society being irrevocably placed upon the individual and upon an isomorphism between the psychological needs of the individual and the functional needs of the society.

We have seen that Durkheim did not reject psychology but directed his critique against theories that sought to reduce social explanation to areas of psychology and biology that were not known at the time, and most of which are still not known. Such "reductionism" to the unknown is indeed a shallow gambit, similar to reference to God, cause or character, to paraphrase Simmel. Moreover, it also seeks to explain particular cultural facts by reference to general human proclivities. Thus, it may explain polygyny as a result of masculine sexual acquisitiveness, the heritage of the primate herd leader, but this explanation would have validity only if everybody was polygynous or at least wanted to be polygynous. Such ideas were rife during Durkheim's time, and they precluded social explanations as well as being very bad psychology and biology.

Most social scientists and psychologists could accept my limited and moderate interpretation of Durkheim's position, but some anthropologists have taken his strictures on psychological explanations to mean that the latter have no place at all in a social science. They argue that there is a psychic unity of mankind that allows us to take psychology as a given—this is a negative formulation of the older doctrine of psychic unity that went on to state that the laws and stages of progress of the intellect, the order of emergence of ideas, would therefore be everywhere the same. What is advanced is a view of human nature that is negative. With the disclaimer that it attributes uniformity to human psychology, it actually attributes nothing to it. It is not so much that men are vessels filled with much the same liquids as that they are empty. Behind the rejection of the relevance of psychological processes, there is a clear psychological assumption, that man is infinitely malleable and plastic, so thoroughly shaped by his social milieu that his influence, singly or in aggregates, can be discounted.

The culturologists and others of an "antireductionist" persuasion take the human psychological factor as a given and treat it as a constant, thus allowing them to study culture *sui generis*. But we never know what exactly is being held constant; we have a k to which no values can be assigned because it is not thought to be a critical factor. It is like multiplying all elements in an equation by 1. In actual practice, an insistence upon the absolute primacy and autonomy of the cultural leads to the "cookie cutter" theory of enculturation. This treats man as a *tabula rasa* who has been made into a "culture bearer" and who can be assumed to do pretty well what custom dictates. According to this view, people are passive. Culture makes people do things, and the most profitable pursuit is, therefore, to forget the people and investigate the impact of culture upon culture. In effect, the culturological position is an idealistic one that goes beyond its disavowal of psychological determinants and overlooks the entire arena of social action. This is the logical conclusion for a view that can claim that "culture causes culture."

Curiously, since they differ in so many other ways, the view held by the culturologists is not too far away from that held by Parsons. The former accomplishes the negation of human strivings and attempts at rationality by ignoring the problem, while the latter achieves the same result by an elaborate social psychology that appears to draw heavily from Freud. Parsons' "voluntaristic theory of action" can be viewed as a vast sponge that soaks up other theories and redistributes them in bits and pieces throughout its cellular structure. Parsons has done this to the thought of Durkheim, Weber, Pareto, Mannheim, and others and, on a smaller scale, to psychology. The earlier stages of his general theory relied heavily on both experimental behaviorism and Edward Tolman's research on purposive behavior. It was only in the 1950s that Parsons gave his greatest attention to the work of Sigmund Freud; his synthesis leaned on Freud's *Ego and the Id* because of that work's attempt to more fully account for the social. Significantly, however, Parsons maintained the centrality of the Oedipal episode in the human career.

For Freud, the Oedipal transition is of paramount importance in the socialization of the child, as it is the primary renunciation of libidinal gratification and, therefore, a major step toward the management of reality. The encysted world of the child is smashed, and he must reach out through more extensive social relations into the broader universe to which he must adjust. A principal part of this process is identification with the father and his introjection into the personality of the child. This is the essential element in Freud's mythical killing and cannibalization of the father. Part of the significance of the father is as a social figure, as the surrogate of the society. The incorporation of the father is then at the same time the incorporation of the rules and standards of the society, which the father, in his turn, had obtained in his own identification process and subsequent life experience. It is important to note that Freud saw the introjection process as formative not only of the superego but of the ego.[2] Norms become at once part of the conscience and a component of the individual's equipment for dealing with external reality. It is not necessary to the identification process that the young subscribe wholly to and believe completely in the dictates of the society, for this would endow the superego with a far greater coercive power than Freud envisioned. Rather, it is essential that the young be made aware that the norms are a very real part of the real world. To Freud, socialization was not just the imposition of the worldly mold—it was, additionally, the acquisition of worldly wisdom. The rules of society can also be

[2] Parsons (1964, pp. 22–23) interprets Freud to mean that there is a strict separation between the ego and the superego, the former distinguished by reality coping and the latter by internalization. In actuality, Freud acknowledges that the extent of this differentiation is variable (Freud 1922, pp. 69–70), and it is abundantly clear in his work that the ego, as well as the superego, functions to govern the id, and that cognition of rules is part of the equipment of the ego.

used as weapons by their supposed victims. In any event, internalization was always a sloppy, incomplete, and tension-fraught process to Freud, for it is in eternal contradiction to the asocial component of man's nature.

A curious thing happened to Freud in his transmutation into the general theory of action. The resultant product looks a bit like him, for we may read of the Oedipal complex, the anal phase, oral dependency, and so forth. The basic developmental paradigm is there, but it is only a skeleton, a ragbag of words that barely conceals Freud's demise. It would be tedious and far beyond the requirements that motivated this discussion to analyze in detail the transformation of Freudian theory in the series of papers that Parsons authored in the 1950s, and I will try only to provide a few critical examples. Parsons is, of course, absolutely entitled to depart from orthodox Freudian teaching, and one would not cavil for a moment at anybody's efforts to criticize Freud or revise him; some very eminent people have done just this. What troubles one in Parsons' work is that he seldom states that he is revising or criticizing, and the reader may accept the interpretation as conveying Freud's actual intent or, at the very least, being a translation of essentially Freudian concepts into a framework suitable for sociology. The latter was indeed Parsons' aim, for he writes in his first paper on the subject that his main task is to spell out the convergence that took place between the theories of Durkheim and Freud and to formulate the common ground between psychoanalysis and sociology (Parsons 1964, pp. 17–20).

The most important concept that Parsons borrowed from Freud is that of internalization, for it is central to his entire treatment of socialization and the relationship between the cultural and personality systems. He uses internalization far more extensively than did Freud, however, placing it as the central dynamic in the formation of the personality. Indeed, it would be quite accurate to say that this emphasis was effected at the cost of the process of repression, the cardinal element in

Freudian psychodynamics. Parsons' developmental theory proceeds on two theorems:

The first of these is that the primary structure of the human personality *as a system of action* is organized about the internalization of *systems* of social objects which originated as the role-units of the successive series of social systems in which the individual has come to be integrated in the course of his life history. His personality structure is thus in some sense a kind of "mirror-image" of the social structures he has experienced (though not of the momentary and not so much the presented as the perceived social system). [Parsons and Bales 1955, p. 54, italics theirs]

It is not just moral standards, the coercive elements of society embodied in paternal authority, but the entire culture that is incorporated (Parsons 1964, p. 23), a process that is more absorptive than reactive. His indebtedness to George Herbert Mead is properly acknowledged by Parsons, and this quote may be instructively compared to the following from Mead:

The individual experiences himself as such, not directly, but only indirectly, from the particular standpoints of other individual members of the same social group, or from the generalized standpoint of the social group as a whole to which he belongs. For he enters his own experience as a self or individual not directly or immediately, not by becoming a subject to himself, but only insofar as he first becomes an object to himself just as other individuals are objects to him in his experience; and he becomes an object to himself only by taking the attitudes of other individuals toward himself within a social environment or context of experience and behavior in which both he and they are involved. [Mead 1967, p. 138]

If anything, Parsons is more sweeping than Mead, for roles, values, style, and content are all absorbed in the internalization process and firmly embedded in the superego as well as in the ego system. It is the entire learning process written in the métier of personality theory.

Freud saw socialization as an interaction process between the individual and his milieu, but he saw the milieu clashing at every significant phase of development with the asocial proclivities of biological man. The central point of this theory is that the instincts, which are highly diffuse and generalized energies, are transformed, redistributed, and made specific through the dialectic of organism and society. The resultant personality is synthetic in this sense, for it differs from both the organism and its environment—and therein lies its humanity. Parsons, however, delibidinized Freud and thus shore the theory of one of its dynamics. His second theorem expresses this adequately:

The second theorem is that this structure of personality develops, not *primarily* by a process of the modification of "primary drives" or "instincts," but by a process of differentiation of a very simple internalized object-system. . . . into progressively more complex systems. A hypothesis which is secondary to this theorem, but none the less important, is that the principle of differentiation is that of binary fission. [Parsons and Bales 1955, p. 54, italics theirs]

Apologists will be quick to point out that Parsons and his associates qualified this statement with the word "primarily" and even stressed its usage. This should not, of course, mislead other scholars for a moment, as we are all experts at leaving the back door open.[3] His theory, as it actually emerges, would have been more aptly described if the qualifier were deleted completely.

This can be seen in the intellectual process by which Parsons translates the dark and raging thrusts of the id into the sociable, amiable, and warm qualities of "affect," a word with all the semantic connections of "affection," "affable," and even "affec-

[3] One could well compile a thesaurus of escape clauses, including a few used in this book. Among the more useful ones is, "Let us assume for heuristic purposes . . . ," which is generally the means by which Parsons posits the structural necessity of a consensus of shared and internalized values and Radcliffe-Brown assumes universal functionalism. Such operational procedures have a habit of losing their origins and becoming axioms.

tation." Using Freud's theory of symbolism as a point of departure, he hypothesizes that the symbolic guise within which the id impulses appear in the conscious mind should be understood as the emotional life of the ego, which is symbolic and socialized (Parsons 1964, p. 31). What Freud saw as illusion, then, is to Parsons the substance of the emotions. He continues, "This may be felt to be a relatively radical conclusion—namely that emotions, or affect on the normal human adult level [a key, but undefined phrase], should be regarded as a *symbolically generalized* system, that it is never 'id-impulse' as such" (ibid., p. 31, italics his). What then is the substance and nature of this id that Parsons retains in his scheme? We are not given a sure answer, but we are told instead that it is not as asocial as Freud would have it. Rather, it is object-cathected, but the relations cathected are those that stem from an earlier stage in the socialization process. Moreover, it is oriented, he states, "to the person's own organism as object"; that is, it is essentially narcissistic (ibid., p. 110). This leads to a fascinating conclusion in his brief discussion of narcissism.

Narcissism is an appropriate vantage point for examining the social nature of the psychic life because of its seeming contrariness to sociability. To Parsons, however, narcissism derives from social interaction, as does every aspect of personality. Narcissism is the turning in on the self of the relationship of the mother toward her child.

The internalization of the nurturant "caring" mother includes the internalization of the object of care. It is only on such an assumption that turning of "libido" on to the self becomes understandable. Then we must say that in so far as the orally dependent child has internalized the mother as nurturant, he has also internalized "secondarily" her concept of himself as object of nurturance. [Parsons and Bales 1955, p. 74]

This would seem to concur exactly with Freud's own views as expressed in his contribution to the theory of sexuality:

It is not without good reason that the suckling of the child at the mother's breast has become a model for every love relation. Object-finding is really a re-finding. [Freud 1938, p. 614]

This passage, however, is footnoted as follows:

Psychoanalysis teaches that there are two paths of object-finding: the first is the one discussed in the text, which is *anaclitic,* i.e., it follows the early infantile prototypes. The second is the *narcissistic,* which seeks its own body and finds it in someone else. The latter is of particularly great significance for the pathological outcomes, but does not fit into the relations treated here. [Ibid., fn]

Narcissism is not, then, a refound relationship, another example of an id that is manifest only in symbolic and socialized forms. It is rather a peculiarly autochthonous tendency of the id impulses. It is one side of the struggle within human personalities between those forces and requirements that pull outward and those that bespeak and promote the isolation of the inner being. Norman Brown builds upon this Freudian theme to see the love of others as an extension of self-love: "Thus the human libido is essentially narcissistic, but it seeks a world to love as it loves itself" (Brown 1959, p. 46).

Let us now consider where Parsons' reverse line of reasoning has brought us:

1. The id is narcissistic.
2. The id is object-cathected and differentiated through the internalization of an early social relationship.
3. Narcissism is the internalization of the mother-child relationship. It turns inward the libidinal attachment of the child toward the mother and also captures the maternal libido and turns it upon itself. Narcissistic *energy* is thus the totality of the mother-child relationship.
4. The id is, therefore, maternal love.

It should now be clear that even the forces of the id are derived from mother love and that Parsons' personality system has no more autonomy than does his social system. Just as the social system appears as the action manifestation of the cultural system, so also is the personality simply a microcosm of social relations and the culture that mediates them. Man is pre-eminently socialized, for it is not enough to say that his natural drives are *molded* by society; instead they are *created* by society.

Dennis Wrong, in a brilliant critique of Parsons, wrote, "To Freud man is a *social* animal without being entirely a *socialized* animal" (Wrong 1961, p. 192). He finds that Parsons, to the contrary, has "an oversocialized conception of man." Wrong attributes this in part to the almost total neglect of innate human biopsychological tendencies. "And certainly their [contemporary sociological theorists] view of man is sufficiently disembodied and nonmaterialistic to satisfy Bishop Berkeley, as well as being desexualized enough to please Mrs. Grundy" (ibid., p. 191).

Both Emile Durkheim and George Herbert Mead have suggested that the individual may be looked upon as a small society, although neither carried this idea through to fulfillment. Parsons has. In his interpretation of the identification process, roles as well as personalities are introjected, and internalization also includes cognitive frames of reference, expressive symbolism, morality, and evaluative standards. More than this, the child undergoing socialization internalizes the integrative structures that bind all of these elements of the cultural environment together. Parsons claims that the personality system is nonetheless independent of the social system because it must be oriented to the needs of the organism, but, since these are in the main, derived from the cultural and social, the autonomy of the personality is illusory. If he means simply that social systems do not eat or copulate and that the integration of activities on that level will therefore be different, then we must agree, with the reservation that we have not learned very much.

Psychoanalysts, on the other side, have often, and rightfully, been accused of looking at societies as blow-ups of psyches. There is a tendency toward this in any theory that attempts to find the main determinants of any system from a system at another level of analysis, and it reaches its logical conclusion when whole societies are characterized as being "anal" and so forth. Freud himself was well aware of the direction of this line of thought and introduced a note of caution:

I would not say that an attempt of this kind to carry psycho-analysis over to the cultural community was absurd or doomed to be fruitless. But we should have to be very cautious and not forget that, after all, we are only dealing with analogies and that it is dangerous, not only with men but also with concepts, to tear them from the sphere in which they have originated and been evolved. [Freud 1962, p. 91]

But, it might be said, if such notable figures from the sociological side as Durkheim, Mead, and Parsons can see the microcosm of society in the person, and leading theoreticians in psychoanalysis can see societies and their cultures as the macrocosm of the psyche, they may all be right: one position is, after all, the corollary of the other. This, perhaps, is the import of the convergence seen by Parsons.

The premise falls apart, as does Parsons' attempt to reconcile his theory with Freud, on an elementary issue. Parsons approaches the psychic life from the standpoint of positivistic, functional sociology. Both personality and society are seen as *organizations,* and he sets himself the central task of discovering the ways in which the two kinds of organization are interrelated. Freud, whom we will revisit in a later chapter, did not approach his study from this direction at all; he is, to the contrary, consistently nonstructural and nonpositivistic. What makes the personality what it is are its "hang-ups," not its modalities: its contradictions and not its complementarity of relations. Freud, as both Herbert Marcuse (1955) and Norman Brown (1959) have eloquently argued, was a dialectician, and he treated the personality as a series of transformations that are at once the negations of previous states and the becoming of new ones.

Parsons' effort to bring him within the framework of contemporary sociology ignored the *dynamism* of psychoanalytic theory.

Lest my remarks on Talcott Parsons' work be construed as being unduly harsh, it must be stressed again that I have examined some aspects of his theory in detail because they represent logical conclusions of structural-functional thought. What is merely implicit in much of social theory is made highly explicit in the general theory of action. His ideas are pervasive not solely because of his personal influence but because his synthesis was largely successful. As is to be expected in any integration of disparate trends, Parsons has been selective in the incorporation of certain theorists and even of certain aspects of their theories. Moreover, these theories have been modified, sometimes radically, as they have been accommodated to each other and to the total architecture of Parsons' Hydra. Nonetheless, to the extent that our field rests on such figures as Durkheim, Weber, and Freud, and to the extent that we have all made a rudimentary synthesis of their ideas in our own minds, we encounter ourselves in Parsons. It is perhaps because of this, and not despite it, that reaction to his theory is often so virulent.

This is especially true of the psychological assumptions underlying contemporary structural-functionalism. Much as we may question the results, it is to Parsons' credit that he has spelled out in detail his view of the mechanisms by which social requirements become embedded in individual motivation. His kind of "Freudianism" is not at all unique to him but is typical of the products of the so-called neo-Freudians, and neo-Freudianism has been one of the strongest influences within anthropology. It is predominant in Malinowski, whose psychological functionalism is oriented around the theme of anxiety and the analysis of institutional means for its reduction. One can find the same theme, mixed with a crude behaviorism, in Radcliffe-Brown's treatment of the economy of affect in the family (cf.

Radcliffe-Brown 1952, pp. 15–31), a train of thought that has been picked up by George Homans and David Schneider (1955) in their discussion of cross-cousin marriage.

The major shift represented by neo-Freudianism is toward a greater emphasis on the social nature and milieu of the personality, a trend that we should, as social anthropologists, seemingly applaud. The net contribution, however, has been the peculiar view of man as the social, malleable, and plastic animal who swallows society in order to buy the acceptance of his fellows. Social science has bought this view of human nature. If man has urges, they are rechanneled and restrained: if he deviates, there are sanctions or he is referred to some form of institutionalized deviation. The feedback of his behavior into the system is generally conceived of as being functional; social conduct is equated with social process. Norms guide behavior, and behavior reaffirms the norms. As Dennis Wrong said of the Parsonian conception of the personality and social systems, "The oversocialized view of man of the one is a counterpart of the overintegrated view of society of the other" (Wrong 1961, p. 190).

PART
II

The Negative Attitude

3

Negativity
and Illusion

The fundamental methods and epistemology of social anthropology and sociology have had mixed results. The successes have been many. First and foremost is the accumulation of an enormous compendium of cultural and social data at a major turning point in world history. We are presently in the critical payoff period of the technological revolution, and new social forms are struggling to emerge that will transcend and replace the contemporary varieties of social order. It is as if the centuries that saw the decline of feudalism and the rise of capitalism were compressed into a space of a half-century with many times the available information on the transition. The new technology will terminate peasant societies, just as the older technology has succeeded in the destruction of primitive life. Exotic types of society, in all their beauty and nastiness, will be finally and irretrievably lost, but we will be left with a record of their existence. Until very recently, modern society has, in a sense, lived in proximity to its own history and has been able to see its past conditions in the present circumstances of other peoples. This will very shortly end, and all the billions of people on earth will live only with the future, standing on the cold threshold of inevitable and accelerating change, increasingly unable to contemplate even their immediate world because of its complexity.

If the literature of anthropology provides us with no guidance, it may at least prove to be a comfort.

The methods of social science have also given us a way of reducing phenomena to facts, thereby allowing us to view our social surroundings in a consistent and orderly manner. The facts have been single-dimensional and the observations incomplete, but the tradition of positivistic social science has enabled its practitioners to see things in roughly the same light, making their observations comparable. The same kinds of normative and institutional data have been collected in the field and, although raw behavioral observations have tended toward a corroboration of the power of norms, such direct observation has become a hallmark of the anthropological method. This is the tradition established by Malinowski and strengthened by his successors, which calls for a minimum of a year's residence among the people they are studying. We have seen what the world is supposed to be like, and we have made some sense of behavior insofar as it may strain toward realizing these ideal constructs. Finally, social science has placed in suspension the notion of society as the creation of rationality and has substituted the idea of rationality as a creature of society. If certain tendencies in contemporary theory are correct, we may have been overenthusiastic and overoptimistic in this conclusion, but the assumption has been a necessary first step in analysis. And it is in the development of basic analytic procedure, taking societies apart, that social anthropology has been most successful. But, however productive this natural science phase has been, it should, perhaps, be looked upon as a necessary first step toward a science that is oriented to a man who is sapient as well as natural.

The tradition of positivism has been to assume a homology, if not a unity, between the phenomenology of the mind and that of the world external to it. Human thought was fitted neatly into an environment that presumably molded it. The discrete categories that form the content of the mind, and which become even more concrete in language, were taken to be the content of social life—external things that the mind, as receptor, comprehended. Mind and society marched to the same drummer, and the task of the social scientist was to record this common beat.

The positivistic mood was in radical contrast to an older philosophical tradition that saw mind and its environment to be joined yet opposed, and that searched for total comprehension of the human situation in an understanding of this antiphony. It posited man as a given factor—not as a totally dependent variable—whose nature was contradictory to that of society. This is a viewpoint that has been revivified in recent social science theory. In the parochial confines of Cambridge, Massachusetts, it is known as the argument between Skinner and Chomsky. The mechanical behaviorism of B. F. Skinner, the Harvard psychologist, is certainly in stark contrast to the work of Noam Chomsky, the linguist at the Massachusetts Institute of Technology, who sees the infra-structures of language to be reflective of universal mental structures, but this is only one episode of a great historic debate.

The crux of the issue is whether man possesses some degree of autonomy from society. The proponents of the anti-positivistic view operate on the premise that he does, that the human mind everywhere has certain properties that are either innate or due to the existential similarities of the human experience. The relationship between mind, or the totality of the psychic life, and society is not, then, unilaterally causal, but is one of interplay and conflict. In this oppositional setting, neither mind nor society emerges wholly victorious, for each is a product of the struggle and neither is completely reducible to the other. Social life is not a mechanism, or even an organism, but a dialectic.

Subject and Object

Dialectical reasoning is both ancient and ubiquitous, and it is sufficient commentary on the influence of Karl Marx that it has been almost completely preempted by him and funneled down to us through the medium of his writings. It is as if Hegel had existed only to be set upright, for his primary relevance today is to the development of Marxian thought. Hammered on one side by the French positivists and the English empiricists, and on the other by Marx and Engels, little is left of German idealism other than the memory that poor old Hegel saw the realization of Truth and Freedom, the unification of Subject and Object, in the German State. It would, however, be just as misguided to measure Hegel's philosophy by the Third Reich as to measure Marx's history by the Soviet State, for there was more fond wish than hard prediction in both men. Their chief sin was optimism. Weber, a pessimist, was a better prophet than either Hegel or Marx. Crystal-ball gazing, however, is neither the responsibility nor the measure of a science of man—the understanding of man's condition and not of man's fate is our charge.

The total tradition of dialectical thought is much broader and looser than the limited Marxian version. Much of Marxian history was quite positivistic, and his dialectics have been rigidified by his commentators into the rather mechanical notions of the change of quantity into quality and a temporal sequence of thesis-antithesis-synthesis. In Marx's hands the use of the dialectic was restricted to macro-history. It is a form of history, to be sure, but it is also a philosophy of mind, an ontology, and an epistemology. Its employment as a logic encompassed all of these aspects and served to integrate them into a metaphysic. In its entirety, it comes to constitute a total world view, a way of looking at existence and reality, and of conceiving man's position within it. It is not the invention or property of one or another school but has been with us throughout the known history of systematic thought in the West, a fact that Hegel himself well knew. (Hegel 1892, p. 149) Some anthropologists indeed hold that dialectical reasoning is a basic property of all human mental process. They find it expressed in Zen as well as in Hegel, in myth as well as in Marx. It is all the more wonderful that it has been considered an arch-heresy in the social sciences until very recently. Dialectics, often expressed fleetingly or in fragments, have nonetheless been a recurrent minor theme in the social sciences, producing underground movements along with sects such as phenomenology. It has stayed in the realm of sociological fun in the past but, precipitated by some of the events of our age, the strands are rapidly coalescing into serious social science.

The principal characteristic of a dialectic is that it is critical and skeptical of received truth and established fact, an iconoclasm that follows from its premises. The basic issue confronted by dialectical thought is the estrangement of man's existence. This estrangement arises from a dilemma of both mind and external circumstance, in which the unitary processes of human existence become fractured and broken into discrete entities by symbolization. The continuity, wholeness, and movement of the world of practical activity appear in the world of thought, language, and culture as discontinuity, limitation, and fixity. What tends toward universality and oneness is broken into finite and opposed objects; the experienced world may thus be said to become an "objectified" one. The roots of the objectification process were found within the mind by Hegel and within social relationships by Marx, but both saw the concreteness of the experienced world as a limitation on human potential and as dependent upon the "negativity" of its objects. This negativity arises because the delineation of the objective world and the creation of its "things" is accomplished by the exclusion of other aspects of reality from its objects. The latter are thus given life and defined by what they are not, by their opposedness, and experienced concrete reality must always contain within itself a negativeness that will ultimately destroy it. In this sense, a world is created that is removed from phenomenal reality, and man's alienation from the processes of life and history is effected.

It is a world that man created, but one in which he cannot

realize his possibilities, for its falseness has become part of him. His creation has been lost to him and turned against him, and that which he made—whether material, social, or mental objects—has been expropriated from him by himself or by others and has become alien. Contained within the dialectical vision is the story of man's fall from Grace and the promise of his Redemption, but both dialectics and Judaeo-Christian theology are derivative from this pervasive interpretation of the human condition. I have given the humanistic view, of course, but, phrased in much more hardheaded terms, dialectical process is a central question of the social sciences, for it is the antithesis of positivism.

Dialectical philosophy is usually associated with metaphysical systems, which are justifiably anathema to social science, but its chief value is as method and perspective. In the hands of a philosopher it may become a metaphysic, but then so also did mechanics in the hands of Descartes and Spinoza. It is not generally understood by social scientists that not even Hegel was so rigid a systematist as is popularly believed. It is commonly thought outside philosophical circles, for example, that Hegel was responsible for the celebrated dialectical triad of thesis-antithesis-synthesis (cf. Burridge 1967, pp. 92–93; Leach 1968b, pp. 1–2), although this is wholly untrue. The philosopher J. N. Findlay sets the matter in historical perspective:

But, quite obviously, Hegel did not really borrow his triadic scheme from Kant: it had already been read into Kant by Fichte. . . . The terms "thesis," "antithesis," and "synthesis," so often used in expositions of Hegel's doctrine, are in fact not frequently used by Hegel: they are much more characteristic of Fichte. [Findlay 1962, pp. 66–67]

J. G. Fichte, an immediate predecessor of Hegel, may have had the dubious honor of coining the paradigm, but it was subsequently adopted by the Marxists and made part of the Hegelian legend.

Although thesis-antithesis-synthesis has the merit of being easily rendered to memory by undergraduates, the equation was far too mechanistic for Hegel. Insofar as it breaks transformation and becoming into discrete units, it corresponds only to what Hegel would call understanding, or the immediate perception of opposed entities. The logical trinity is analytic in nature and, as such preliminary to the dialectic exercise of transformation and reconstitution. Hegel's procedures were tripartite, as is best shown in his chapter headings and in such well-known triads as being-nothing-becoming, but his triads were parts of a unity and not a sequential arrangement of things.

Walter Kaufmann goes further than most students of Hegel in refuting the idea of a rigid, closed dialectical cosmogony:

What do we find if not a usable dialectical method? We find a vision of the world, of man and of history which emphasizes development through conflict, the moving power of human passions, which produce wholly unintended results, and the irony of sudden reversals. If that be called a dialectical world view, then Hegel's philosophy *was* dialectical—and there is a great deal to be said in its favor. This is certainly an immensely fruitful and interesting perspective, and from the point of view of pedagogy, vivid exposition, and sheer drama it may be unsurpassed. But the fateful myth that this perspective is reducible to a rigorous method that even permits predictions deserves no quarter, though by now half the world believes it. [Kaufmann 1966, p. 161]

Most of what Hegel said is not relevant to our enterprise, and it is hardly my intent to write either an essay on Hegel or a Hegelian anthropology, if such a thing were even possible. A dialectical play of the mind does not require that one be a Platonist, Hegelian, or a Marxist—let us remember that Plato, Hegel, and Marx are all dead—but only that one is willing to draw upon their better insights and to allow oneself to transcend the limitations of the given and the obvious. Our task should be understood as an attempt to break out of a closed system of thought and not to adopt one. The total impact of a dialectic is destructive of neat systems and ordered structures, and compatible with the notion of a social universe that has neither fixity nor solid boundaries. It is the mood and style of dialectics more than sets of dogma that can inform social anthropologists.

One of the most basic questions raised by dialectics is the epistemological one: assuming that objective reality indeed exists, how do human subjects comprehend it? This is a somewhat different question from the philosophical inquiry into how we can know the truth or essence of anything, or form "notions" of things in Hegel's terms, but it is essentially the same problem phrased for our own material. Positivism, which Herbert Marcuse calls "the philosophy of common sense" (Marcuse 1941, p. 113), sees social facts as given within the natural order, perceivable and verifiable intersubjectively and possessing an autonomy and existence of their own. They are describable and quantifiable by their positive attributes, and they are authoritative—one does not question the facts.

Positivism was supposed to have delivered us from the kind of idealism, thoroughly discredited today, that claims that since the world is known to us only through mental images, mind is therefore the ultimate reality. Hegel adopts this extreme position in his treatment of the history of the world as the history of mind. But it is not necessary to become a "close-your-eyes-and-it-doesn't-exist" idealist to detect a certain simplistic vulgarity in positivism. The mind is not a template that faithfully registers events. One could more profitably compare it to a computer that has been preprogrammed or, perhaps, shortcircuited. The objective world does indeed have an existence and reality of its own, but its impact upon the observer is a subjective one. People translate phenomena into experience, and the translation process is prone to all the vagaries of the subject's prior experience, seen either individually or culturally. There is reality, but there are also representations of reality, which are very real to those who live with them. The two are not at all the same. Thanks to life in society, however, the images of the mind are not completely individual fantasies, for people tend to share the representations of reality and thus to legitimize and reinforce one another's interpretation of it. This gives rise to collective fantasies (and, therefore, no longer fantastic), which we anthropologists call "culture."

This theme has antecedents in a basic Hegelian principle, one of the main sources of its so-called negativism, that states that the history of man has been shadowed over by an estrangement and tension between mind and its objects. The reality that we receive through sensory perception appears to us as fixity and independence, but this is more a quality of the perceiving mind than of reality itself. The phenomena themselves strike the individual as transient, fleeting, and indeterminate excitations of the sensory organs, but mind interposes itself and our conception of reality is a result of the interaction of mind and sensation. The subject may be said to "constitute" the object; its objectivity arises in the mind.[1] This objective world, falsely conceived of by man as wholly independent of his mind, is a universe of finite and "other" things whose very existences are permeated with a negativity that is generated by their limitations. It is a world that is artificially alienated from mind and from reason, according to Hegel, but it pushes toward the realization of reason, which is freedom. This in turn is the recognition of the unity of world and mind, the actualization of "World Mind," and the manifestation of mind in institutions that reflect and conform to this essential freedom. Until this millennial development, which Hegel thought was about to occur, human consciousness occupied a "false world" that was, paradoxically, of its own making,

---

[1] Language is, of course, a central aspect of the objectification process, and this was recognized by Hegel, Marx, and Durkheim, to name only a few. Conceptualization cannot, however, be subsumed under language. The interrelations between word and concept raise problems far beyond the scope of this book, and I will only note that among the most instructive ideas ever generated by a linguist was Edgar Sturtevant's hypothesis that the origin of language was in deception. (Sturtevant 1947, pp. 48–49) If the spoken word indeed first served to misrepresent reality, then we can agree that things have not really changed much.

but accomplished without knowledge that mind itself was, in the final analysis, the object of its own thought.

To Hegel, mind has always been, in essence although not substance, free and infinite, but it has had to deal with things that are finite and determinate, limited by what they are not. The self-realization of the mind and that of history are inseparable, and the evolution of both mind and society are characterized by the oppositions between finite things and their otherness and the resolution of these contradictions in the birth of something new. Ideas may be the ingredients and results of Hegelian dialectics, but the motive force of the process is will and passion:

A *second* element must be introduced in order to produce actuality—viz., actuation, realization, and whose motive power is the Will—the activity of man in the widest sense. It is only by this activity that the Idea as well as abstract characteristics generally, are realized, actualized; for of themselves they are powerless. The motive power that puts them in operation, and gives them determinate existence, is the need, instinct, inclination and passion of man. [Hegel 1956, p. 22]

Mind realizes itself, and history too, by going beyond the contradictions set in motion by human will and the particular ideas related to it. It emerges from these conflicts a step nearer knowledge and freedom: "This may be called the *cunning of reason* —that it sets the passions to work for itself, while that which develops its existence through such impulsion pays the penalty, and suffers loss" (ibid., p. 33). In each major step of history, the clash of special interests and particular ideas is resolved through their being absorbed into and made part of a more general thesis. The relentless push toward Truth is thus a process by which the particular becomes universalized.

Hegel sought to destroy the traditional philosophical separation of consciousness and reality as independent entities by demonstrating the subjectivity of the objective world in which all men believe and with reference to which they act, and showing that its essence is in becoming rather than in being. The world is false to man because he does not know it, and he does not know it because he does not know himself. He sees only the finitude of the world, which is a negative reality by definition. It is only through reconstituting its dividedness into higher orders of ideation that progress is attained, but this is an exercise of thought, working upon the broken products of will and passion. Hegel believed that reality was inseparable from the way men thought about it, but, since man has always thought about it imperfectly, it has always eluded him. The external circumstances of man's life are related to his mind but are out of harmony with its underlying structure.

Negativity and Nonthings

The Hegelian metaphysic teaches that the estrangement between Subject and Object derives from the Subject's failure to understand that the locus of reality lies in the mind—that Subject and Object are one and that, although sensory experience does arise from outside the mind, the essences, or Truth, of the objects of experience are subjective. Truth, like evil, lies in the eyes of the beholder. It is an extreme sort of idealism, but one that is far more worldly than would appear. Traditional philosophy, especially as expressed within the tradition of German idealism, insisted upon a separation of mind from reality, encouraging withdrawal from the world into the labyrinthine realm of internal discourse and contemplation. Empiricism returned philosophy to the world but at the expense of the autonomy of the mind, which became linked through the senses to the world as is and constrained by it to the function of receptor of reality and not its creator. Hegel's was a far more radical philosophy than either empiricism or traditional idealism, for, by uniting world and mind and asserting the primary reality of thought, he set the mind's task as the transformation of a false world to conform to the inner truth revealed by reason. As

Herbert Marcuse (1941) has argued, despite his apotheosis of the German State, Hegel's was a revolutionary philosophy that called for the dissolution of common-sense appearances and the common-sense basis of the status quo, and for the reordering of external reality to effect freedom. The mind is not free unless it recognizes truth and *exists within* the truth of a rational social order. This "truth" is reached only by challenging the given and fixed and transcending it. As Engels said, "But just there lay the true significance and the revolutionary character of Hegelian philosophy . . . in that it, once and for all, gave the coup de grace to finiteness of results of human thought and action" (Engels 1906, p. 41).

A dialectical critique of common-sense reality does not deny that the things of sense-experience exist or maintain that experience is wholly chimerical. Rather, it need only hold that the reality of the senses is fleeting and transient. Sight, hearing, taste, touch, and smell all give us aspects of the real world, but each is partial and the five together do not provide the totality of subjective experience. The integration of phenomena into experience is accomplished through thought, and true comprehension of experience must take the first step of examining in entirety what is presented to the senses. Mere common sense orders and categorizes experience into fixed things and according to the kinds of laws of identity that are employed in syllogistic reasoning. It is based upon the validity of the common-sense here and now, and it generalizes upon phenomena by seizing upon certain selected external attributes of them. Dialectical thought, on the other hand, denies the objectivity of the here and now through the assertion that both disappear, or negate themselves, upon being considered in time.

The method, and the epistemology, of dialectics is contained in this process of negation. According to the doctrine, time and force are more real than substantive things, and the essence of reality is the process of transformation of perceived reality. Things are not to be understood as fixed entities but are in a continual state of transition into other forms of themselves. The structure of reality is a structure of oppositions, of elements that contradict each other and limit each other's possibilities. Out of this clash of antagonistic tendencies, new forms arise that incorporate the opposing elements, albeit in altered form and with their contradictions now resolved. States of being contain their contradictions as a condition of their existences, and they realize their possibilities by transcending these limitations and passing on to another phase. But the latter is also found to breed its own opposition, and the resultant world view is one of continual movement and transformation. Underlying the oppositions of the sensate, phenomenal world, then, there lies another, deeper reality, which is the process through which the contradictions are contained within a unity—a transcending of their mutual negation through synthesis, which is a "negation of the negation." Hegel summarizes dialectics as a philosophical method:

There are three aspects in every thought which is logically real or true: The abstract or rational form, which says that something is; the dialectical negation, which says what something is not; the speculative-concrete comprehension: A is also that which it is not. A is non-A. These three aspects do not constitute three parts of logic, but are moments of everything that is logically real or true. They belong to every philosophical Concept. Every Concept is rational, is abstractly opposed to another, and is united in comprehension together with its opposites. This is the definition of dialectic. [Hegel 1959, p. 82]

The method finds its most basic expression in Hegel's trinity of Being, Nothing, and Becoming. He argues that pure, indeterminate Being is opposed to any determinate and particular Being, just as the latter concept is also opposed to Nothing. Being and Nothing, though opposites, are therefore identical; they pass from one into the other. But in this mutual dissolution of Being and Nothing lies their "truth" and a synthesis of the contradiction. The truth, to Hegel, is that their passage, itself, is a higher reality. They both thus resolve into Becoming. The reality of the world is its flux, says Hegel: " 'To become' is the true expression for the resultant of 'To be' and 'Not to be'; it is the unity of the two; but not only is it the unity, it is also inherent unrest . . ." (Hegel 1892, p. 166)

As for states of determinate being, they are similarly negated by their own finiteness and limited identity—they gain reality and definition through their otherness. The definition of a phenomenon does not lie in an inner quality that endures and gives substance to the phenomenon; it derives from its boundaries or limits, the parameters beyond which it becomes something else. Things have no independent and autonomous existence but exist only in their relationships to other things. This is not the same as the idea, common to structural-functionalists, that the relationships of anything are determinate of its nature because of the requirements of complementarity or conformity to the organic whole. Rather, it is a statement of how anything attains a definable existence and how we know it as such. Moreover, it sees the limitations, the finiteness, of things as their negations, and it sees the recombination of the contradictory elements as a negation of their opposition. Things are continually pushing against their opposites, the latter reacting as contradiction, and in going beyond these oppositions go beyond themselves into a new state. Functional relationships, in the usual sense, take place only in space; dialectical ones occupy both time and space. One might say: positivism destroys time to assert common-sense reality; dialectical reasoning destroys common-sense reality to assert time. In the process, the locus of reality shifts from the things of the positivists, which are unidimensional and timeless, to relationships and processes, which convert the supposedly fixed in time into the temporally variable.

Hegel's idealism ultimately becomes transcendentalism, for his underlying reality—the Truth toward which men strive, the Reason that is immanent in the world and that history will actualize—is "World Mind." World Mind is the essential totality of consciousness and reality, of man and God. That his metaphysic conceals a theology does not, however, render the entire enterprise futile. There is indeed a world outside the mind, but there is also a mind that stands outside the world, and their union is the crux of the question. What is important to us is the mood and spirit of dialectical discourse. Its very nature is question, challenge, and skepticism. It asks us to look quizzically at the neat categories and clichés of common-sense reality and impels us to use thought to discover whether the evidence of the senses, as mediated by culture, is complete and final. It teaches that reality is paradoxical and that culturally given truths may be false, in themselves, but that they may be at the same time one side of a larger truth. Reality is fraught with contradiction, for the nature of its presentation to us contains within it its very negation. It is not enough to say that every thesis has an antithesis, for this is a vulgarization of the dialectic. Properly, it should be said that every thesis *contains* and *is* its antithesis. Everything is the seed of a nonthing and reality is bestowed equally by the attributes of the thing and its relations to what it is not. The apparent world is in a state of phenomenological flux, which humans attempt to overcome by the imposition of categories upon phenomena and through which process they convert phenomena into experience and subjective perception into objective, alien things. Stability is attained through the falsification of reality, but underlying this apparent reality is its contradictory nonreality and beyond that is the fusion of the opposites in a restless push toward new forms. Stated in another way, everything in life has a set of possibilities, and things transcend themselves and realize these possibilities only through their own destruction. It is this general attitude of dialectical thought that Marx retained, while curing Hegel of his idealism.

Marx

Marx and Hegel both found the active element in history in man's "interests," the impelling drive for gain and power, and the push toward fulfillment of his needs. Moreover, both found that through the contradictions born of the realization of these limited ends, man served the general purposes of history. To Hegel, these purposes were the advancement of reason to a state of absolute knowledge and self-consciousness of man's essential freedom and its embodiment in a society that permitted its fullest expression. The highest interests of the individual and of the society would be unified. To Marx, the purpose of the historical process was the production of higher social forms that emerge from the contradictory elements generated by previous ones. The culmination of the process also was to be the achievement of a society in which the true interests of the individual and the collectivity would be one. History was not the history of mind but the history of man and his institutions, begotten by labor upon nature. The cunning of reason was replaced by the cunning of history, for mind was its product and not its genitor.

To understand the acrobatics by which Marx turned Hegel right side up, it is necessary to consider their common ground. Hegel did derive reality from consciousness, whereas Marx reversed the order, but Marx did not divorce the two nor did he see mind as a passive reflection of reality. Thought does not stand independent from reality, but absorbs reality and works through objects. This is the basis of one of his critiques of Feuerbach:

The chief defect of all materialism up to now (including Feuerbach's) is, that the object, reality, what we apprehend through our senses, is understood only in the form of the *object* or *contemplation;* but not as *sensuous human activity*, as *practice;* not subjectively. Hence in opposition to materialism the *active* side was developed abstractly by idealism—which of course does not know real sensuous activity as such. Feuerbach wants sensuous objects, really distinguished from the objects of thought: but he does not understand human activity itself as *objective* activity. [Marx 1947, p. 197]

History grinds on inexorably, producing results that are neither intended nor comprehended by men, but their consciousnesses are most surely involved in and are part of the process. Most anthropologists would agree with the latter statement, but there is a further tenet of Marxian thought with which most would disagree. This is that man *mis*apprehends material social activity in the process of thinking about it and that these representations, when attaining the level of ideology, are commonly inversions of reality:

Consciousness can never be anything else than conscious existence, and the existence of men is their actual life-process. If in all ideology men and their circumstances appear upside down as in a *camera obscura,* this phenomenon arises just as much from their historical life-processes as the inversion of objects on the retina does from their physical life-processes.

. . . The phantoms formed in the human brain are also, necessarily, sublimates of their material life-process, which is empirically verifiable and bound to material premises. Morality, religion, metaphysics, all the rest of ideology and their corresponding forms of consciousness, thus no longer retain the semblance of independence. They have no history, no development; but men, developing their material production and their material intercourse, alter, along with this their real existence, their thinking and the products of their thinking. [Ibid., p. 14]

The representations of the mind are related, although not directly, to the praxis, or totality of social activity, of the society in which mind is immersed. In class-structured societies, according to Marx, ideology is conceived to serve the purposes of the ruling class, but this is not the genesis of its inversions and illusions. This seems to arise in the first instance from the finite, limited, and restricted character of man's relationships to nature and to other men (ibid., pp. 16–21), a thesis that brings Marx very close to Hegel's notions on the objectivity of the perceived world. In a very revealing passage, Marx writes; "It is self-evident, moreover, that 'sceptres,' 'bonds,' 'the higher being,' 'concept,' 'scruple,' are merely the idealistic, spiritual expression, the conception apparently of the isolated individual, the image of very empirical fetters and limitations, within which the mode of production of life, and the form of intercourse coupled with it, move" (ibid., p. 21). Man, it would appear, dissembles his own existence in order to transcend its limitations and to resolve the contradictions that are inherent in these limitations. Hegel said that we lived in a false world, and Marx said that we lived with a false consciousness.

The significance of Marx's theory of knowledge was in the statement of the primacy of action over idea, a premise that many social scientists accept today. Consciousness, however, does not spring solely out of productive relationships but out of social action in a general sense. His emphasis on production to the exclusion of most other forms of action arose from the practical requirement that ideology be linked with class structure, which, in turn, was the crux of his political theory and program. But it is in the political program that consciousness asserts itself and the ideal intrudes itself into "historical materialism." Although mind is not independent in any formal sense, the basis of revolution is the self-consciousness of a class, as such, and a consciousness of the true interests of the members of a class. This grasp of Truth is not realized mechanically but comes about through *conscious* revolutionary activity—the attainment of true self-consciousness is predicated upon struggle, which, in turn, is predicated upon some degree of realistic and nonrefractory thought. Henri Lefebvre states it to be a dialectic of consciousness and activity:

It is on the basis of conscious revolutionary praxis that thought and action are articulated dialectically, and that knowledge "reflects" praxis, i.e., is constituted as reflection on praxis. Until then knowledge was characterized precisely by its failure to "reflect" reality, namely, praxis, could only transpose it, distort it, confuse it with illusions—in short, knowledge was ideological. [Lefebvre 1969, pp. 86–87]

If an independent consciousness is a necessary factor in the transformation of society, can it be said to be wholly contingent? And what do our ideological mirages do when they are not employed in the interests of a ruling class? These are questions upon which Lévi-Strauss touches and to which we will later redirect our attention.

Anthropological Doubts and Historical Relativism

Marx's theory of the determination of thought by human life processes is not a sociological determinism of the kind that we reviewed in the preceding chapter. The first principle of sociological positivism is that social "things" are real and that the mind reflects, even if in highly symbolic form, the constitution of the society. Mind is essentially passive, and the social system need only take account of the instinctive-emotional life, shaping it to its requirements, for it, too, is malleable. The mind is an active factor in Marxian theory, despite the primacy of *praxis,* for it transforms social action into object, image, and ideology. Mind does not just receive but reworks the external world. In making it subjective, it is commonly erroneous, but it is nonetheless doing something.

Mind produces illusions of the world, which by becoming social have an empirical reality of their own. The levels of culture and social action are, therefore, nonhomologous because of a continuing dialectic between mind and society. The precondition of such a dialectic is a psychic structure that has a measure of autonomy although it must exist *in and through* social life; it also presupposes a social system that has its own requirements, although it, too, must operate through a system of symbols and the activities of sapient and sentimental individuals. The sociological separation of the cultural, social, and personality systems assumes that the three together form the totality of social life, but that each is an expression of the other on a different *analytic* level. We would suggest that it might be more worthwhile to consider them as a unity, but a *dialectical* one. Rather than being expressions of each other, they are transformations of each other, and the totality of social life is a product of their clash (cf. Geertz 1957). This is an untidy and conflict-prone model, but we may ask whether or not it indeed represents the world as we know it.

The vision of a mind that is estranged from the realities of the world raises a series of methodological problems for scientific observers of the social scene. Kant, for example, believed that there were basic mental categories that organized experience, making the essences of phenomena forever elusive to the observer. Hegel accepted part of the notion of transcendental consciousness, but he attempted to escape its ultimate skepticism by demonstrating that the categories of the mind, if allowed their dialectical development, were the same as the truth of the world. Social science has done little more than ignore this problem by subsuming consciousness within society, but it has created, thereby, other dilemmas. By making the sociological assumption that mind is society writ small, custom and socialization are seen as the means by which society is perceived and comprehended: it is, moreover, a means that has as its end the maintenance of the continuity of the society. For the idealists, society is teleological to mind; for the social determinists, mind is teleological to society. If the subjects of our study are social beings whose ideas and acts promote social equilibrium, then how do the observers escape this relativism? It would seem that for both the positivist and the dialectician, there is a gap between the practical activity of the world and our comprehension of it.

Anthropologists have always been aware of the potentiality for bias inherent in their methods. How indeed does one keep his own personal quirks or cultural shackles from imposing themselves upon the selection and evaluation of data? How does one develop a structure that is neither the structure of his own mind nor the self-interpretation of the society under study? How does one prevent an ethnography from becoming the autobiography of the ethnographer, his subjects or both? Clifford Geertz states the anthropologist's dilemma with elegance:

His personal relationship to his object of study is, perhaps more than any other scientist, inevitably problematic. Know what he thinks a savage is and you have the key to his work. You know what he thinks he himself is and, knowing what he thinks he himself is, you know in general what sort of thing he is going to say about whatever tribe he happens to be studying. All ethnography is part philosophy, and a good deal of the rest is confession. [Geertz 1967, p. 25]

The importance of the observer as a variable has been well documented by studies carried out by different investigators in the same society. The most famous instance of these, of course, was the investigation of Tepoztlán, Mexico, by Robert Redfield, followed twenty years later by Oscar Lewis' research. Redfield (1930) discovered all of the amiable qualities of the "folk culture" in Tepoztlán. The community was family oriented, its life was permeated with a sense of the sacred, and social relations were embedded in a general communality. Lewis (1951), on the contrary, found factionalism, suspicion, materialism, and isolationism among the same people, and the time difference of twenty years between the two studies could not adequately account for the disparate results. There were, of course, differences of personality and background between the two ethnographers, but were these dissimilarities of sufficient magnitude to account for the radical divergence in simple description? This would seem unlikely on the face of it, for even if one can see Lewis' America in Tepoztlán, it was essentially the same America as Redfield's. At the very least, Redfield's U. S. A. resembled

Lewis' more than it did his own description of Tepoztlán. Other students of Mexican peasantry have found a resonant note in Lewis' description that is lacking in their reading of Redfield, so we may perhaps conclude that Redfield was wrong. But did a trained investigator fail to document the most important aspects of the life of a town in which he had lived for months? Faced with these contradictions, we could profitably consider whether both Lewis and Redfield were right. Most students of Mexican culture have agreed that Lewis was accurate; his monograph was a sensitive presentation of the actual quality of social relationships in Tepoztlán, in all their grubby meanness. On the other hand, it can equally be acknowledged that Redfield obtained the official version of Tepoztecan culture, as the people liked to think of it and as they probably interpreted it to themselves and each other. "We're just plain folks here, one big happy family," or at least so goes the rhetoric through which a fractured way of life is made whole in the minds of its inmates. Although their conclusions were diametrically opposed, both Redfield and Lewis were right. And because of their incompleteness and one-dimensionality, they were both wrong.

The Lewis-Redfield debate over what was Tepoztlán was a disturbing experience for anthropology for very obvious reasons. If Redfield and Lewis had written autobiographies, what assurance did any ethnographer have that he had comprehended a society. Sociologists, secure in the belief that method is a sufficient inoculation against subjectivity, have apparently not been deeply troubled by this dilemma, although one increasingly hears the maxim "garbage in, garbage out" (garbage in, theory out, and so forth) applied to those who feed the computers. Historians, on the other hand, grappled with the problem for the last forty years or so, and it was explicit in both Hegel and Marx. The premise that knowledge is "relative" to, that it is contingent upon and covariant with, the investigator and his social milieu became hardened into a doctrine of "historical relativism," which holds that the criterion of the validity of a history is its relevance to the times in which it was written. It would follow, then, that the writing of history is a continuous process that must be repeated for each era as new insights and new canons of relevance are developed. Nobody can write *the* history of any period, unless he were to accomplish the impossible task of total recapitulation. One can only write *a* history, but one must be prepared to see it superseded and hope that he will live long enough to witness its reinstatement as relative truth.

Historical relativism starts from the historiographic axiom that events are, in part, fabrications of the historian's mind, for it is he who selects out of the time flow a "happening" that he can delimit temporally and to which he can assign dramatis personae and their scripts. History really took place, to be sure, but "histories" take place in the mind of the historian. He not only finds the events, but he must select out of the mass of available material those events that he considers significant for events (similarly created) that follow.

The criteria of relevance and significance are commonly those that present themselves to us through the medium of our own society, in part because we are products of that society, and in part because we look upon the past as teleological to the present. The selection of facts is also influenced by our theories, which are transient enough, and it would seem that the nearest approach to the absolute in what is historically significant is the measure of gross magnitude. Wars, kings, and revolutions are important: these are Big Facts. Work, family, and habitation are less unique to their times and less exciting to our imaginations: these are Little Facts. And it is for this reason that, although every skirmish in the French and Indian Wars has been worried to a frazzle, historians are only beginning to form an accurate picture of the family in colonial America. The vast bulk of historical "facts," like ethnographic ones, are thrown out by historians, and for every history that is published many nonhistories are discarded. But one man's, or one epoch's, nonhistory is another's history, and the almost infinite possibility for "new interpretations" gives confidence that histories are just as inevitable as History.

The issues in the debate over historical relativism were lucidly presented over thirty years ago in Maurice Mandelbaum's *The Problem of Historical Knowledge* (1938), but the problem is still unresolved. There were howls of anguish from professional historians a couple of decades ago, when Allan Nevins published a new history of the Standard Oil Company on the implicit grounds that Ida Tarbell's account was a dated perspective. As it turned out, Nevins took a kindlier view toward Standard Oil than did Tarbell, drawing the criticism that he was writing apologetics rather than history. And at the time that I write this, there is a very substantial "revisionist" movement among young historians centering on the interpretation of the origins of the Cold War. History is not at all as hard and factual as the layman thinks, nor is it the ultimate human discipline. Lévi-Strauss, in his critique of Sartre's canonization of history as the complete study of man wrote that historical facts are constituted and not given, a statement equally applicable to ethnographic facts. Anthropology has suffered less from these doubts only because the magnitude of its task and the small number of its practitioners have kept them busy always studying something new. The recently discovered tribe is priceless, the merely unstudied one only a bit less valuable. And it is considered to be in poor taste to study a group that is in the process of being studied by somebody else or was only recently the subject of research. Is it because there is thus less danger of being forced into a confrontation with ourselves?

The cases of the historians and anthropologists cited are similar in that both involve the Subject-Object quandary—the alienation of reality from image of reality and the variable interpretations of social life that result from this estrangement. This offers small comfort to the simple positivistic faith in the reality of the social facts and in the method by which they are treated as hard things in natural systems. The debate among the historians centers on the relativity of historiography itself; the historian does not stand as an absolute in relation to his data, but is himself a creature of history and a variable of social circumstance.

There is also a strong element of this relativism in the Redfield-Lewis disagreement, and it manifests clearly the complication that the same kind of subjective biases are present in the sources of information themselves, a problem that is also central to historiography. The question of the folk sociologist was raised in Chapter One in my commentary that everybody is a sociologist as a condition of his life in society. People have and share set views of the nature of the universe, of man and of social relationships, and these views are both normative—they establish what should be done—and cognitive—they dictate modes of perception of reality. Both consist of relatively fixed sets of ideas; they are mental constructs. It has been one of the operating assumptions of social anthropology that activity follows from these constructs or at least strains toward coherence with them. A movement has developed in recent years in France and in the United States to treat these cognitive aspects of culture as a kind of mental code, according to which the mind arranges reality. One of the salient failings of these scholars has been the neglect of social action, which, presumably, is what they are trying to understand, but this very separation of mind and social action has reintroduced doubt about their unity. I will turn to this subject in greater detail in a later chapter. For present purposes, some of the earlier writings of Lévi-Strauss will suffice to define the problem.

Models and Reality

Claude Lévi-Strauss, as the most consistent and methodical of anthropological dialecticians, has never looked upon facts as either hard or authoritative, as the final irreducible bed of reality. He confounded my generation of graduate students with the cryptic comment that, "The term 'social structure' has nothing to do with empirical reality but with models built up after it" (Lévi-Strauss 1963a, p. 279). The present generation of students is equally bemused by this passage. They point out that it contains a contradiction, and they are not at all assured by the answer that they have thus taken the first step toward understanding the Master. As I have pointed out elsewhere (Murphy 1963), Lévi-Strauss's structures are not isomorphic with social reality but are dialectical transformations of that reality. Their stuff is not the actors and groups and the positive ties that are empirically presented, but the differences between them, arranged as sets of contrasting relations that follow a logical order. These logical orders underlie the empirical diversity of entire ranges of society, and they, in turn, can be subjected to further transformations that can further reduce this diversity. Like Hegel, Lévi-Strauss finds ultimate realities in the universal, which can be reached only through reason. If this becomes rather heady and ethereal, it cannot be said that Lévi-Strauss does not warn us, for he writes that, "I believe the ultimate goal of the human sciences to be not to constitute, but to dissolve man" (Lévi-Strauss 1968a, p. 247).[2]

Structures exist, for Lévi-Strauss, on a number of levels of abstraction, but they are not completely creations of thought, although they are accessible only by thought. Anthropologists certainly think about social structures and attempt to describe and make sense of them, but they are not alone in this enterprise, for their subjects of study are busy thinking, as well. And

[2] For those who do not recognize the provenance of this thought, it derives in spirit from Hegel's *Logic* and is most clearly summarized in Marcuse's exegesis:

"The process of dissolving and destroying the common-sense stability of the world thus results in constructing 'the Universal which is in itself concrete;' concrete, for it does not exist outside the particular but realizes itself only in and through the particular, or, rather, in the totality of particulars" [Marcuse 1941, p. 127].

what the subjects do not arrive at cognitively, they often arrive upon by intuition. Lévi-Strauss calls the results of this folk sociology "the conscious model," or "the informant's model," of the system.[3] More materialistically oriented social anthropologists operate, as had been said, on the implicit assumption that they can discard and ignore the fact that the people they study are thinking, plotting, and scheming for the future and attempting at all points to "psyche" the system. It is far tidier and intellectually easier to see man as helpless in the grips of history and of institutions that are less of his making than the results of culture working upon culture according to natural laws. Primitive men, however, are no more prisoners of custom than are moderns. They are no more "traditional" than modern man is "rational" in any absolute or qualitative sense. Both primitives and moderns are, however, rationalizers; they all play off activity against norm and use values as scenarios as well as guides. Primitives and moderns, alike, attempt to develop coherent schemes, or conscious models of society, that give meaning and order to activities, but their thoughts strain in the direction of distortion and mystification because of self-involvement and the limitations of human conceptual ability. Their ruminations do much to fill up the free time that hangs so heavily in primitive society, but they also have the very serious function of producing standardized rationalizations of a way of life.

The informant's conscious model attempts to give coherence to social life by providing a systematic framework of the principal values and rules of conduct of the society as well as of the bodies of meaning that make these rules and values intelligible and consistent. This model, along with material at a lower level of abstraction, is part of the cultural yield of ethnography.

[3] One makes a 'model' by reducing any kind of system to that limited number of related elements that can still explain and account for the greatest range of facts. A 'model' of a market system can thus be created by evoking the law of supply and demand, or a mechanical system can be represented by a model that presents its components and their connections in mathematical terms.

Underlying the conscious models, however, are mental infrastructures, or unconscious models, which are the mainsprings of human thought and which are isomorphic with the structures underlying social phenomena. These unconscious models are frequently obscured, according to Lévi-Strauss, by the conscious models, which may appear to the anthropologist, as well as to his informant, to give sufficient explanation of the phenomena being studied (Lévi-Strauss 1963a, p. 281). He argues this to be a pitfall, for the conscious model functions to perpetuate the system of social relationships, and it does so by simplification, by partial falsification, and by obscuring the inconsistencies and contradictions of actual social life. The conscious model patches up the untidiness of society and produces the appearance of order. It also reduces the flux of social life to objective categories and thus makes it thinkable. As such, the conscious models present a limited and finite view of reality which may produce truncation and inversion as easily as replication. The anthropologist's task is to reach beyond this screen to infrastructures that are at once explanatory of both the culture, including the conscious model, and of the system of social action.

One of the limitations of any empiricism that refuses to go beyond its data is that the data must form the basic elements of its structural models. If there is a norm of affective conduct between the mother's brother and the sister's son, then the avunculate becomes one of the dyadic units within the total architecture of the structure. The anthropologist may then relate it outward to other norms—in this case patrilineality would be the first step—until he has an entire description of an empirical social system, or, at least, of a system of norms. Lévi-Strauss rejects this procedure because it courts the peril of unwitting acceptance of the informants' models. He says of the dual organizations commonly found among Brazilian Indians: ". . . the descriptions of indigenous institutions given by field workers, ourselves included, undoubtedly coincides with the natives' image of their own society, but . . . this image amounts to a theory, or rather transmutation, of reality, itself of an entirely different nature" (Lévi-Strauss 1963a, p. 121). He continues:

The dual organization of the societies of central and eastern Brazil is not only adventitious, but often illusory; and, above all, we are led to conceive of social structures as entities independent of men's consciousness of them (although they in fact govern men's existence), and thus as different from the image men form of them as physical reality is different from our sensory perceptions of it and our hypotheses about it. [Ibid., p. 121]

To briefly summarize Lévi-Strauss's analysis of Brazilian dual organizations, he finds among the Sherente, the Bororo, and, less clearly, other groups that the dual organization that is expressed in spatial symmetry and exogamic rules is apparent and obvious but unreal. The Sherente, who have exogamous, patrilineal moieties, each containing four clans, correspond to his type of "restricted exchange," as presented in his classic *Les Structures élémentaires de la Parenté* (1949). It corresponds to the model of a closed system dichotomized into two groups that exchange women. Ideally, this should be expressed in the idiom of bilateral cross-cousin marriage and should appear in the kinship nomenclature in the form of rigid exclusiveness of kin terms to one moiety or the other. Neither of these conditions is actually encountered, for cross-cousins are not only terminologically distinct from one another but there is a preference for marriage with the father's sister's daughter, as opposed to the mother's brother's daughter. This produces the patrilateral form of "generalized exchange" in Lévi-Strauss's scheme and he finds the kinship terminology to be congruent with it and not with a moiety system. Through analysis of certain kin relationships, especially between a bridegroom and his bride's maternal uncle, he discovers that the system is only possible if there are actually three descent groups—Ego's, Ego's wife's, and Ego's wife's mother's—the minimal number required for generalized exchange. These are operating in latent and subinstitutional form but they explain the working of the society as the moiety model cannot.

The Bororo present another contradiction between the apparent, conscious reality and the underlying, unconscious structure. Here again, we encounter an order in which territory and marriage are conceived of as dual but that contains a triad beneath the obvious dyad. In the case of the Bororo, however, the triad is composed of three endogamous groups, as distinguished from the latent system of generalized exchange found among the Sherente. This is accomplished through the trichotomization of each of the Bororo clans into groups distinguished as High, Middle, and Lower. Although the rule of moiety exogamy prevails, Highs can only marry Highs and so forth, yielding a system of three closed units between which there is no kinship and each of which is split into marriage halves.

In a subsequent publication, Lévi-Strauss attempts to repair the seemingly irreconcilable breach of the Bororo through the interjection of another moiety division that precisely bisects the exogamic moieties (Lévi-Strauss 1963a, pp. 132–163). The argument in this article suffers from exasperating gaps of data and from a lack of sufficient connective reasoning, not all of which are the author's fault, and one is left with the impression that the Bororo, like Humpty-Dumpty, will never be quite the same again.

Aside from the problems posed by the fractionation of the Bororo, the essay poses the question from which it takes its title: Do dual organizations exist? Through a comparative examination of certain Indonesian and American Indian societies, Lévi-Strauss decides that they do not, at least not in the neat symmetrical form that is empirically evident. The latter, which he calls "diametric dualism," is the conscious and common-sense model of simple binary opposition between two equal halves, expressed residentially among the Bororo by assigning each moiety to a separate half of the village. But there is another form of dualism just below these surface phenomena. The village can be conceived as consisting of two circles, one inside the other. The inner circle contains the men's house, the sacred precincts, and the dancing ground, while the outer circle is formed by the dwellings. The latter is the realm of the women and of domesticity; contrary to the sacred inner ring, it is the spatial expression of the profane. Lévi-Strauss refers to this form of dyad as "concentric dualism." Unlike the diametric type, it is asymmetrical and hierarchical. Moreover, concentric dualism contains an implicit triad. The Bororo arrangement of the inner village circle is illustrative, inasmuch as the men's house is divided between the opposed moieties and this opposition is mediated by the communal dancing grounds. He finds the same triad within concentric dualism among the Winnebago Indians who divide their space between an inner village circle, an intermediate cleared area, and the outer environ of forest. The triadic element within concentric dualism is the mediator between simple diametric dualism and the deeper structure of triadic division among the Bororo—it stands as a social and a logical step in a dialectical transformation. Dyads and triads are transformations of each other and are part of the same general structure:

. . . it follows that triadism and dualism are inseparable, since dualism is never conceived of as such, but only as a 'borderline' form of the triadic type. We may then examine another aspect of the problem, which concerns the co-existence of the two forms of dualism—diametric and concentric. The answer is immediately apparent: Concentric dualism is a mediator between diametric dualism and triadism, since it is through the agency of the former that the transition takes place between the other two. [Ibid., p. 151]

The informant's conscious model is different from the structural model produced by the anthropologist, but it cannot be ignored. It is a primary datum of cultural experience and the proper starting point from which other models are developed. It contains the truth but in veiled form, and it is the anthropologist's task to cast the conscious model against the mode of operation of the society—particularly in the forms of exchange that take place—to reveal the transformation. And, of great importance, Lévi-Strauss believes that the infra-structures of society correspond to the unconscious infra-structures of the human mind; the informants thus often express the underlying structure in metaphor, proverb, and myth. Indeed, Lévi-Strauss looks upon their cogitations as being often superior to those of his empiricist colleagues (Lévi-Strauss 1969a, 450).

Not all of man's thoughts about his societies are illusory and inaccurate by any means, and every anthropologist has encountered some very hard-headed thinking among his informants. Allen Johnson reports a high correspondence between his own interpretations of ecological and economic relations among Brazilian peasants and those of his subjects (Johnson 1968). In my own experience, certain quite intelligent Mundurucú Indians were able to see that their spiraling desire for manufactured goods had placed them at the mercy of white society (Murphy 1960). And a Tuareg once told me that slavery was ending in his society because it was cheaper to hire a laborer than to feed and clothe a slave. Most of these interpretations, however, exist at variance with other representations of the social system. Moreover, they are quite commonly individual views within a broad spectrum of opinion of varying degrees of perspicacity. They lack the symbolic formulation and delineation of the normative as well as the commonality and pastness of norms, and they may be best regarded as ideas on the way to becoming culture. It would seem that, when culture is measured against activity, it is a mixture of accuracy and misrepresentation. Perhaps it is this quality that makes all of it at once believable and yet highly suspect.

Lest the verbiage of model-building lead us astray, we should recapitulate what all of this means. Reduced to elementals, Lévi-Strauss is saying with the Hegelians and with the early Marx that thought and reality may contradict each other; their relationship is necessary but negative. The conventional view of social reality contains falsifications of the actual state of affairs and functions to perpetuate it. It does not perpetuate it by positive feedback, by the accommodation of behavior to norms, but by providing the illusion of a superior, and simpler, order. Ongoing life has a structure, but our ideas of it make it palatable and comprehensible. The world and man's objectification of it are discordant, but this is not the product only of particular times and circumstances. It is, rather, a necessary part of the human situation and an existential condition of society. Lévi-Strauss's dialectic has led him to generalize the notion of false consciousness.

4

The Human Dilemma

The Dialectics of the Individual Life

The dialectic finds its proper dimension in time, because it is above all the study of becoming and transformation. It is for this reason, and because Hegel and Marx specifically addressed themselves to historical problems, that it has largely been applied to the study of changes in the institutional orders of societies, to historical analyses of broad scope and great depth. Whether history is seen as the fruition of the idea of freedom or as the fruition of the social conditions of freedom, the focus must be upon ideology of the most general sort and upon the course of civilizations. But what of our interest in the societies of the unknown and the unlettered, where history does not exist and freedom is hardly an issue? And what of our study of the mean and drab, but equally temporal, routine of everyday life, where, in the final analysis, we must look for understanding of the essential condition of social man? These have been the private preserve of positivism, neglected by the dialecticians of recent years, who have subsumed their energies and their talents to ideological warfare in the revealed belief that their role was to change the world and not understand it. But it is exactly at this level of fundamental social theory and the study of mundane interaction within short time spans that the persistent impulse to question, to disbelieve, and to contradict has been reintroduced. Paradoxically, these new trends in anthropology are not the result of a Hegelian or Marxian renaissance, but have been awakened by a positivism and an empiricism so thorough that it has destroyed its own premises.

The dialectical exercise is simple in the extreme, for it requires only that the analyst of society question everything that he sees and hears, examine phenomena fully and from every angle, seek and evaluate the contradiction of any proposition, and consider every category from the viewpoint of its noncontents as well as its positive attributes. It requires us to also look for paradox as much as complementarity, for opposition as much as accommodation. It portrays a universe of dissonance underlying apparent order and seeks deeper orders beyond the dissonance. It urges the critical examination, in the light of ongoing social activity, of those common-sense guidelines to behavior and common-sense interpretations of reality that lie at the core of our cultural systems. It enjoins us to query the obvious and given truths of both our culture and our science. The result of all of this may fall far short of revelation and the discovery of general social laws, but it will at least impel us to ask new and fresh questions. And the measure of a science lies as much in the questions it asks as in the answers it obtains.

A good many of our society's clichés have become translated into scientific fact, just as many of our research findings have become popularized into clichés. Edmund Leach of Cambridge University manages to annoy his colleagues and the public alike by his penchant for turning many of these received truths on their heads to produce counterclichés that prove themselves to be just as true as their opposites. It is commonly thought that moral systems provide not only guides to behavior but cognitive frameworks by which we may perceive activity as a precondition to judging it. But Leach tells us that morality is deceptive by nature: "So long as we allow our perception to be guided by morality we shall see evil where there is none, or shining virtue even when evil is staring us in the face, but what we find impossible is to see the facts as they really are" (Leach 1968a, pp. 54–55). Having thus disposed of the unity of truth and goodness, Leach moves on to the family, which we all know is the font of security and love. "Far from being the basis of the good society," he writes, "the family, with its narrow privacy and its tawdry secrets, is the source of all our discontents" (ibid., p. 44). He continues his pursuit of popular self-delusion with a thought on youth: "So what we have to consider is not 'why are the young so disorderly?' but 'why do the old imagine that the young are so disorderly?' . . ." (ibid., p. 37). This is a most likely question for the time at which I write, for the majority of the American public were clearly more frightened and disturbed by the campus demonstrations that followed the April 1970 invasion of Cambodia than by the invasion itself. By their clear disposition to generalize from a quite limited number of violent demonstrations to an entire generation, they hinted at something else. This is that the American adult population, which has been typified as youth-oriented and as permissive and indulgent toward their own offspring, does not really like kids in general. Nobody should be surprised at this. The kids knew it all along.

We live in a topsy-turvy world, and it makes sense to turn many of our questions upside down, to examine the consequences of a reversal of the obvious. This reversal of common sense and the conventional interpretation of reality may appear to be only intellectual gymnastics and a method of disputation. It is indeed possible to call it sophistry, and this would not be too far wrong. In fact, the refutation of obvious and received truth and counterargument of the contradictory proposition was a characteristic of those Pre-Socratic philosophers who are generally classed as "Sophists," a term that has carried over into modern usage as a pejorative for people who indulge in facetious and fallacious argument.

Hegel differentiated his dialectical method from Sophistry, which he said gives "authority to a partial and abstract principle, in its isolation, as may suit the interest and particular situation of the individual at the time" (Hegel 1892, p. 148). But, he continued, "From this sort of party-pleading Dialectic is wholly different; its purpose is to study things in their own being and movement and thus to demonstrate the finitude of the partial categories of understanding" (ibid., p. 149). The Sophists, nonetheless, merit some attention. They were far less concerned with metaphysics than were the philosophers of subsequent periods, and they placed the focus of their study upon man and society. They did not reject the thesis that reality is truly out there, as is commonly believed, but believed only that reality was also subjective to the observer. They were, in a sense, early phenomenologists who maintained, as do the modern phenomenologists, that observation is just as phenomenal as the phenomena observed and is part of the total phenomenal field. Observers attach meanings to phenomena, which are not autonomous and objective, but are subjective and part of the situation in question. This is also recognizable as Max Weber's main epistemological thesis and as a central element in social-science relativism. But above all, the Sophists spoke in dialectics and, in keeping with the tradition, were critics of established orders as well as of received truths. They questioned morality and doubted the gods, attitudes toward which anthropologists should be sympathetic.

Whereas the Sophists devoted their attention to the human situation and to the relation between thought and reality, other Pre-Socratic dialecticians were concerned with the natural order and the development of a metaphysic. They are not an ultimate concern of this book, any more than are the Sophists, and only enter our narration through their influence upon Sigmund Freud. One of the more overstated clichés about Freudianism is that it is fine therapy but bad science—we may yet reverse that view to state that it is dubious therapy but brilliant science, however different it may be from the tradition of empirical scientific research. Freud's triumph, it should be stressed, was not gained *despite* his failure to adhere to the norms of positivistic science, but *because* of this departure. Modern science traces part of its ancestry to Aristotle, but Freud went further back in time to the pre-Socratic dialecticians, specifically to the natural philosophers, for inspiration.

Freud was far more concerned with opposition and dissonance in human affairs than even Marx. Where others would look for identity, congruence, and function, Freud consistently sought out processes of conflict and contradiction; where others would look for structure in personality, Freud sought the restlessness of self-realization and becoming, the struggle of the psyche to realize its possibilities through the transcendence of its built-in limitations. He dealt in duality, like many Western thinkers, giving his theories a cast that seemed to fit into Parsons' general scheme of binary differentiation as the principal mode of development. Parsons, however, sees binary differentiation as productive of entities that stand in a structured relationship to one another in a situation of evolving complexity. The entities that emerge are new and, although organically related to others, they have an independent existence of their own. The binary units split again; they do not synthesize. It is an essentially mechanistic theory. Freud's dualisms on the other hand, are inherent in life and are immanent in the basic contradiction of a mind that is rooted in an organism, the body, but which has become alienated from it. Its differentiations are fragile formations that clash with each other and then pass on into something else. They also continually struggle to recoalesce and to reassert their primal unity, but another dialectic, that between the self and others, forces them apart. There are two countervailing tendencies. The first is to drift back into the depths of one's own organism, and the second is to drift into immersement in others. Both are alike in that they are destructive, and the essential career of the mind is to resolve these tendencies through the development of

the autonomous ego. The compromise between the instinctual
(in the broadest and most general sense) and the social is
accomplished through alienation from both—this is at once
man's agony and man's victory over nature.

Struggle is the principal dynamic in Freudian theory rather
than the molding of plastic affect and cognition into a socialized
personality system. The main mechanism of the conflict lies in
repression, and one of its principal diagnostics is ambivalence.
The former constitutes the means by which man maintains his
transcendence over nature. According to the theory of sublima-
tion, repression generates the energy for culture-building, but at
a minimal level it serves as the differentiator of mind and body.
To Freud, it is at once the source of our humanity and of our
illnesses. We may agree with Norman Brown that the essential
truth about man is that he is a sick animal with the simple
modifier that some sicknesses are socially useful or, at least,
successful. Ambivalence is the psychological expression of the
struggle in the form of contradictory attachments to the same
objects. But ambivalence is not a "this or that" choice. Rather,
the opposing elements are always present because they define
each other. Love and hate, if not the same, are the possibilities
of one another. The existence of one is predicated upon the
other, and in real life they transform themselves into each other.
Most of Freud's antitheses have this characteristic of inter-
changeability: love-hate, object libido-ego libido, sadism-maso-
chism (which are quite basically the same), and even Eros-
Thanatos. This is an important aspect of dialectical thought. It
does not simply separate things as conceptual opposites, for the
essence of the process is that the opposites are in an active
relationship of mutual contradiction. They negate each other
through moving into each other; they are opposite sides of the
same coin, but their clash and fusion produce new forms. This,
and not binary differentiation, is at the core of the Freudian
view of human nature.

The Oedipal situation provides a good example of Freud's

antagonistic model of the psyche. It was not through whim that Freud found its genesis in a mythic parricide, for he saw the Oedipal phase, whether in history or ontogeny, as the means by which man breaks out of the undifferentiated state of nature into a higher phase of development. Freud's myth brings out something else in his theory that has not been sufficiently stressed. This is that there is something teleological about man's struggle with other men and within himself. His theory is deterministic, to be sure, but he also sees man as striving to realize his possibilities, as forced to transcend his present state, whatever it may be. His only choice is to press forward; fixation is not only illness but it is at the very edge of the abyss of regression. There is no such thing as a stable personality, for this would be a contradiction in terms.

Freud started out with the shocking premise that infantile life is sexualized, a notion that was received with horror by some and disbelief by others. Everybody knew that sexuality is a biological drive that appears only at the onset of puberty. Where it was before then was never questioned, although it was well known that all of the organs connected with sexuality are present from birth. It was also well known that babies and little children exhibit rather peculiar behavior for an age of innocence. Male infants did indeed have erections before Freud's time as well as after; they played with their genitalia; they smeared feces on nursery walls; they engaged in embarrassing conduct with each other; they learned early the basic comparative anatomy of males and females with the same mixed feelings; they were, and still are, really quite awful by Victorian standards. We may marvel today that people really believed children to be asexual, but "common sense" and the evidence of the senses are not exactly the same. Conversely, it is not always necessary to defy the evidence to reverse common sense, for it can be done by examining the facts more closely.

The distinctive character of infantile sexuality in Freudian theory lies in the undifferentiated nature of the libido. The fusion of object libido and ego libido is at the root of the oceanic feeling of oneness with the world that is attributed to the infant, and it constitutes the true innocence of the child (Freud 1962, p. 11; cf. Brown 1959, p. 32). It is also the necessary prelude to the onset of the Oedipal complex, which finally and decisively shatters this unity. Freud's earlier statements on the Oedipal situation were at once deterministic and thoroughly dialectical. The attachment of the child to the mother, which is initially expressed in total unity and later in complete possessiveness, comes into conflict with social reality in the form of the father. The father effectively blocks the desires of the son, appearing to him as a threatening and forbidding figure. The interjection of the father between the son and the mother is emasculating in itself, given the libidinal nature of the child's attachment, and the paternal authority sometimes becomes more specifically emasculating through the threat that sexual expression of any kind will draw the punishment of castration. The child resolves the contradiction by an identification with the father, repression of the incestual urges, and the introjection of the regulatory aspect of society. He also transcends his former state of dependency by breaking out of his enclosure within the family and developing a semi-autonomous ego. He has learned the reality game—by suppressing the truth.

The later Freudian theory develops the teleological qualities of personality development. It was only a question of time in a male-dominated society before it was discovered that males are not at all important in the life process except to help sustain it through their work, and this is what happened to man in Freudian theory. Essentially, it was found that all the necessary elements of contradiction were present in the child's relation to the mother—it was not the father who threatened castration but the woman, nurturing and protective, on one hand, and enveloping, incorporating, and hostile on the other. There is the placental mother, and there is the mother of the vagina dentata theme, both of them products of the ambivalence that develops toward the child's primary love object. The child attempts to overcome this ambivalent conflict by obtaining mastery over the mother. Or, as Norman Brown interprets it, he attempts to defeat death, in the form of the passive relation to the mother, by becoming father to himself and by achieving domination of his family universe. The Oedipal situation is an event generated by the child as he transcends himself in the dialectic of life and death:

The Oedipal project is not, as Freud's earlier formulations suggest, a natural love of the mother, but as his later writings recognize, a product of the conflict of ambivalence and an attempt to overcome that conflict by narcissistic inflation. The essence of the Oedipal complex is the project of becoming God—in Spinoza's formula, *causa sui;* in Sartre's, *être-en-soi-pour-soi.* By the same token, it plainly exhibits infantile narcissism perverted by the flight from death. At this stage (and in adult genital organization) masculinity is equated with activity; the fantasy of becoming father of oneself is attached to the penis, thus establishing a concentration of narcissistic libido in the genital. [Brown 1959, p. 118]

If ambivalence is a negation, then the Oedipal resolution is the negation of this negation. In the later Freud, the dynamic of the process lies in the child, who creates the conflicts out of his own necessities for maturation. This seems rather teleological but it is only so because we are looking at the process retrospectively. Seen in itself, the process consists of the conflict of the ambivalencies and their further interplay with the immediate objects of the child's expanding world.

It would be possible to trace these dialectic movements in Freud through all the ontogenetic phases, the dream theory, the trilogy of id-ego-superego, and so forth, but this is now a familiar story. Brown summarizes its place in Western thought as follows:

It is one of the great romantic visions, clearly formulated by Schiller and Herder as early as 1793 and still vital in the systems of Hegel and Marx, that the history of mankind consists in a departure from a condition of undifferentiated primal unity with himself and with nature, an intermediate period in which man's powers are developed through differentiation and antagonism (alienation) with himself and with nature, and a final return to a unity on a higher level of harmony. But these categories—primal unity, differentiation through antagonism, final harmony—remain in the romantics arbitrary and mystical because they lack a foundation in psychology. The psychoanalytic theory of childhood completes the romantic movement by filling the gap. [Ibid., p. 86]

The anthropological reader will also recognize within this "romantic vision" the structuralism of Lévi-Strauss, but this is a subject for a later chapter. At this point, we can digress a bit to briefly consider the implications of the later Freudian theory for anthropology. Many anthropologists are unaware of these shifts in the psychoanalytic school and still consider the Malinowskian critique, which questioned the universality of the Oedipal complex on the basis of variations in family form, to be correct for the reasons stated by Malinowski. He argued that the institutions of matrilineality and avunculocality among the Trobrianders removed the father from the role of jural authority, and indeed physically removed the boy to the home of his mother's brother, modifying the Oedipal complex so as to shift the center of ambivalence to the uncle and the focus of repressed desire to the sisters. There were problems with this argument even then, for the child did not really come under the authority of the uncle until after the Oedipal crisis should have passed, and Malinowski's evidence for a displacement of attachment from the mother to the sisters is shaky at best. Nonetheless, many social scientists read into the Trobriand material a complete refutation of Freud or, at the very least, a revision of the theory in the direction of the plastic man of sociological relativism. But the critique depended on Freud's original postulation of the nurturant, loving mother and the patriarchal father who monopolized the mother and threatened the son with castration. (It would help a great deal in understanding Freud if "castration" were read as the fantasy representation of the fear of passivity and, in a general sense, emasculation—nobody has to threaten a child with cutting off his genitalia for him to imagine it). The later Freudian theory, however, removes the father from involvement, something that novelists had already anticipated, and only predicates that there should be a loving female—perhaps just any female, loving or not. Moreover, the contradictions of psychological development are not totally imposed from the outside, for they are also rooted in the innate psycho-biology of the species. To state the theory as radically as possible, *the family is within the child just as much as the child is within the family; the childhood experience is the eternal recreator of the family.* From this point of view, Malinowski was right in concluding that the middle-class Viennese family structure was not necessary for the Oedipal syndrome to occur, but he was wrong in thinking that the complex was very different in the Trobriands.

The later Freud offers a way out of a series of theoretical binds that have afflicted the study of personality and culture. If I may utter an anthropological heresy, the early theory probably overstressed the importance of culturally specific child-training patterns and variable family structures in determining the course of personality development. This led us down the trail of studying weaning, sphincter training, swaddling, and so on, and it has always been a surprise, given these basic premises, that people were really so similar everywhere and that statistically significant summations of personality, characteristic of particular cultures, were so difficult to establish. What were interpreted as personality clusters in different societies sometimes turned out to be more easily attributable to culture—variations in style—and the remarkable range of customary exotica that we have collected seemed to have no counterpart of variation in psychic process. Perhaps the answer is that the basic constellations established in infancy are everywhere quite the same, granted that postpubescent personality development may show great cross-cultural variation. (This question has ramifications that cannot be treated here.) There would be two reasons for this. The first, the extent to which the transitions are autochthonous, has already been covered; it is implicitly known by all parents who have discovered that their children decide when to toilet train (cf. Brown 1959, p. 120). The second reason is possibly that we have looked at the child's environment through the eyes of an adult, and we have read into it implications that may not be terribly significant to the child. The infant's world, we must remember, is largely within his body, and its external extension can be measured in inches; we have measured in feet and yards. Just as innate infantile biological and intellectual endowments do not show significant mean variation from one society to another, so also is the infantile experience everywhere much of a piece. There is a vast difference in being an American as opposed to being a New Guinean, but there is not as much difference in being an American baby, as opposed to being a New Guinean baby.

This, at last, gets us back to the question of the oversocialized image of man to which I referred in the last chapter. Early personality development has a career of its own that is not the helpless pawn of an interplay between heredity and environment. Psychic processes are instinctually determined in only an amorphous and general way, and the *peculiarities* of cultural milieu have a minimal impingement upon infancy. Our early experience may be an American one, or a Trobriand one, but it is preeminently a human one. These are the generalized influences upon which the dialectics of ontogeny operate, and the net effect is *not* to produce an elemental personality structure that is the society miniaturized and embedded, but rather to produce a being that is, distinctively, only partially socialized. In this sense, the totally socialized androids of the science-fiction writers are as antithetical to humanity as are the beasts. The essential condition of man is that in many important respects, he stands apart from and opposed to his society. He is weak, embattled, neurotic, but he is *sui generis,* although betrayed and compromised by his postchildhood life experience. His later surrender to the demands of living is not, however, total, and his relation to his life and times embodies alienation and contradiction more than isomorphism.

Dialectical thought is manifest in the Freudian vision of the psyche as an imperfectly socialized thing that stands somewhat apart from its own body and its society, although in both, and alienated from its fellow man, although straining toward union with him. Above all, the commonality of the infantile experience produces certain basic psychic processes and configurations in all men that cut across cultural differences and yield a least-common denominator of human personality. Later experience builds upon this residuum, but it does so in conformity with directions already established. Freud's procedure was not that of positivistic science. Freud saw the personality as a series of oppositions, and he assigned to the ego the function of dealing with reality through a resolution of these internal antagonisms and through mediation between society and the requirements of the individual. In the Freudian view, personality, itself, evolves through a series of contradictions that are resolved through repression. As in Hegel, nothing is lost in the transformations of the personality. Rather, the repressed material is conserved in the unconscious, but it is negated by being made a part of a higher phase of development. The transcendence of the self and the movement to autonomy and maturity are, however, in continual struggle with the wish to return to the blissful early stage of undifferentiated existence. Infancy is the prototype of utopian thought; it is a period in which mind and body are one, in which the self and the object are unitary, in which struggle has not yet begun. It is the model of Rousseau's state of nature and Marx's primitive communism, and is equally unreal. This is a theme that is common in human views of the past and is part of the mythology that every society maintains about itself.

Freudian psychology, in both the early and late versions, depicts man as pitted against society. The controls built in during the socialization process are, at best, only partially effective, and the ego is seen as that part of the psyche that achieves a temporary compromise with reality. Its task is to bring an accord between the self-assertions of the individual and the rules of society, and it does this through evasion, subterfuge, deception of both self and others, and rationalization and projection as well as by conformity. Norms, after all, can be manipulated to personal advantage, and they can serve to mask activity as well as determine it. This is to say that the same ambivalence that pervades all human attachments pervades man's relationship to his fellows and to culture, as an abstracted set of norms. The demands of the maturation process create the loneliness and sense of estrangement that are a constant quality of life among primitives as well as among moderns. It is the attempt to overcome this loneliness, to rediscover undivided attachments, that accounts for human sociability. Perhaps man is sociable because he isn't social.

The Individual and the Group

Buried in a postscript at the back of Freud's *Group Psychology and the Analysis of the Ego* is the suggestion that love, the closest of human relationships, is a form of withdrawal from group life. (Freud 1922, p. 121) Pushed to its limits, the impulse toward union with others produces involution and the contradiction of the impulse. Close personal attachment begets isolation, just as overattachment to a collectivity begets the loss of the ego. This insight is closely paralleled in the writings of Georg Simmel, the German sociologist and philosopher, whose works have undergone a strong revival in recent years.

The unmistakable similarity of Freud and Simmel, in both the style and content of their writings, stems from the fact that both found the key to the human condition in alienation and struggle, in the paradoxical frustration of man's possibilities as a prerequisite to his humanity. Simmel's adherence to the tradition followed by Hegel and Marx is insufficiently noted in this country, although European scholars have almost taken it for granted. American commentary has been centered about Simmel's "formalism" without proper attention being given to the relationship of his sociology of forms to his dialectical method. Simmel excited some interest in the United States in the early part of this century, but the contemporary resurgence of his work has been greatly facilitated by the translations and commentaries of Kurt Wolff and Lewis Coser, who received all and part of their educations, respectively, in Europe. Coser, especially, has drawn attention to Simmel's dialectical method in his book, *The Functions of Social Conflict* (1956), and in a series of essays by himself and others edited by him under the title *Georg Simmel* (1965). The historic sources of Simmel's theories are also treated in Rudolph Weingartner's *Experience and Culture* (1962).

Simmel attempted to produce a sociology by reconciling the school of German idealism with Marxian philosophy. He inherited from Kant and Hegel a concern with the individual and a feeling for the pervasive and existential quality of dialectics, and he took from Marx the primary emphasis upon social relations. He was a materialist to the extent that he believed that interaction and group relations had a life of their own and were partially determinate of mind. But Simmel was also an idealist in that he assumed that mind as well had its own life and its own possibilities. Above all, the two elements were in constant interplay and opposition with each other. The dialectic of consciousness and society was not just a matter paramount in the generation of class-linked ideology or revolutionary self-consciousness but was a central factor in all social interaction. This is brilliantly illustrated by a passage from Simmel's discussion of secrecy:

Every relationship between persons gives rise to a picture of each in the other; and this picture, obviously, interacts with the actual relation. The relation constitutes the condition under which the conception, that each has of the other, takes this or that shape and has its truth legitimated. On the other hand, the real interaction between the individuals is based upon the pictures which they acquire of one another. Here we have one of the deep-lying circuits of intellectual life, where an element presupposes a second element which yet, in turn, presupposes the first. . . . Both are inextricably interwoven. In their alternation within sociological interaction, they reveal interaction as one of the points where being and conceiving make their mysterious unity empirically felt. [Simmel 1950, p. 309] *

The "pictures" are not objective and complete. Individuals in their interaction have skewed and partial ideas of the other that are laden with illusion and ignorance as a precondition of the association. The formulated and standardized relationship, commonly a cultural one, between individuals is, then, a synthetic product of interplay between the mind and the reality of activity. The representation of the relationship is isomorphic with neither mind nor reality, but serves to bring their discordances together.

To Simmel the totality of social life is encompassed in this interaction, and it pits man against the cultures that he creates. Simmel starts from a conception of the nature of man as a set of potentialities, rather than as a fixed group of characteristics. In a passage remarkably resonant of Freud, Simmel writes that human nature is:

. . . that into which the psyche can develop at all; [it] already lies in any given state as something that urges on; it is etched into the psyche as with invisible lines; despite the fact that in regard to its content it is often unclear and realized only fragmentarily, it still constitutes a positive directedness." [quoted in Weingartner 1962, p. 74]

* Reprinted with permission of The Macmillan Company from *The Sociology of Georg Simmel* by Georg Simmel. © 1950 by The Free Press.

The ideal direction of the life process is toward the unfolding of these individual possibilities to produce a unitary personality, a wholeness that integrates and thereby actualizes the various "invisible lines." But, in a theme that Simmel develops in his essay "On the Concept and the Tragedy of Culture" (Simmel 1968, pp. 27–46), he concludes that the products of the psyche, crystallized in culture, defeat the very processes of creative self-realization that gave rise to them.

In order for the actualization of man's nature to occur, it must be transformed and given substance through the incorporation of the objects of the external world. Simmel uses Hegel's term "objective spirit" to denote these external objects, but anthropologists would call them "culture." Human potential is thus, in part, a capacity for partaking in cultural activity. The objects of culture, being made by humans, are assimilable by man, but they are nonetheless alien to him. There are a number of reasons for this. First, they were made by other men, in other times, and they reflect other subjectivities, a separation that is made greater by the fact that so much of culture is the product of multiplicities of people. Individuals assimilate culture, but the objects that become theirs do not contribute to their self-realization because they pertained to the actualization of others. Secondly, since there is much more in culture than can be incorporated by any one person, the realm of culture becomes oppressive, incomprehensible, and estranged. In a passage that is an even better epitaph for our own time than for his, Simmel wrote:

Thus, the typically problematic situation of modern man comes into being: his sense of being surrounded by an innumerable number of cultural elements which are neither meaningless to him nor, in the final analysis, meaningful. In their mass they depress him, since he is not capable of assimilating them all, nor can he simply reject them, since after all, they do belong *potentially* within the sphere of his cultural development. [Simmel 1968, p. 44]

The tragedy of the individual in society is not, however, limited to modern man but is inherent in the human situation: it is truly existential. Simmel states that in the subject-object dualism that constitutes the process of development, "the subject becomes objective and the object becomes subjective" (ibid., p. 31). The essential qualities of objectivity and subjectivity pose a "radical contrast: between subjective life, which is restless but finite in time, and its contents, which, once created, are fixed but timelessly valid" (ibid., p. 27). Simmel's fundamentally dialectical position is made still clearer in his delineation of the essential subject-object contradiction:

. . . the deep estrangement or animosity which exists between the organic and creative products of the soul and its contents and products: the vibrating, restless life of the creative soul, which develops toward the infinite contrasts with its fixed and ideally unchanging product and its uncanny feedback effect, which arrests and indeed rigidifies this liveliness. Frequently it appears as if the creative movement of the soul was dying from its own product. [Ibid., p. 31]

Finally, the mind's alienation from its products is accomplished by the fact that the objects of creativity have a life and career of their own. Culture, external to the mind and objective, has its own requirements, its own manner of integration, and follows historical paths that are determined by what Simmel calls "an immanent logic of development" (ibid., p. 42). He wrote, "The 'fetishism' which Marx assigned to economic commodities represents only a special case of this general fate of contents of culture," a passage that incidentally, accentuates the limited application of dialectics in Marx (ibid.). Man is caught up in the logic of an external and alien world, and he becomes its tool. Instead of culture becoming a part of his personality and its integration, he becomes an epiphenomenon of the culture. Its objectivity and its divisions pull him apart rather than tie him together. The contradiction between the flow and development of life and the forms that it produces is insoluble. The philosopher Rudolph Weingartner summarizes Simmel's sense of tragedy:

Life is more-life—it is a process which pushes on, seeking to follow its own developmental laws. But life is also more-than-life; it is formative and produces objects that are independent of it. For life as process to continue, it requires the aid of form which, in its stability, is the antithesis of process. Hence, life as process stands the risk of being shattered on the surface of the very object it has produced. [Weingartner 1962, p. 83]

Here is Marx's concept of self-alienation and Freud's specter of the destruction of the ego by the group. But by not holding out a smidgen of hope, Simmel retained a realistic outlook toward life and divested the dialectic of its overburden of political rhetoric.

Simmel's dialectic of the self and culture emphasizes the continual concern throughout his writings with the freedom, autonomy, and self-actualization of the individual. This preoccupation arose in part from his personal values, but it was also a central part of his sociology. The theme is found throughout his work, and it is only possible to touch upon a few highlights of it. The conflict between the individual and society does not derive from a view of man as being totally outside society, but is exactly a function of the fact that society becomes embedded in certain ways in the individual to produce the "divided self" (cf. James 1902, Lecture VIII). Simmel wrote,

For man has the capacity to decompose himself into parts and to feel any one of these as his proper self. Yet each part may collide with any other and may struggle for the domination over the individual's actions. This capacity places man, insofar as he feels himself to be a social being, into an often contradictory relation with those among his impulses and interests that are *not* preempted by his social character. In other words, the conflict between society and the individual is continued in the individual himself as the conflict among his component parts. Thus, it seems to me, the basic struggle between society and the individual inheres in the general form of individual life. It does not derive from any single, "anti-social," individual interest. [Simmel 1950, pp. 58–59] *

Man has an inward orientation toward himself as a totality, but he is pulled outward by his necessity to become a part of a collectivity and to serve its requirements. Simmel goes beyond the social psychological implications of his position to see this as a central problem in the evolution of society, which is "an attempt at saving the unity and totality of society from disruption by the autonomy of its parts" (ibid., p. 239). The principal impetus of social life is not toward equilibrium but toward its transformation.

Both the individual life and the social life are precarious and highly temporary compromises; one gets no sense of mutual adjustment and balance of the two spheres from Simmel. The respective interests are irreconcilable, and the forms of social life are transformations of the opposition between them. These forms are fragile and are maintained by a series of mechanisms that underlie interaction and are universal to it. Among the most important of Simmel's insights is the recognition that differentiation and separation are an integral part of "sociating" and relating. Closeness to some requires distance from others and the active assertion of difference and opposition are ways of relating. The preservation of the individual from total self-alienation requires that he reserve a "private sphere." It is also a necessary mode of defense of the self, for knowledge of people bestows power over them. This would seem to be contradicted by the social role of the servant, who has more knowledge of the master than the latter has of him, but it is for this very reason that servants are treated as invisible and nonpersons. Social roles are defined negatively as well as positively by Simmel; they denote the individual by socially significant attri-

* Reprinted with permission of The Macmillan Company from *The Sociology of Georg Simmel* by Georg Simmel. © 1950 by The Free Press.

butes, but they also function to impart only that information necessary to the relationship and no more. This is true even of the marital union, which allows considerable self-revelation but which, concomitantly, defends all the more strongly the residual area of privacy. If Simmel were to have drawn up a Social Contract, it would have contained a principal clause that "allows the right to question to be limited by the right to secrecy" (ibid., p. 329).*

Privacy and reserve do more than defend the ego, for the dialectic delineates the form of social relationships. Life and activity grate against each other and against other life and activity, shaping the culture that enfolds them and makes them communicable. People play roles, and the roles they play are made possible by their restriction to a stage occupied by actors having related parts within a hall occupied by an appropriate audience. The subject has several such parts to play and he plays them in dramas involving casts that overlap somewhat but not completely. And he plays them before different audiences. But if he is to play any of them effectively and credibly, he must divorce each part from the others, acting them out before different audiences and with different casts. This is the dramaturgical model of Erving Goffman and a problem that has been investigated by Robert Merton in his discussion of segregation of roles, but the inspiration derives from Simmel. The dilemma of the individual as a holder of multiple roles requires that they be isolated from each other. The actors behave in a certain way before the audience and in quite another way backstage. The extension of a part of the self automatically entails a withdrawal of the rest.

One way that this differentiation of the self from the collectivity and the various aspects of the self from inappropriate aspects of the collectivity is accomplished is through secrecy and illusion.

* Reprinted with permission of The Macmillan Company from *The Sociology of Georg Simmel* by Georg Simmel. © 1950 by The Free Press.

With an instinct automatically preventing us from doing otherwise, we show nobody the course of our psychic processes in their purely causal reality and—from the standpoints of logic, objectivity, and meaningfulness—complete incoherence and irrationality. Always, we show only a section of them, stylized by selection and arrangement. We simply cannot imagine any interaction, or social relation or society which are *not* based on this teleologically determined non-knowledge of one another. This intrinsic, *a priori*, and (as it were) absolute presupposition includes all relative differences which are familiar to us under the concepts of sincere revelations and mendacious concealments. [Ibid., p. 312] *

What is true of interpersonal relations is also true of the symbolism, or the cultural expression, in which they are conducted. Lie, illusion, and ignorance are essential to society, for ". . . in view of our accidental and defective adaptations to our life conditions, there is no doubt that we preserve and acquire not only so much truth, but also so much ignorance and error, as is appropriate for our practical activities" (ibid., p. 310). The objects of culture are not only overwhelming in number and alien in provenance, they are distortions of the flow of social life.

Groups have the same differentiation requirements, and Simmel emphasizes that the very inclusiveness central to the definition of the group bespeaks its exclusiveness. They are defined by their nonmembership as well as by the rules of membership and by the information that is kept privy to them as well as by that which is passed within their ranks. Individuals come into conflict with groups to preserve their individualities, and this conflict is central to the nature of the group and its potential for change and flexibility. But groups, by coming into conflict with each other, also define and preserve their boundaries, obtain a modicum of internal solidarity, and sometimes combine and transform each other. Group conflict is not necessarily destructive, for only withdrawal is antithetical to society. Rather,

---

* Reprinted with permission of The Macmillan Company from *The Sociology of Georg Simmel* by Georg Simmel. © 1950 by The Free Press.

conflict is a necessary counterpart of positive sociation, a pervasive dualism that Simmel found in human nature and in the sociology of collectivities:

This same dualism also causes sociological relationships to be determined in a twofold manner. Concord, harmony, co-efficacy, which are unquestionably held to be socializing forces, must nevertheless be interspersed with distance, competition, repulsion, in order to yield the actual configuration of society. The solid, organizational forms which seem to constitute or create society, must constantly be disturbed, disbalanced, gnawed at by individualistic, irregular forces, in order to gain their vital reaction and development through submission and resistance. [Ibid., p. 315] *

Simmel's formal sociology distinguishes "form from the heterogeneity of content, and purpose from the variety of interests—be they material or ideal—which actuate human beings" (Coser 1965, p. 8). It was in this sense that he was a "formalist" (a "dirty" word in contemporary sociology), but he never divorced form from content. Indeed, his adherence to dialectics provided Simmel with the method by which he continually saw form and content as joining synthetically. Durkheim attacked Simmel's formal sociology as being "philosophical variations on certain aspects of social life" (in Coser 1965, p. 49), but Coser defends him from the charge of being a trafficker in abstractions: ". . . Simmel is often misunderstood: he was not asserting that forms have a separate and distinct existence, but that they inhere in content and have no separate reality. Simmel was far from a Platonic view of essences" (ibid., p. 8). Indicative of the basic miscomprehension of Simmel's theory, Pitrim Sorokin wrote in 1928; "Simmel himself has shown that even such a 'content-condition' as the number of members of a group decidedly influences the 'form of the group' " (ibid., pp. 146–147). Sorokin is here referring to Simmel's discussion of the

* Reprinted with permission of The Macmillan Company from *The Sociology of Georg Simmel* by Georg Simmel. © 1950 by The Free Press.

differences between the relationships of two parties as opposed to groups having three, the celebrated essay on the dyad versus the triad, which has very little to do with what Simmel meant by content. In fact, if we take content to mean the cultural mode of expression and distinctiveness, as opposed to the structural, then the problem of numbers, which is pancultural, can hardly refer to content. Rather it refers to certain formal, structural problems that underlie cultural variation and that should constitute the core of the problem of action structures as well as the basis of cross-cultural comparison.

Simmel was not given to simplistic formulations by which quantity passes into quality (Simmel 1950, pp. 115–17), and his essay on numbers concerned itself with the radical structural (or formal) changes that occur when a shift is made from two-part to three-part (or more) interaction systems. Dyads are symmetrical and depend upon pure reciprocity. Triads, by the introduction of a third element, automatically become asymmetrical and hierarchical as "each one operates as an intermediary between the other two, exhibiting the twofold function of such an organ, which is to unite and to separate" (ibid., p. 135). In place of the completeness of the relation of the two, each pair within the triad has an incomplete relationship that can only be filled by the third. Reciprocity exists between the three, or more, elements, but it is indirect.

Simmel said in another way and with reference to other data (or just his own life experience) what Lévi-Strauss was to state decades later in his *Les Structures élémentaires de la Parenté*. In the latter work, the author distinguished between the "restricted exchange" of women that goes on between moiety pairs and the "generalized exchange" that takes place between three or more kin groups having an asymmetrical marriage rule (i.e., marriage to the mother's brother's daughter, as opposed to the father's sister's daughter, or vice-versa). Lévi-Strauss's models of the two types of exchange gave direct reciprocity, egalitarianism, and relational closure as the criteria of restricted exchange, and indirect reciprocity, hierarchy, and relational openness as the qualities of generalized exchange.

It is interesting, in light of the review in Chapter 3 of Lévi-Strauss on "conscious models" that he found consciously formulated dyads overlaying unconscious triads and concluded that perhaps there were no purely dyadic forms in society, although such simple binary oppositions are common in the human conceptual apparatus. We might say the same for Simmel's dyads, for his choices of marriage and friendship as type cases cannot be said to illustrate the total isolation of a pair. The very essence of marriage, following Lévi-Strauss, is that it goes beyond simple mating by the introduction of a third party—the society and its surrogates. Dyadic relations also have audiences that guarantee the validity of the performance, and, even within the greatest possible seclusiveness, some third party in the form of a reference group constricts the freedom and pure reciprocity of the interaction. It makes a difference whether the third party is concrete and explicit or whether it is implicit and outside the immediate arena of interaction, but dyads always hint at a triad. Perhaps this is necessary, as all simple oppositions may well be just what are apparent and obvious, their binary character having already been resolved into an order at once more general and higher, but hidden and less "empirical."

Simmel's empiricism, or rather his lack of it, was a common theme in the early critical commentary of his work. It is interesting, then, to note that while this book was being written a young linguist, Susan Bean, showed me a paper that she had written that explained the differences between the intimate usage of the singular form of the second-person pronoun as opposed to the formality of the plural second-person pronoun (*tu* versus *vous*) by reference to Simmel's theory of dyads and triads (Bean 1970). Her paper embodied the lucidity of Simmel and the empiricism of structural linguistics in a small gem of analysis, but it was hardly the first empirical research stimulated by Simmel. One could indeed compile a very respectable bibliography of Simmelian data analysis, and the briefest inspection of this would reveal the products to be just as "hard-headed" as anything written from the functionalist position.

My own interest in Simmel derives completely from my attempts to understand bodies of ethnographic data. His ideas on conflict illuminated my own efforts in analyzing Mundurucú warfare (Murphy 1957), but I really discovered Simmel, and the relevance of dialectics to ahistorical problems, as a consequence of fieldwork among the Tuareg of Saharan Africa. The Tuareg present a number of structural anomalies that do not yield to ordinary functional analysis and that are accompanied by some rather exotic cultural forms. The most notable of these is the custom whereby the Tuareg woman, unlike women in some Moslem societies, go unveiled and unsecluded, yet the men wear veils which cover the face from the bridge of the nose to below the chin.[1]

The ethnography of Tuareg veiling is intriguing. It accomplishes much more than mere protection from dust and sand or a way of humidifying the hot, dry air of the Sahara, although it is obviously useful in this regard, for it is employed differentially and expressively and serves as a mode of "silent language." Not all males wear the veil. Boys below the age of seventeen or eighteen go about with their faces exposed at all times, and the few men who have made the *hajj* to Mecca go unveiled. The Tuareg say, in effect, that the boys are too unimportant to use the veil, and the *hajji* is too important. Those who have not yet become full social persons and those who have transcended their status as social personages through becoming sacred are both excused from the obligation to wear the veil. There is, then, something special about mundane adult social status among the Tuareg.

The key to understanding the veil is contained in the Tuareg's

[1] A full analysis of this practice has been presented in an article entitled "Social Distance and the Veil" (Murphy 1964).

consciously expressed attitude toward it. They say that they would be ashamed to be seen uncovered and confess to feelings of exposure and vulnerability when unveiled before their own people. It has been compared to being seen in public with one's genitalia exposed. An unveiled man is ludicrous, without demeanor and deprived of status. But these sentiments apply only to Tuareg audiences, and the properly veiled man would quite commonly lower his veil when only in my presence. There are other, more important, situational and status differences in the use of the veil. Slaves ordinarily wear the veil in a lowered position, its upper edge passing across the end of the nose or just below it. Nobles and vassals usually raise their veils to about the middle of the nose, but here there are some interesting variations. In any sort of asymmetrical relationship between two men, the person occupying the upper position will maintain his veil in his customary intermediate position, but the low-status holder will raise his veil until it leaves only a slit for vision. Thus, a man will raise his veil quite high when confronting a chief, but will raise it to the maximum extent when in the presence of his father-in-law or mother-in-law.

Tuareg veils, then, are means of maintaining symbolic reserve, of separating while relating, in Simmel's sense. They operate to shield the individual from the perils of interaction through covering a major part of the expressive and communicative zones, and they thus defend the "inner sphere." The special attention given to veil decorum among the Tuareg with senior in-laws bespeaks its use as a social distance-setting device, but we must additionally ask why such symbolism must be extended to all social relationships. I find that the explanation lies in certain structural features of Tuareg society. Despite an openly expressed preference for marriage with the mother's brother's daughter, the Tuareg are preferentially endogamic. Actual marriages include all categories of cousin, first cousins and more extended ones, and unions are sought within the tribal section, in general. This results in a cross-cutting of ties of consanguinity and affinity that is rather different from the situation in other societies that allow or encourage marriage with relatives. In many of the latter, cross-cousin marriage (i.e., with the mother's brother's daughter or the father's sister's daughter or either) coupled with a rule of unilineal descent, or a tendency toward one, sorts out the kin group into which one is born and holds membership from those kinsmen whom one may marry. Even if no such neat division is made, the rule that prohibits parallel cousin (father's brother's or mother's sister's daughter) marriage minimally segregates out the "we," whom one may not marry, from the "they," who are eligible partners. The absence of such a division among the Tuareg results in a very extensive overlap of bonds of descent, or blood, from those of alliance, or marriage. All Tuareg social relationships tend to be ambivalent, certainly more ambivalent than in most societies, and there is a lack of the neat dichotomization of the commitments that one has toward his fellows in exogamic societies.

Social life is indeed a series of contradictions, but the contradictions of Tuareg society are deeper than most. The resolution for the individual is a withdrawal of the self, and the culture provides the means for this. But the withdrawal is not complete by any means. The Tuareg are sociable folk, gregarious, outgoing, and full of humor. They are tender in love, expressive in music, and thoroughly amiable, except when they are killing their enemies. They are able to be like this because they wear veils. The veils hide symbolically significant portions of the self while allowing the rest of the person to be engaged. This is a phenomenon that is not restricted to the Tuareg. Simmel comments on the "de-personalization" that is achieved by masking that allows the masked to carry out acts ordinarily forbidden (Simmel 1950, p. 374). Masking is a common practice during festivities, especially those connected with behavior normally considered licentious. This is true of various kinds of saturnalia, and its recent occurrence in England, when a prominent personality appeared nude but masked at a dinner party, was given considerable notoriety.

Simmel's insights were based on the kind of data available to a turn-of-the-century German philosopher, but they are remarkably applicable to societies that he had no knowledge of. He wrote:

The man of nature [primitive man] with his undifferentiated, sensuous conception, cannot imagine a more perfect separateness, such as he wants to emphasize, than for those who wish it and are entitled to it to *hide* themselves, to make themselves invisible. This is the crudest and, externally, most radical manner of concealment: not only a particular act of man, but all of man at once, is concealed—the group does not do something secret, but the totality of its members makes itself into a secret. This form of the secret society is perfectly in line with that primitive stage of mind in which the whole personality is still absorbed in every particular activity, and in which the activity is not yet sufficiently objectified to have any character that the whole personality does not automatically share. [Ibid., p. 364] *

Dismissing Simmel's quaint notions about primitives and allowing for the fact that he is talking about secret societies, the applicability of the passage is clear. He is saying, with Weber, that social relations in primitive society tend to be diffuse, that is, any two people stand toward each other in a variety of different ways. A brother may also be one's work partner, fellowholder of land, residence mate, political ally, and so forth. This "functional diffuseness" is opposed to the "functional specificity" of relationships in societies with an extensive division of labor. The whole person is involved in the contradictions of Tuareg kinship, and the veiling practice, although observed in extreme fashion toward certain persons, carries over into all of one's activities.

A final and noteworthy aspect of veiling is that it is sur-

* Reprinted with permission of The Macmillan Company from *The Sociology of Georg Simmel* by Georg Simmel. © 1950 by The Free Press.

rounded with protocol and punctiliousness: it belongs to the area of etiquette and social ritual. This brings us to Simmel's important essay, "The Negative Character of Collective Behavior" (ibid., pp. 396–401). Simmel argues that "the result of (collective) phenomena is achieved, in several respects, only through negation" (ibid., p. 396). This is a characteristic of larger scale groups, for, to the extent that they unite larger numbers of people and more diverse interests, the norms governing the group must be simpler and less numerous. Simmel states this in the form of a principle:

As the size of the group increases, the common features that fuse its members into a social unity become ever fewer. For this reason (although at first glance it sounds rather paradoxical), a smaller minimum of norms can, at least, hold together a large group more easily than a small one. Qualitatively speaking, the larger the group is, usually the more prohibitive and restrictive the kinds of conduct which it must demand of its participants in order to maintain itself: the positive ties, which connect individual with individual and give the life of the group its real content, must (after all) be given over to these individuals. The variety of persons, interests, events becomes too large to be regulated by a center; the center is left only with a prohibitive function, with the determination of what must not be done under any circumstances, with the restriction of freedom, rather than its direction. [Ibid., pp. 397–398] *

The sparsity and diffuseness of values are thus inadequate to the regulation of the myriad interconnections of social life, and they are recognized and given life only through repression. Nothing results from the observance of the norms, and they are visible only when they are violated.

The applicability of Simmel's ideas to, for example, criminal law are clear. The body politic does not reward a person for not having murdered anybody that day, but the law is swift when he does. But general codes of values and interpretative models of society are another matter. These are commonly not the sub-

* Reprinted by permission of The Macmillan Company from *The Sociology of Georg Simmel* by Georg Simmel. © 1950 by The Free Press.

ject of repressive laws or other social sanctions. How does one violate them? Simmel is unclear on this point, and we return to it in the last chapter, for it is of consummate importance. For the present, we should note that the negativeness of the general leads him to stress the positive quality of the particular norms, which, he says, "hold small groups together, positively give their members character and distinction" (ibid., p. 400). Simmel adds:

On this situation rests the practical utility of social courtesy forms, which are so empty. Even from their most punctilious observance, we must not infer any positive existence of the esteem and devotion they emphasize; but their slightest violation is an unmistakable indication that these feelings do *not* exist. Greeting somebody in the street proves no esteem whatever, but failure to do so, conclusively proves the opposite. The forms of courtesy fail as symbols of positive, inner attitudes, but they are most useful in documenting negative ones, since even the slightest omission can radically and definitely alter our relation to a person. [Ibid., pp. 400–401]

Simmel points to the daily irrelevance of general norms and the corresponding attention that is given to the rituals of conduct. There is a dialectic here, and not a paradox, for what universalizes becomes negative and what particularizes becomes positive, a reversal of Hegel. Performances find their objectivity in nonperformances, and form takes precedence over content. This is reminiscent of Erving Goffman's work on the implicit structures that determine conduct and his emphasis on the rules of etiquette. Goffman's sociology takes small account of systems and of values; his actors are not governed by the norms but thread their way between them. It is the analysis of man as the eternal loner endlessly working his way through scenes and encounters, betraying others but always betraying himself as well. Etiquette is not the froth, but the stuff, of social life, for Goffman writes: "The gestures which we sometimes call empty are perhaps the fullest things of all" (Goffman 1956, p. 497). It is a world in which the insane are "transgressors of the ceremonial order" and the adjusted are simply well-mannered. The general form of social relationships is given positive affirmation in highly particular and meticulously observed rules of conduct, and the outward appearances of social life are a shadow play of its material transactions. This is Simmel's message. In the final analysis, he must be understood not as a Marx but as a Jeremiah—and thus a more authentic hero for our times.

Toward a Sociological Skepticism

We have understood for a long time that actions have consequences that were wholly unintended by the actors. Freud built a science on the principle, and Simmel hinges one of the cornerstones of his sociology on the notion of antiknowledge. The idea is also explicit in Marx's analysis of the labor process and in De Mandeville's *Fable of the Bees,* and we could go far beyond these for other examples. It underlies all of the sociological distinctions between function and purpose, or manifest and latent functions, and it can be argued that it is the principal *raison d'être* of the social sciences; if society followed rational intent, it would be so transparent that sociologists and anthropologists would all be out of jobs. The eventuation of the unpredictable and the unplanned in social life has generally been treated in the social sciences as providential and serendipitous, the net effect being the perpetuation or maintenance of social systems that are not rationally understood by members of the society. The very existence of the concept of "dysfunction" does more to prove than to refute this statement. It is an idea, however, that is instructive only when the facts are abstracted from history. Sociological awareness that history is accidental and adventitious to those experiencing it and orderly only to those who recall it has a significance beyond "latent functions." It is another aspect of the divorcement of image and reality, and an instance of the social process by which ideas and activities work against each other. The gap between purpose and result can perhaps best be understood as the product of a course of action that proceeds from a blemished set of premises regarding a situation and pushes on to an outcome that may be contradictory of these premises, or at least, quite different from them. This is an admittedly skeptical view of the given truths of society, but it is a peek through the looking glass at an inverse world that is hinted at by the study of religion.

We know from Durkheim and our own investigations that participation in communal religious activity promotes social solidarity and reinforces certain values. But the True Believer believes that there is a God, and he goes to church because he loves the God, or is afraid of Hell or both; we may doubt that he is trying to promote social solidarity. Objectively, we can state that the True Believer is misguided—there are in all probability no gods, spirits, heavens, or hells—but that he is doing something socially useful. It really does not make any difference for the analysis whether or not there is a God or a Hell, for collective worship would still have the same consequence for society whether or not these beliefs are delusions. Following Durkheim's discussions in *The Elementary Forms of the Religious Life,* we can conclude that chimerical though the objects of belief may be, the beliefs are *social* realities.

Supposing, however, that we reverse the proposition and look at the matter from the point of view of the Untrue Believer. We proceed by hypothesizing people who consciously and deliberately engage in collective devotion in order to endow their lives with meaning and to assign some absolute values to their activities. They believe that they are furthering the unity of their families and integrating themselves into their communities by church attendance. Conversely, it is felt that persons who do not engage in worship lack commitment to the values of the society, producing no small suspicion as to the validity of their loyalties to family and country. Now, it can be further hypothesized that the Untrue Believers do not take the intricacies of dogma too seriously. They may hold that there is some kind of

God who does not interest himself in human affairs, a First Cause that can thenceforth be forgotten, but they are dubious of the hereafter and incredulous of virgin births and other such wonders. Nonetheless, their activities, whatever their purposes, have the latent function of perpetuating the gods. This is also good Durkheim: "The gods also have need of man; without offerings and sacrifice they would die" (Durkheim 1965, p. 53).

Now this is a bit more than intellectual sport, for the Untrue Believer is very real in modern society, as is the religion of sociability. Yet, do we say that social solidarity is chimerical in substance but real in its contribution to the maintenance of an idea? Underlying this trick of inversion that history has played on us is a possible unity: in each case, the object of the religious activity, God or solidarity, does not exist or cannot be known beyond dispute to exist. Perhaps, then, it makes some difference whether God has an objective existence, for, if this were empirically demonstrable, it is doubtful whether God would be venerated. Both the True Believer and the Untrue Believer pursue will o' the wisps, and this is what lends fervor to their pursuit. If this is the case, we can agree with Lévi-Strauss that the truth of a cultural premise is a vital element in structural analysis (Lévi-Strauss 1963c, p. 11). Granted that we may not establish what is absolute Truth with regard to many of the ultimate questions that man asks, we may do so with regard to his interpretations of society and its ways. For just as man spins fabrications into the cosmos, so also does he into his everyday affairs. His culture equips him with a framework upon which to hang his social life. It comes complete with values, norms of conduct, and models of the social system, but it is a framework that is belied at many critical points by what is really going on. Culture *is* a kind of social reality, of course, but it is not the only level of social reality. Perhaps our consciously held values are so fiercely defended because, like the gods, they are chimerical on the level of the objective reality of social action. The South American myths that recount the mistaking of shadow for substance are an allegory of social life; but the error is also at the root of comedy (cf. Lévi-Strauss 1969b, p. 109).

The thesis that there is a common discontinuity between idea and act is, as we have said, central to the dialectical theory of knowing. It implies that people *re*act to normative systems and that their behavior may be *systematically* noncongruent with the norms. Their ideas of the social world do not correspond with its phenomenology but are part of the phenomenology. The matter goes beyond the purely speculative and believing aspect of mental activity and the fact that people, not being omniscient sociologists, do seemingly irrational things that find their rationality in the social system. It calls into question the objective validity of the operational premises that people have about their own conduct and that of others. It raises the specter that the work of the world often gets done through misunderstandings, dissonant mutual expectations, and false images of the social system. This is implicit in Lévi-Strauss's conception of "conscious models" as falsifications of behavioral reality that mask that reality and thus permit its persistence. It is quite explicit in both Freud and Simmel.

One source of skewing in the conventional perception of the world is that it is teleological, or oriented to canons of relevance that are in themselves part of culture, and it is on this point that a thoroughly naturalistic science of society becomes a dubious enterprise. Alfred Schutz the sociological phenomenologist, found the problems of the physical and social sciences to diverge because of the radical differences in their subject matter (Schutz 1962, pp. 5–6). The natural scientist, he noted, deals with an order of phenomena upon which he bestows meaning and interpretation; that these are not the meanings and interpretations of his subject matter is hardly a question, for the atoms and the molecules do not think. These, then, are unmediated phenomena, whereas those of the social scientist are mediated by virtue of the fact that human events are influenced by the meanings and interpretations bestowed upon their own behavior by the subjects of study. The mental constructs of the human subjects are, of course, within the social scientist's realm, insofar as they are part of a culture, and he commonly erects his own constructs, his own set of meanings and interpretations upon them. In Marvin Harris' terms, the social scientist adopts the "emic" point of view, or the subjective images of social life that are held by his subjects (Harris 1968, pp. 568–604). The result of such procedures is that the social scientist develops what Schutz calls "constructs of the second degree, namely constructs of the constructs made by the actors on the social scene" (Schutz 1962, p. 6). He finds himself attempting to understand these social phenomena by using the very same phenomena as analytic categories.

A more elegant and pithier summary of Schutz's view may be found in Simmel, who writes of man as an object of knowledge that: "No other object of knowledge can reveal or hide itself in the same way, because no other object modifies its behavior in view of the fact that it is recognized" (Simmel 1950, p. 310).

The dialectical questioning of the common-sense categories of experience has an analogue in the phenomenological notion of "multiple realities," of which the common sense world is only one. Schutz suggests that the "naturalistic attitude" characteristic of the latter reality may be maintained only through public consensus as to its validity:

Phenomenology has taught us the concept of phenomenological *epoché,* the suspension of our belief in the reality of the world as a device to overcome the natural attitude by radicalizing the Cartesian method of philosophical doubt. The suggestion may be ventured that man within the naturalistic attitude also uses a specific *epoché,* of course quite another one than the phenomenologist. He does not suspend belief in the outer world and its objects, but on the contrary, he suspends doubt in its existence. What he puts in brackets is the doubt that the world and its objects might be otherwise than it appears to him. We propose to call this *epoché* the *epoché of the natural attitude.* [Schutz 1962, p. 229, italics his]

Whether the concern is with attention to the phenomenological stream or to the otherness of the world of sense-perception, the phenomenologist and the dialectician both stress the conventionality of our images of everyday activity and state that this level of reality is warped, bounded, and incomplete.

The acceptance of the negativeness of the perceived world does not require a metaphysic but it does encourage a critical attitude to the data received from our subjects of study. Verbally expressed norms and values are indeed data, but they should be treated as shadows until they can be empirically demonstrated to be substance. The idealized representations that any society has of itself must be examined at each and every point in terms of the contradictions posed by other representations and by the concrete happenings of social life. Take our own times as an example. It is possible to state that the *ideology* of democracy and freedom is strengthening every year in this country and elsewhere in the world. Populations, or segments of populations, are making demands for autonomy and self-determination that were unmentionable only two or three decades ago, and they are getting at least part of what they want. Despite this fact, government is becoming increasingly omnipotent and omnipresent; it touches upon the citizen's life at points where it never did in the past, exerting its guardianship through a variety of means extending from the latest electronic devices to the powerful fiscal controls of the welfare state. One could easily argue both sides of the question "Are we becoming more democratic?" and be perfectly right, and wrong. But we resolve this antimony by seeing "democracy" as simply another aspect of social control. It derives part of its effect in mass societies because it gives the illusion of participation in the process of governing and thereby derives committedness from the population. Socialism may become a higher form of the same process, for it gives the illusion that the citizen joins in the ownership of the means of production as well as in the decision of the central polity. Through the involvement and co-optation of the citizenry in a process that they are controlled by far more than they control, the citizen is given less a sense of power over than of responsibility for the actions of government. Ambivalent though his attitude may be toward the state, the citizen tends to justify its acts ideologically. In this curious sense, the doctrine of collective responsibility may also result in a fiction of corporate innocence. But our own society provides examples of the thesis of this book that are too blatant and evident, and those from primitive society are, therefore, more intriguing and conclusive.

One of the principal characteristics of structural-functionalist social science is that it lacks this sense for paradox and contradiction and, although analytic in method, is uncritical in spirit. Alvin Gouldner, a sociologist, used the occasion of a review of a book of essays on the sociology of American society, edited by Talcott Parsons, to characterize Establishment Sociology as the purveyor of a myth:

. . . a myth of a progressive society, whose very disturbance is a sign of progress, of the America blessed by George Washington, where democracy goes hand in hand with affluence. It is a myth made persuasive by a number of techniques. One is the technique of calling the partly filled glass of water half-filled, rather than half-empty; where American Blacks are described as one-third middle class, rather than two-thirds miserable. It is a myth consecrated by the strategy of the Great Omission. For in all this there is scarcely anything about war, not an echo of the new revisionist historiography; indeed, the word "imperialism" does not appear in the index, and there is nothing about the relation between democracy, affluence and *war* [Gouldner's italics]. But myths are not merely narrative tales that begin with "Once upon a time" and end with "They lived happily ever after." Most powerfully of all, *myths are incorporated invisibly into the total view of social reality by the entire structure of language and conceptualization* [my italics]. When the bloody struggle to register Blacks in the South becomes the frictionless "extension" of the franchise, a mechanical way of viewing *all* [Gouldner's italics] social change is implicitly communicated. [Gouldner 1968, pp. 248–9] [2]

Underlying the disciplines is an epistemology and a method that begets its own results; the language of the social sciences is directed toward its unproven assumptions. It has often been said that dialectics is a bag of tricks by which one simply restates propositions and data in a different idiom. It may well be, but the same may be said about contemporary positivism.

The negativity of the world of common sense is not a mystical concept but a reminder that our categories are incomplete and one-sided. Facts do not stand out by themselves as things either in nature or in Durkheim's reduction of the phenomenal world to ideal things. Boundedness and determinateness are given by opposition and otherness as well as by intrinsic properties, and the critical attitude is one that examines what constitutes and lies beyond the parameters of any series of events that we wish to treat as a fact. Social systems may be defined as networks of relations between the conceptual entities of society—roles and groups—but social systems are orders of differences between these entities as well. Relatedness always implies a universe of nonrelations, and membership rules are predicated upon rules of exclusion. Contained in every opening outward is a tendency toward closure inward, and in every bond a series of alienations.

[2] Gouldner has developed this critique of contemporary sociology in a book (1970) that was published after this work had been written.

PART
III

Structures

5

Structuralism
and Opposition

Social anthropology has come far from the time when it was considered admissible to rely upon verbal information from one old informant, or even a few. Some of this kind of work was, of course, necessary because of the total disruption of traditional activity or because the ethnographer was in search of esoteric information that was closely guarded by the society. But even in the heyday of plumbing individual minds as the source of social reality, it was understood that informant consensus was elusive and that one man's truth was another's fiction. Not even the wisest old Indian could be accepted as the final arbiter and authority on traditional lore, for it is part of the nature of all societies that there should exist within them alternate and mutually contradictory patterns of ideas. The search for essential and correct culture foundered on the fact that all culture expressed by informants (barring outright deception, which is also factually significant) is correct, just as all language use is considered "proper" by the linguist.

The need for long, systematic, and broad observation as well as questioning was taught to us by Malinowski, but it did not completely originate with him. Alfred Kroeber's classic study of Zuni social organization (Kroeber 1917) drew attention, for example, to the existence of variant uses of kinship terminology

157

in the group. Kroeber had a skeptical attitude toward the sociological utility of the study of kinship nomenclature, as did Malinowski, and liked to annoy his colleagues by saying that people "played" with the systems. This hardly fitted in with the burgeoning functionalism of the time, and several attempts have been made to correlate these alternate usages of kin terms with situational variations in social relationships (cf. Schneider and Homans 1955) as part of the general project of demonstrating the homology of norm and action. What is significant in all this, however, is that the unity of idea and deed was laid open to question so long ago. Even Franz Boas noted that they were commonly out of harmony, as in the following passage: "In general we may observe that actions are more stable than thoughts" (Boas 1928, p. 164). The separability of concept and conduct was also central to W. Robertson Smith's theory that ritual, as action, was prior to belief, as idea, in both time and derivation. Beliefs, to him, were the rationalizations of activities and not merely another aspect of their substance.

The question of the priority of norm versus activity is another form of the idealism versus materialism argument, and it suffers from the same oversimplicity, commonly falling to the level of the question of whether the chicken or the egg came first. But the chicken and the egg have a complementarity that is lacking in the relation of image to act, and I have argued that although ideas are generated by action, they are not merely a reflection of that activity or a restatement of it in symbolic and ideal form. Rather, ideas, including ones that are normative in a society, may deny behavioral reality, they may reinterpret it according to other frameworks of meaning, they may simplify and distort it, or they may be in open and conscious conflict with social action. This does not mean that the normative system is unrelated to conduct, for ideas are the precondition of activity. The very distortions of human images of reality are what make social life possible.

A basic canon of modern social anthropological method has

been that there must be intensive observation of activity in the communities that we study. It is not enough to collect idealized patterns of behavior from the verbal responses of informants, for these ideas must be studied against the setting of ongoing activity. The study of interaction itself has involved quantification of the most elemental sort. There may be a rule of residence that stipulates virilocality in a patrilocal household, but detailed information must also be gathered on where couples actually go after marriage and on the compositions of the households in which they are incorporated. With what frequency do married couples reside in the household of the bridegroom? Are these households really patrilocally composed, or do their memberships indicate past variability? Is the residence choice permanent, or do couples commonly move from their first postmarital location? Is the residence in the actual household of the groom or the bride, or is it simply proximate or in the same community (cf. Carrasco 1963)? Can we determine a range of acceptable modes of residence and an opposed range of unacceptable ones? What is the degree of incorporation of the foreign spouse into the household and community? Is there internal variation in residence depending upon the status of the spouses or their kin? Is there variation contingent upon seniority within a sibling group? This is only a start toward delineating the full scope of inquiry, but it is sufficient to indicate that the increase in empirical detail will lessen the utility of typologies based upon actual choices and situations. Each society tends to approach uniqueness, and it is only through a wealth of behavioral information that the actual workings of the social system can be properly studied.

As our data improved in quality and quantity, it became apparent that the formal, conscious models of society held by its members provided far less than a complete picture of its workings. In 1940, E. E. Evans-Pritchard published his noted study of the Nuer, which described a society having elaborate values for patrilineality. Patrilineages of varying depths of genealogical reckoning form the essential structural elements in Nuer society, and these, in turn, are contained within larger aggregations born of the same principal. According to the Nuer world view, one could draw a social map of their country by superimposing it upon a genealogical grid, for territory and time are also encompassed within the dogma of agnation. But underlying this system of order, the picture of the Nuer that emerges from his masterful description is that of a society in which there is enormous internal movement of people, in groups or as individual families. Settlements are extremely eclectic with regard to kinship, and camps contain considerable numbers of Dinka and other "strangers." Contrary to ideology, the basic and binding ties between people arise from territorial contiguity and coresidence, which entail cooperation in war and economy, and these bonds are translated into the language of kinship. Evans-Pritchard gives instances of the uses of matrifiliation in forging political alliance and of genealogical manipulation as a means for encompassing shifting political fortunes within the seemingly rigid framework of agnatic kinship. He nonetheless sees kinship as the dominant principle:

Kinship values are the strongest sentiments and norms in Nuer society and all social interrelations tend to be expressed in a kinship idiom. Adoption and the assimilation of cognatic to agnatic ties are two ways in which community relations are translated into kinship relations: in which living together forces residential relations into a kinship pattern. A third way is by mythological creation of kinship fictions, and this way is appropriate to relations between dominant lineages and stranger and Dinka groups, living with them in the same tribal segments, which are too large and occupy too distinct a territory for incorporation by either of the other two methods. It is the way in which large pockets of strangers and Dinka are incorporated into the conceptual scheme of a tribe. [Evans-Pritchard 1940, pp. 228–229]

The reader may well question the strength of Nuer kinship values as sentiments, if not as norms, for they seem to be less a guide to action than a misconception of it. The Nuer image of their own society lends a stability and coherence to it that is contradicted by social reality, a discrepancy that does not interfere too much with social life because of the malleability of their ideas. False though the Nuer premise about their social structure may be, it provides them with the metaphorical rationale for their actions. Despite the contradiction between ideology and on-the-ground relationships, the society works and the opposition finds unity in that. Evans-Pritchard's discussion of values and norms corresponds to Edmund Leach's usage of ritual and myth:

The structure which is symbolized in ritual is the system of socially approved "proper" relations between individuals and groups. These relations are not formally recognized at all times. When men are engaged in practical activities in satisfaction of what Malinowski called "the basic needs," the implications of structural relationships may be neglected altogether; a Kachin chief works in his field side by side with his meanest serf. Indeed I am prepared to argue that this neglect of formal structure is essential if ordinary informal social activities are to be pursued at all.
Nevertheless if anarchy is to be avoided, the individuals who make up a society must from time to time be reminded, at least in symbol, of the underlying order that is supposed to guide their social activities. Ritual performances have this function for the participating group as a whole; they momentarily make explicit what is otherwise a fiction. [Leach 1965, pp. 15–16]

Although Leach's usage of ritual and instrumental activity differs somewhat from my own distinction between the cultural topics of norms, values, meaning, and aesthetics on one hand, and the realm of social action on the other, the applicability of his remarks to my thesis is evident. This is hardly fortuitous, for Leach, as a prominent member of the profession but a principal renegade from anthropological orthodoxy, has been a major source of this book. The message of his *Political Systems of Highland Burma* is that people in diverse societies do rather similar and prosaic chores in life but express them in remarkably different ways. To understand their social systems, we must study the practical action of their daily lives as well as the metaphor in which they express it. These are not the same thing on different analytic dimensions but systems in their own right, each of which must be studied. Furthermore, the ritual and the activity systems are not amenable to a neat empirical fit, for at a certain point in the analysis the contradictions between them must be stated and reconciled through the logic of the investigator.

Leach and the early Lévi-Strauss pursued this goal in the face of no small resistance from other social anthropologists, and their contributions will be reviewed in a later section of this book. What has otherwise been noteworthy in anthropology has been the tendency to split the two realms of culture and social interaction into separate areas of investigation. The study of culture has tended in many instances toward a kind of formalism that has borrowed heavily from linguistics in the search for both syntactic and transformational grammars of symbolic domains. The formal analysts attempt to tell us how the natives "think" of kinship terms and firewood, but they never descend to the prosaic level of what the natives do. Social relationships are either assumed to follow from these categorical systems or they are left unspoken. On the other side are the pure interactionists and behaviorists, students of nonverbal activity and discoverers of the regularities latent in mundane speech and motion. The two groups are hardly able to communicate with each other, which would bode ill for the profession but for the fact that most anthropologists are still engaged in quite orthodox functionalism. Hope may also be found in the fact that such meticulous attention is now being given to both conceptual systems and to behavior, but a full social theory depends upon their being united. When this does happen, however, it will be found that they do not fit the way they were supposed to. Finally, I would venture the guess that the disjunction between the studies of norm and activity has come about just because of the fact, generally unnoticed, that the two realms do not reflect each other, as was assumed. This discovery has in turn come about because of the radical improvement in our data. In a very curious way, when empiricism is pushed far enough, it tends to undermine its own naturalistic basis.

Durkheim and Opposition

The ideas of opposition and contradiction are not foreign to the structural-functional tradition, although they were most clearly expressed by its founders and least developed by its perpetuators and custodians. Emile Durkheim's work, to which we now return, is most illustrative because of its resort to a series of binary distinctions and also because his central thesis has a dialectic movement hidden within it.

Durkheim's sociology, we have said, was one of categories rather than actions, and it is this that connects him with the entire European philosophical tradition. The categories are group products, the result of "collective thought," and these collective representations are impressed upon individual minds in the form of such basic concepts as space, time, class, and totality, which, in turn, encompass lesser orders of conceptualization. These too are collective in nature, but they are structured by the basic categories, for: ". . . the function of the categories is to dominate and envelop all the other concepts; they are permanent moulds for the mental life" (Durkheim 1965, p. 488). The categories themselves are neither *a priori* nor the immediate outcome of individual experience but represent the collective experience of the group, according to Durkheim:

A collective representation presents guarantees of objectivity by the fact that it is collective: for it is not without sufficient reason that it has been able to generalize and maintain itself with persistence. If it were out of accord with the nature of things, it would never have been able to acquire an extended and prolonged empire over intellects. At bottom, the confidence inspired by scientific concepts is due to the fact that they can be methodically controlled. But a collective representation is necessarily submitted to a control that is repeated indefinitely; the men who accept it verify it by their own experience. [Ibid., p. 486]

This group experience, in Durkheim's theory, generates basic categories and ideational concepts out of the social order. The process is manifest to Durkheim in the field of religion, where he sees the categories to be communicated to members of society through the medium of rite and belief. Rite and belief, in turn, are symbolic representations of society itself and of its modes of differentiation. Thus, mental category, religion, and social structure refer to the same reality but are expressed in different metalanguages.

Now it is here that Durkheim's theory of knowledge runs into difficulty. Durkheim continually refers to the fact that ongoing reality on the rawest empirical level is a nonrepetitive stream of activity. Orderly perception becomes possible only through the collective representations of the society:

In order to make a law for the impressions of the senses and to substitute a new way of representing reality for them, thought of a new sort had to be founded: this is collective thought. If this alone has had this efficacy, it is because of the fact that to create a world of ideals through which the world of empirical reality would be transfigured, a super-excitation of the intellectual forces was necessary, which is possible only in and through society. [Ibid., p. 270]

But if socially meaningful and communicable constructs of reality depend completely upon the categories of the society, then how can the same mental faculty act as a receptor and critic of these categories? The same question has been raised many times with respect to the origin theory of society contained in Durkheim's work on religion: how can primal man form mental categories out of social categories unless he at least has the capacity and tendency toward classification? Or as Rodney Needham phrases it in the introduction to his translation of Durkheim's and Mauss's *Primitive Classification,* ". . . the social 'model' must itself be perceived to possess the characteristics which make it useful in classifying other things, but this cannot be done without the very categories that Durkheim and Mauss derive from the model" (Durkheim and Mauss 1967, p. xvii).

Durkheim's problem lay in his attempt to formulate a causal explanation that enunciated priorities of both significance and time. This line of reasoning produces the internal contradiction between the mind that derives its rationality from society and the mind that first perceived the rationality in society and continues to reformulate it. It is also responsible for the paradox by which the religious attitude is generated by society and at the same time is responsible for society. Durkheim's attempted answer to these questions can be found in his apotheosis of the collectivity and the assumption that it is collective thought that apprehends the social order and not individual mentality. Individual thought is excited into a "state of effervescence" by an intensification of social life, which occurs primarily in religion, and it is under these altered circumstances that individual mind is transformed into collective mind. Thus, Durkheim's theory of knowledge depends upon a theory of the sentiments, common in the French sociological tradition, which sees group activity as productive of radical alterations of subjective states.[1]

Sentiment and sensual perception are the irreducible and nonsocial elements of the individual life, and these elements are in contradiction with the requirements of society, which call for both conformity and orderly ideation. It is collective thought, in Durkheim's theory, that mediates between the two and trans-

---

[1] Lévi-Strauss (1963b, pp. 69–71) refutes Durkheim's thesis on the human priority of sentiment by deriving sentiments from the ritual attitude.

forms them. Man becomes rational and social, and society becomes ideal—the negativity of each is negated, and the distin-
guishing fact of social life is that it is moral: this is Durkheim's
dialectic.

Durkheim believed that his epistemology effected a compromise between Hume and Kant, for he treated his categories
and concepts as *a priori* to individual experience but rooted
within the collective experience:

The rationalism which is immanent in the sociological theory of
knowledge is thus midway between the classical empiricism and
apriorism. For the first, the categories are purely artificial con-
structions; for the second, on the contrary, they are given by nature; for us, they are in a sense a work of art, but of an art
which imitates nature with a perfection that is capable of increasing unlimitedly. [Durkheim 1965, pp. 31–32 fn.]

The collective consciousness is, paradoxically, both transcendental and part of the natural order. It is characterized by generality and impersonality, but it is forged upon sentiment and
aggregations. Man goes beyond himself through group life,
but the very process of transcending the sentiments transforms
society. This is Durkheim's great effort to synthesize "the contradiction which is realized in man" (ibid., p. 494).

The Elementary Forms of the Religious Life is indeed a departure from the spirit of *The Division of Labor* and *The Rules
of the Sociological Method,* but in the final analysis Durkheim
opted for naturalism and positivism. The *Elementary Forms*
raises a series of oppositions: real and ideal, reality-class, in-
dividual-social, sentiment-impersonality, and sacred-profane.
Durkheim finds the latter to be the elemental discernment of the
collectivity and its constraints, and above all its externality, or
objectivity. Out of it comes the basic attitude of religion, but it
is also fundamental in bestowing upon thought its binary and
oppositional quality. Contrary to Levy-Bruhl, who speculated
that one quality of primitive thought was its propensity to

merge what is contradictory, Durkheim believed that the basic thought processes are the same for all men, although there may be differences of category and concept. He wrote:

Every time that we unite heterogeneous terms by an internal bond, we forcibly identify contraries. Of course the terms we unite are not those which the Australian brings together; we choose them according to different criteria and for different reasons; but the processes by which the mind puts them in connection do not differ essentially. . . .

Thus between the logic of religious thought and that of scientific thought there is no abyss. The two are made up of the same elements, though inequally and differently developed. The special characteristic of the former seems to be its natural taste for immoderate confusions as well as sharp contrasts. It is voluntarily excessive in each direction. When it connects, it confounds; when it distinguishes, it opposes. It knows no shades and measures; it seeks extremes; it consequently employs logical mechanisms with a certain awkwardness, but it ignores none of them. [Ibid., pp. 271–272]

Although Durkheim attributed a kind of dialectical thought to savage and civilized folk alike, he attempted to shun its ultimate conclusions in his own work. To those who would compare his derivation of thought and religion from society to Marx's distinction of substructure and superstructure, he replied that the collective consciousness was not a simple outgrowth of the material conditions of man but a unique synthesis of it, which, once emergent, has a life of its own.

In order that the [collective consciousness] may appear, a synthesis *sui generis* of particular consciousnesses is required. Now this synthesis has the effect of disengaging a whole world of sentiments, ideas and images which, once born, obey laws all their own. They attract each other, repel each other, unite, divide themselves, and multiply, though these combinations are not commanded and necessitated by the conditions of the underlying reality. The life thus brought into being even enjoys so great an independence that it sometimes indulges in manifestations with no purpose or utility of any sort, for the mere pleasure of affirming itself. [Ibid., p. 471]

Durkheim's remarks were made specifically with regard to religion, but he also stated that there is great similarity between the religious representation of a society and the society's ideal conception of itself. It is all the more perplexing, then, to find the following passage:

A society can neither create itself nor recreate itself without at the same time creating an ideal. This creation is not a sort of work of supererogation for it, by which it would complete itself, being already formed; it is the act by which it is periodically made and remade. Therefore when some oppose the ideal society to the real society, like two antagonists which would lead us in opposite directions, they materialize and oppose abstractions. The ideal society is not outside of the real society; it is a part of it. Far from being divided between them as two poles which mutually repel each other, we cannot hold to one without holding to the other. [Ibid., p. 470]

Just as in his treatment of the collective consciousness as both natural and transcendental, Durkheim seems to want it both ways at once. In one passage he says that the collective consciousness follows its own course, and in the other he sees it as continually and isomorphically related to the realities of social existence. Perhaps there is a problem of semantics here, for despite his references to social reality, Durkheim actually looks upon the ideal categories and concepts contained within the collective consciousness as being "real"; what most of us would call real life is transient and ephemeral to him, saved from becoming pure illusion by the imposition of a higher order upon it. It is only by deriving this order from society that Durkheim can regard the collective representations as falling into a natural domain and therefore accessible to the methods of positivistic science. This is manifest in his entire analysis of Australian totemism.

Durkheim never resolved the contradictions inherent in his theories, but part of his greatness must surely rest on the fact that he raised them. He never took proper account of that sector of social life that he terms "the mass of individuals who compose it, the ground which they occupy, the things which they use and the movements which they perform" (ibid., p. 470); and he did not give proper attention (his *Division of Labor* notwithstanding) to the organizational requirements of social action per se. Furthermore, Durkheim probably underestimated the inherent cognitive capacity of the human mind, and he certainly ignored completely the relationship between this capacity and the complexities of the emotional life, which he loosely grouped under the rubric of the "sentiments." This, in turn, led him to underestimate the degree to which man has what he himself recognized as "this aptitude . . . of living outside of reality" (ibid., p. 471). Durkheim's positivism called for the socialized man, the man whose rationality and conceptual equipment are wholly derived from society, for only under these circumstances could the common-sense facts of the normative order be regarded as a reality *sui generis* and as a part of the vast mechanics of nature.

But lurking behind Durkheim's positivism there is an undercurrent of dialectics and the shadow of a doubt. Do the rites and beliefs of religion faithfully record the categories of society and translate them into the dimension of wonder? Or does it transform them in the process of translation, depicting a state of affairs related to the temporal order but reversed? We can agree with Durkheim that the conceptualization of a society is necessary to its social life, but we may ask, as does Lévi-Strauss, whether the concepts are directly, albeit symbolically, representative of that life. Durkheim concludes that the philosophers' perception of the concept of Truth derives from their apprehension of the categories of collective thought in all their universality, impersonality, and absolutism (ibid., p. 485). It will be remembered that Hegel, too, sought to reconcile the gap between mind and reality by equating pure reason with the

Truth of the natural and human world. But where Durkheim regarded the received categories of mind, referred to by both Hegel and Durkheim as "sense-perceptions," as social, natural, and, therefore, relatively true, Hegel's Truths were transformations of these apparent categories. Durkheim indeed attributed such a transformation function to the collective consciousness, but he finally chose to regard it as a template of society.

Radcliffe-Brown and Contrariety

There were two Emile Durkheims. The first was the positivist from whom we have derived so much of our social-science heritage, and the second was the almost-dialectician who, like Marx, charted the relationship between society and states of consciousness, between the collectivity and the individual. The second Durkheim was by far the more controversial, but he was also by far the more brilliant. Durkheim pursued his sociological method to its logical conclusion and, if he ended in puzzlement and incompletion, it was only because he asked ultimate questions. This is perhaps the reason why it is the elder Durkheim (and the younger Marx) who is studied most closely today. Durkheim's ideas on the social nature of time have inspired some of the best of Leach's essays (Leach 1961). And Durkheim's emphasis on the pervasiveness of dualism has had a remarkable renaissance in recent years, as evidenced by the revival of Robert Hertz's essay on right-handedness (Hertz 1960), and the work of Needham (1960), Yalman (1963), and others.

This revival is largely a result of the influence of Lévi-Strauss, whose contribution to dialectical thought in anthropology is more extensively discussed later in this chapter. It was Lévi-Strauss, however, who first told us that there were also two Radcliffe-Browns, something that many people claimed to have known all along but had somehow kept to themselves. In his book, *Totemism* (1963b), which is dedicated to the thesis that totemism [2] is not a thing in itself but rather an exemplification of a way of thinking, Lévi-Strauss had occasion to review the major theories regarding it. That he covers a good deal of social anthropological thought in the process is predictable, for every major theorist has devoted attention to the phenomena of totemism and it has had the curious power of bringing out the underlying premises of their theories; it is in this sense that thinking about totemism is very much like totemism. Lévi-Strauss builds his final argument around two papers by Radcliffe-Brown. The first, "The Sociological Theory of Totemism," was published in 1929 and, according to Lévi-Strauss, was a model of naturalism and social utilitarianism. Radcliffe-Brown took issue with Durkheim's position that animal and plant totems were purely emblematic of the unity of the clan and that their actual designation was arbitrary and a matter of cognitive availability. Radcliffe-Brown concluded that totemism is not a "projection of society into external nature" (Radcliffe-Brown 1952, p. 131), which is Durkheim's view, but is rather the incorporation of nature into society as an integral part of a total universe that is characterized by a moral order. As such, totemism is a special form of the universal processes of religion.

There then remains the problem of why this special form in these societies? Here, Radcliffe-Brown borrows a bit from Boas and a bit from Malinowski, and concludes that totemism is found in societies that have segmentary groups and that rely for their subsistence upon the products of the natural environment. The first condition stipulates the kinds of kinship units associated with totemism by customary anthropological definition; it is thus tautological. The second stipulates that objects in which man has a lasting and critical interest will be used as totems; the objects in this instance are from the subsistence

[2] Totemism refers to the use of animal and plant names as group emblems. In the case of kin groups, it often includes a belief that descent is shared with the totemic species.

realm. Lévi-Strauss summarizes Radcliffe-Brown's first theory to read that "an animal only becomes 'totemic' because it is first of all 'good to eat' " (Lévi-Strauss 1963b, p. 62).

Radcliffe-Brown's 1929 paper on totemism is a splendid example of his continual effort to build up ever higher orders of organic unity that progressively encompass broader ranges of phenomena. Nothing seemed to him fully explicable unless it could be analyzed within the framework of a larger total system. This inevitably pushed him beyond the empirical realm of social action into levels of abstraction that could only be conceived of as essences arranged in logical orders: the entire universe becomes a moral system; there is a principle of "unity of the sibling group" (which is less a statement of actual sibling solidarity than an attempt to present an economical statement of the logic of kinship typology); unilineal descent may be derived from a social law that requires continuing and precise definition of rights over persons and things. There is an awesome gulf between principle and activity that provides a link between Radcliffe-Brown and Lévi-Strauss, although they are opposed in that Radcliffe-Brown always saw the principle as being directly distilled from the data.

Radcliffe-Brown's 1929 paper, by pushing beyond totemism to the general structure of society, went a step further than was indicated by Lévi-Strauss's analysis of it. In expressing his disagreement with Durkheim, Radcliffe-Brown wrote:

The totem, for him, is primarily the means by which the clan recognizes and expresses its unity. But the matter is much more complex than this. The clan is merely a segment of a larger society which also has its solidarity. By its special relation to its totem or totems, the clan recognizes its unity and its individuality. This is simply a special example of the universal process by which solidarity is created and maintained by uniting a number of individuals in a collective relation to the same sacred object or objects. By the fact that each clan has its own totem there is expressed the differentiation and opposition between clan and clan. [Radcliffe-Brown 1952, p. 128]

This statement poses, in a general way, the thesis that Lévi-Strauss terms "Radcliffe-Brown's second theory." The latter is found in Radcliffe-Brown's paper on "The Comparative Method in Social Anthropology" (Radcliffe-Brown 1958, pp. 108–129) in which he turned attention from the earlier problem of "why animals" to that of "why *these* animals?" He found that the totems of pairs of social segments in turn formed logically opposed pairs because of certain contrary features they had vis-à-vis one another. Their contrariety was thus a symbolic expression of the contrariety and distinctiveness of the social groups with which they were associated. Whereas Radcliffe-Brown's first theory stressed the utilitarian interest in the totems, the second placed emphasis on their logical and denotative significance: the totemic animals are "good to think." Animals and humans are not merged but kept apart in totemism; the totems represent differentiation and not unity. As Lévi-Strauss states it in his inimitable oracular language: "it is not the resemblances, but the differences, which resemble each other" (Lévi-Strauss 1963b, p. 77).

Lévi-Strauss believes that the later Radcliffe-Brown attained the "structuralist" (i.e. Lévi-Strauss's anthropology as opposed to Radcliffe-Brown's structural-functionalism) integration of form and content, which, in this instance, is accomplished by viewing the immediate, and opposed, meanings of the respective totems as an inherent part of a contrastive structure. Parenthetically, this union of form and content is also Lévi-Strauss's defense against the charge of formalism.

Radcliffe-Brown dealt with opposition and contrariety in other ethnographic contexts, his thought showing a similar progression toward purely dyadic formulations and ideational polarities. Two papers, "On Joking Relationships" and "A Further Note on Joking Relationships," which were reprinted in his *Structure and Function in Primitive Society* (1952), served as vehicles by which Radcliffe-Brown developed Durkheim's ideas on binary categories. In the first article, Radcliffe-

Brown took the well-known customs of institutionalized familiarity and avoidance, and analyzed their functions within social
systems. He found them both to be specific types of expression
of more general relationships of "alliance," or "consociation,"
between groups or categories of persons who are separated in
certain ways by the social structure but between whom there
exist enduring ties. The lines of structural differentiation that
set aside the groups or persons from one another also produce
basic differences of interest that can serve as points of conflict.
Joking or avoidance are means by which ties can be maintained
in the face of potential conflict, through the imposition of highly
stylized relationships that set people somewhat apart from each
other by a narrowly defined sociability. Radcliffe-Brown distinguishes this kind of relationship from contractual relations
and those "set up by common membership of a political society
which are defined in terms of general obligations, of etiquette,
or morals, or of law" (ibid., p. 104).

Radcliffe-Brown's second paper was a response to Marcel
Griaule's criticism of his first essay. Radcliffe-Browne reaffirmed
the primacy of the comparative method, but, characteristically,
the push toward greater generality inherent in his comparisons
forced him into a more strictly ideational dimension, a path
upon which he was also impelled by Griaule's Gallic preoccupation with mental categories. The four modes of consociation of
the previous paper and the three-part distinction between contract, membership, and alliance are given less prominence, and
in their place we find a basic distinction between bonds of
"friendship" and those of "solidarity." This reduction was actually indicated by the first article, because of his four kinds of
consociation, only blood brotherhood stood out as a truly independent one; certainly, gift exchange, intermarriage, and joking
are commonly found to be part of the same complex of affinal
relations. The second article adds the further structural observation that "friendship" (i.e., alliance, or consociation) ties are
generally the result of the establishment of jural bonds between

individual members of distinct groups: "The relationship may be said to be one that expresses and emphasizes both detachment (as belonging to separated groups) and attachment (through the indirect personal relation)" (ibid., p. 110). There is thus a basic, binary opposition between alliance and solidarity, which finds its best, although not by any means the only, expression in the opposition of ties of blood and marriage. Turning to Griaule's explanation of Dogon-Bozo joking relationships as derivative from their cosmological belief that twinship is the basis of order, Radcliffe-Brown states that both joking relations and Dogon beliefs in the special status of twins are epiphenomena of a more pervasive dualism in human society. This principle can be found in the Dogon differentiation of the masculine and feminine as universal categories, Heraclitean philosophy, and the Chinese concepts of *yin* and *yang*. These oppositions, however, are not detached and eternally separated but are part of a larger unity, and it is in this way that higher order emerges out of division.

Radcliffe-Brown's use of oppositions falls far short of a dialectical view. His opposed entities do not generate each other, they do not cut against each other, they do not clash, nor do they pass into each other in the process of being transformed into something else. They are not necessary to each other except on the level of conceptualization; they just exist as empirical entities within a whole.

Radcliffe-Brown skirts around the question, "Why do they specifically joke and avoid?" Exaggerated familiarity and respect are clearly separating, or distance-setting, forms of behavior, as he suggests, but they hardly exhaust the inventory of possible expressions of detachment. He states with regard to affinal links that it is common to observe avoidance toward a wife's parents and joking toward their siblings because this is congruent with general patterns of respect toward elders and familiarity toward age mates. This, however, tells us only why one pattern is commonly observed toward one group as opposed to the other and leaves one with the impression that the fundamental attitudes toward peer and senior in-law are really much the same. In any event, we still do not know why they joke and avoid except by resort to a functionalism that only takes account of forms and neglects specific content.

I would venture the hypothesis that Radcliffe-Brown is partially right: joking and avoidance are indeed modeled upon the respect and solidarity that one observes toward the co-members of his group of incorporation, but they are actually the inversions of these attitudes. The etiquette that one observes within his own membership group is extended to persons in corresponding generational positions in the group into which he marries; he extends to them, then, the symbols of solidarity. Because of the gross inconsistency of these attitudes with the real situation prevailing, which is one of tension and potential conflict arising from divergence of interests, they acquire a supererogatory character. The ambivalence on the social level impels the original attitude into a caricature of itself; it is an overprotest that ultimately contradicts the original form. What emerges is not familiarity but a highly tentative jocularity that sets up aloofness through seizing upon the negative aspects of the model relationship, itself an ambivalent one. By the same reasoning, respect is transformed into fear of authority and partial withdrawal from a potential threat. Avoidance is less a mode of an extension of the self than a form of protection of it, and of the delicate social relationship with which it is involved. In the beginning, the movement is toward union, but the contradictions inherent in the social situation force an exaggeration of the expression of solidarity and place a wedge of distance between alter and ego. The transformation of the etiquette serves, in its turn, to more neatly define and demarcate the already existent cleavages. It is quite true that in most cases the avoidance or joking comes prepackaged and institutionalized, but the dialectical process sustains the opposition; it also explains its subinstitutional forms, where it is seen only as latent tendency. We can go beyond this to expand the thesis for much of social life. Sociability would thus arise from an inversion of aloneness, and opposition and social distance would follow as a transformation of sociability.

Lévi-Strauss

One of the origins of this book was an article that I wrote in 1963 that attempted to clarify the dialectical, specifically the Hegelian, elements in the work of Claude Lévi-Strauss. I believe that the article was favorably received by some, probably because I took only two pages to state my case, but the general reaction was one of indifference. "Hegel, Schmegel," was the response, "let's get back to this question of Australian eight section systems. . . ." My purpose was to sound the tocsins and shout that something different was being introduced into anthropology, but I mainly succeeded in proving to myself the wonderful capability of the professional mind for absorbing the new into a prior order and context. Surely, if somebody had reported to the Roman authorities that Christ had raised Lazarus from the dead, the only reaction would have been a learned discussion over whether or not to issue him a new birth certificate. Nonetheless, Lévi-Strauss's commitment to the dialectical method is not a conclusion to be inferred from his approach, as had to be done for Durkheim's notion of collective consciousness, but is stated overtly and explicitly throughout his publications [cf. Lévi-Strauss 1963a, 1965].

Lévi-Strauss's work has shown certain shifts in subject matter since the first publication in 1949 of his *Les Structures élémentaires de la Parenté,* but it has maintained a remarkable consistency of method and spirit. The *Structures* took the single, seemingly limited, theme of asymmetrical cross-cousin marriage (preferred union with the mother's brother's daughter *or* the father's sister's daughter, but not indifferently with either) and wove it into a general theory of marriage and of the dialectics of exchange as the basis of social life. It was preeminently concerned with action systems, although it took account of their symbolic representations by the actors, and it celebrated man's transcendence over the natural order by examining the ways in which he expresses the oppositions between culture and nature. It was a sociological treatise in the strictest sense of the word, for it bore upon the fundamental character of social relationships and presented a general theory that would advance the understanding of the particularities of ordinary life as well as of the human situation in the broadest sense.

Within the vast architecture of the *Structures,* however, was a theme that waited to be developed. This is the congruence of the structures of society, language, and thought, a parallelism for which Lévi-Strauss owed much to the writings of the psychologist, Jean Piaget, and the linguist, Roman Jacobson. In his chapter entitled "The Archaic Illusion," Lévi-Strauss turned to the problem of why primitive thinking seems childlike to the outside observer. It had been customary for anthropologists to dismiss this common impression as simple ethnocentrism, whether emanating from Freud or from a missionary, but Lévi-Strauss committed the anthropological heresy of acknowledging it as a truth, albeit a relative one. He added, however, the remarkably acute insight that the civilized person seems to the primitive to behave like a child as well. Following Piaget, Lévi-Strauss stipulates that the categorical content of the child's mind is diverse. The child's thought is differentiated, but it contains a multiplicity of modes of differentiation, and consequently of ways of thinking. These are subjected to a selective process during socialization, which maintains those structures that are homologous with the infrastructures of society and represses those that are not. What we recognize in the primitive, and he in us, are the alternate structures that we all have within us but that we do not use, although our children do. Childhood is emotionally "polymorphous perverse" and intellectually "polymorphous logical."

To illustrate, Lévi-Strauss recounts the fantasy of a four-year-old Egyptian boy who imagined two countries that he called Tana-Gaz and Tana-Pé, the respective homes of his mother and father. To him, Tana-Gaz is a better land than Tana-Pé, which is at times an evil place. Moreover, Tana-Gaz has calm seas that invite swimming, but Tana-Pé's waters are rough and stormy, and one cannot swim there (Lévi-Strauss 1969a, p. 96). Now, this is an Oedipal fantasy, pure and simple, but Lévi-Strauss, without mentioning or refuting this explanation, states that the boy has imagined a moiety that he later repressed because it was contradictory to the structure of urban Egyptian society and, *ipso facto,* fantastic:

The logical requirements and social attitudes expressed in dual organization would have been satisfied normally in an institutional activity conforming approximately to the infantile model. But Johnny grows up in a group which does not use bipolar structures to express antagonisms and reciprocities, except superficially and ephemerally. In it, the model proposed by the infantile mind cannot acquire any instrumental value. Furthermore, in many ways it is contradictory to the selected model, and because of this it must be abandoned and repressed. [Ibid., p. 96]

This raises a critical point. First, the mental structures appropriate to life in a particular society are selected according to their conformity to the social structure, a point that I once made with regard to Freudian symbolism and independently of Lévi-Strauss's theory [3] (Murphy 1959). Second, diverse though these systems may be in the child, they are quite finite. Mental representations are not imposed by and out of the col-

---

[3] In this article, I argued for a common human infantile experience and a pancultural similarity of the reservoir of repressed material from which fantasies, myths, and projective institutions, in general, draw. Cultural differences in the latter could not, therefore, be derived from culturally distinctive and distinctive infantile careers, but from the variant forms of social structure that recall them for expressive use. There is not, therefore, total disparity between Freud's position and that of Lévi-Strauss, despite the former's libido theory and the latter's psychology of the intellect. Rather, they are mirror-images.

lective consciousness of society, as Durkheim would have it, but are pre-existent within the child; the collectivity determines only which ones will be ascendant in individual thought, and it has a limited range from which to choose. Since Lévi-Strauss's later writings clearly indicate that social structures and the structure of thought must be homologous, then mind limits, although it does not determine, the possibilities of social structures.

The members of a society need not be aware of the conformity of their mentality to the social structure any more than they are aware of the grammatical structure to which they adhere—it thus can be said to have an unconscious structure. This can lead the casual reader to assume that Lévi-Strauss is deriving social structures directly from inborn and unconscious mental structures, but the intervention of the social factor saves him from such extreme Kantianism. It introduces other problems, however. It can be asked whether the unused and repressed structures residual from childhood are not also unconscious and do they simply appear as aberrancies, or are they recalled when structural change occurs? And if the latter is the case, then what is the source of this change, for would not this source be an equally potent basis of structure? Lévi-Strauss appears to have struck a curious middle-ground between Hegel's derivation of the world from mind and Marx's derivation of consciousness from the world. Lévi-Strauss's Truth would seem to lie in neither the world nor the mind but in their conjunction. But then, in the final analysis and regardless of the vexing question of priorities, did not Hegel and Marx really arrive at this same conclusion? To Hegel, this was the union of subject and object; to Marx, it was the end of alienation. Marx found Hegel standing on his head and righted him. Perhaps Lévi-Strauss has put them both on their sides.

This poses a major problem in Lévi-Strauss to which we must return after gathering up a few more strands, for in his later writings he further complicates the issue by making it clearer that he is dealing with the structures, and not the products, of thought. The question is further involved with the fact that the *Structures* also elaborated Lévi-Strauss's ideas on the homology of language and social structure, of linguistics and structuralism. Both are concerned with the reduction of their plethora of respective rules to a central few that underlie the explanation of all of them. In another publication, he uses the metaphor of the machine to illustrate his point (Lévi-Strauss 1960, p. 52). The structural-functionalist would describe the structure of the machine through the enumeration and positioning of its various gears and cogs and describe process by their workings; Lévi-Strauss, however, would choose to characterize the structure by giving the mathematical equation for the carefully machined irregularities on its eccentric camshaft. In much the same way, linguistics seeks to formulate for a language a minimal number of rules out of which the entire grammar can be generated, just as his *Structures* sought to generate the elementary kinship systems out of the single factor of harmony and disharmony of the rules of residence and descent.

Lévi-Strauss saw both marriage systems and languages as means of communication and integration, an insight that he found in W. I. Thomas. Both exchange signs—women and words—and both are therefore the media of order. This is evident to him through ethnographic evidence that indicates a common classification in certain societies of immoderate noise and misuse of language with "acts evocative of incest" (Lévi-Strauss 1969a, p. 495). Both, he says, are misuses of signs and are therefore antithetical to structure. There are other similarities between the grammars of language and of mating, but they have a significant difference. Language, in our scientific society, has become profaned and shorn of its "affective, aesthetic and magical implications" (ibid., p. 496). It has become impoverished of value. Women, however, are more than mere signs:

In contrast to words, which have wholly become signs, woman has remained at once a sign and a value. This explains why the relations between the sexes have preserved that affective richness, ardour and mystery which doubtless originally permeated the entire universe of human communications. [Ibid., p. 496]

The language of love is thus a kind of poetry.

The *Structures* stated, without pursuing to their conclusions, some of the basic themes that Lévi-Strauss was to follow in his later writings. The course of his subsequent work showed an increased departure from the study of social relationships in the direction of the analysis of human thought as expressed in cultural symbolism. It would be tangential to our thesis to attempt a review or analysis of the totality of Lévi-Strauss's theory and its sources. It can be noted, however, that Lévi-Strauss was inspired not only by structural linguistics and theories of congruence between language and thought but by the communications theory that emerged in the 1940s under the leadership of Morgenstern, Von Neumann, and Wiener. He visualized an integration of social anthropology with communication theory that would be based upon a common methodology "to deal with objects—signs—which can be subjected to a rigorous study" (Lévi-Strauss 1963a, p. 314). The basis of the study would be the analysis of the consequences of *rules* affecting the communication of the signs and would "have little concern with the nature of the partners (either individuals or groups) whose play is being patterned after these rules" (ibid., p. 298). Social anthropology accomplished the transmutation of people into *persona,* but Levi-Strauss transformed *persona* into signs; from objects of value, they become objects of thought.

From the time of his 1952 article on "Social Structure," from which the two preceding short quotes are taken, Lévi-Strauss's interests have departed from the action realm toward pure culture. This has been most pronounced in the two major projects that he has undertaken since the *Structures,* which deal with totemism and myth, respectively. *Le Totémisme Aujourd'hui* and *La Pensée Sauvage* were both published in 1962, the former serving as an overture to the latter. The two books set out Lévi-Strauss's theory of the structure of human cognitive process, the goal toward which Durkheim and his students had fumbled some fifty years earlier. But where they undertook a "sociology of knowledge," Lévi-Strauss gives an analysis of the means by which the categories of the mind are transmuted into the symbolism of the society—a theory of the "knowledge of sociology," if you will. *Totemism* and *The Savage Mind* can, in turn, be seen as a prelude to a larger project, which Lévi-Strauss first announced in his 1955 article, "The Structural Study of Myth." (Lévi-Strauss 1963a, pp. 206–231) [4] As he later wrote, it takes as its aim nothing less than to prove, through the analysis of mythology, "that there is a kind of logic in tangible qualities, and to demonstrate the operation of the logic and reveal its laws" (Lévi-Strauss 1969b, p. 1). Lévi-Strauss also sought human logic in the language of totemism, but he found myths to be the ultimate vehicle for expressing the categories of mind in that they are man's internal dialogue, said aloud.

There is a continuity in Lévi-Strauss's structuralism that derives from his dialectical method and from his definition of anthropology as a quest for a "better knowledge of objectified thought and its mechanisms" (ibid., p. 13). "Objectified thought" is perhaps as good a summary as can be found of what Durkheim meant by the materialization of the collective consciousness in the collective representations, and Lévi-Strauss thus follows in the Année Sociologique tradition in his attention to the relationship of mental structures to social structures.

One of the more basic differences between Durkheim and Lévi-Strauss, in addition to the latter's systematic use of dialectics, is that Durkheim postulates the essence of man to lie in his sentiments whereas Lévi-Strauss sees it in his thoughts. This brings us back to the very difficult problem of the rela-

---

[4] *The Savage Mind* was also a roundhouse attack on Sartre's *Critique de la Raison Dialectique*. Whatever Lévi-Strauss's reasons for writing the book, however, it fits neatly into the corpus of his work.

tionship between mind, culture, and activity, which we left a short time ago with Lévi-Strauss, Marx, and Hegel all lying sideways. Lévi-Strauss, like Durkheim and Radcliffe-Brown, is not above contradicting himself without noticing it, and it is easy to find passages that seem to prove him to be an idealist. The last sentence of *Totemism,* for example, reads: "If the illusion [totemism] contains a particle of truth, this is not outside us but within us" (Lévi-Strauss 1963b, p. 104). The matter is more complicated, however, for Lévi-Strauss's theory actually has little to do with the power of *ideas,* as such, nor does he purport to tell us what goes on inside men's minds. This is made clear in the introductory pages of *The Raw and the Cooked:* "Mythological analysis has not, and cannot have, as its aim to show how men think. . . . I therefore claim to show, not how men think in myths, but how myths operate in men's minds without their being aware of the fact" (Lévi-Strauss 1969b, p. 12). What he attempts to demonstrate is a homology of structure between myth and mind, and since we cannot literally look into the mind, our only access to it is through its products. If there is an underlying logic, or grammar, through which man exchanges signs, then this logic must also be that of the mind. The ideas embodied in the myths interest him only in the structure of their relations to other ideas in the myths; content has its principal relevance to form. That the structure exists in the first place in the mind does not make this "idealism" in any conventional philosophical sense of the term. Marvin Harris's (1968) usage, "mentalism," is a far more felicitous choice of words, but then "mentalism" in this sense is not the logical opposite of "materialism." In any event, the opposition of materialism and idealism has been clouded by variant meanings can be misleading. It has its chief relevance in the study of man to purely mechanistic theories, phrased in the idiom of causes and effects, which seek to establish temporal priorities of material conditions, as opposed to ideas, and usually tend toward infinite regress. A dialectical theory, even that of Marx, absolutely requires *both matter* (phrased as social relations, simple activity, mode of production, or whatever) *and mind* (whether seen as cognitive process, psychoemotional states, and so forth) in interaction with each other. They are inseparable and their opposition produces the forms of social life, or culture. Phrased appropriately, dialectics negates the opposition between materialism and idealism by making them a part of a new whole. This was supposed to have been the "end of philosophy," but it at least should have been the end of this particular argument.

Lévi-Strauss nonetheless answers to the criticism that he is an idealist and elucidates his method in the process:

Here again I do not mean to suggest that social life, the relations between man and nature, are a projection or even result, of a conceptual game taking place in the mind. . . . If, as I have said, the conceptual scheme governs and defines practices, it is because these, which the ethnologist studies as discrete realities placed in time and space and distinctive in their particular modes of life and forms of civilization, are not to be confused with *praxis* which . . . constitutes the fundamental totality for the science of man. Marxism, if not Marx himself, has too commonly reasoned as though practices followed directly from *praxis*. Without questioning the undoubted primacy of infra-structures, I believe that there is always a mediator between *praxis* and practices, namely the conceptual scheme by the operation of which matter and form, neither with any independent existence, are realized as structures, that is as entities which are both empirical and intelligible. [Lévi-Strauss 1968a, p. 130]

This, like much of Lévi-Strauss's writing, is not self-explanatory; I acknowledge that those who interpret oracles court danger, but the passage begs illumination. Lévi-Strauss is saying that he does not derive culture from mind but from a dialectic that goes on between mind and activity, neither of which is wholly derivative from the other. Marx found the notion of *praxis* to be implicit in Hegel's distinction of "civil society" from "political society," or the organization of the workaday world as opposed to the higher idea of the state and its laws. To Marx,

however, *praxis* became embedded in the idea of the totality of
social activity, especially work and the mode of production. But
this *praxis,* like Hegel's civil society, is already a symbolized,
conceptualized, and communicable world—it has been invaded
by idea. Lévi-Strauss wants to reduce *praxis* to a lower rung,
to sheer matter and content, to raw action. He asks how does
this activity become translated into something that can be conceived and perceived, that has form and delineation, and that
can be employed in the interchanges of social life. The answer
is that it is mind that structures activity, unifying form and content, and yielding ordered, cultural behavior. The latter is what,
I believe, he means by "practices." In real life, of course, form
and content, or mind and *praxis,* are not found apart, but this
is the root of the matter. Neither one can be given priority
because they are a dialectical unity.

The dialectic of *praxis* and mind implies that one is necessary
to the other, if *praxis* is to be human and mind social. The two
should be thought of not as fixed entities, but as possibilities in
search of realization. Both are mutable in Lévi-Strauss's opinion:

I am not disputing that reason develops and transforms itself in
the practical field: man's mode of thought reflects his relations to
the world and to men. But in order for *praxis* to be living thought,
it is necessary first (in a logical and not a historical sense) for
thought to exist: that is to say, its initial conditions must be given
in the form of an objective structure of the psyche and the brain
without which there would be neither *praxis* nor thought. [Ibid., pp.
263–264]

The logical structures, it would seem, are fixed by human neurophysiology, but Lévi-Strauss's previously cited (ibid., pp. 259–
262) remarks on the innate polymorphism of these structures
indicate that the mind also has possibilities. It can be argued
that Lévi-Strauss has not gotten much beyond proving that the
innate structure of the mind is a dialectical one, but the basis
of the theory is at least not a *monistic* "mentalism."

I have said that Lévi-Strauss's theory must be distinguished from a strict idealism, a distinction that becomes more clear when we compare him to Max Weber, who represents another point of deviation from the natural science approach. Weber, starting from the position that the individual is the irreducible element of sociology, asks how does raw behavior become translated into action? His answer is that it is through the bestowal of subjective meaning upon acts that they become "action" and that it is through the involvement of this meaning with the meanings of other actors that "action" becomes "social action." This is very much like Lévi-Strauss's transition of *praxis* to "living thought," for both are ways of stating that man has beaten nature through symbolic behavior. The mind intervenes and transforms activity in Weber's theory but through the imposition of value and idea; it takes the forms of behavior and gives them content. Lévi-Strauss's theory assigns mind the role of formulating behavior through the imposition of its order upon activity; it takes the contents of behavior and gives them form. Meaning is secondary to structure, as the following opaquely suggests:

They [Marx and Freud] have taught us that man has meaning only on the condition that he view himself as meaningful. . . . But it must be added that *this meaning is never the right one:* superstructures are *faulty* acts which have "made it" socially. Hence it is vain to go to historical consciousness for the truest meaning. [Ibid., pp. pp. 253–254, Lévi-Strauss's italics]

Weber tried, unevenly, to erase the Marxian distinction between subjectivity and objectivity of meaning by considering meaning phenomenologically, but Lévi-Strauss attempts to reduce both subjectivity and objectivity (and Marx and Weber) under the general structures of mind. Weber tries to constitute man and Lévi-Strauss tries to dissolve him. The problem posed by the two men is much the same, but they solved it in diametrically opposed fashions. And in "going beyond" Marx, something that very few thinkers smitten by Marx have been able to do, Lévi-Strauss is trying to discover the influences of consciousness upon the infrastructure, without destroying its autonomy.

Our discussion in Chapter 3 of the dialectic of mind and reality, of idea and act, introduced Lévi-Strauss's concepts of conscious and unconscious models, and we pursued the question in this chapter with regard to the fantasy of an Egyptian child. He further writes:

From the point of view of the degree of consciousness, the anthropologist is confronted with two kinds of situations. He may have to construct a model from phenomena the systematic character of which has provoked no awareness on the part of the culture; this is the kind of simpler situation referred to by Boas as providing the easiest ground for anthropological research. Or else the anthropologist will be dealing on the one hand with raw phenomena and on the other with models already constructed by the culture to interpret the former. [Lévi-Strauss 1963a, pp. 281–282]

In the same article, he goes on to discuss "mechanical" and "statistical" models (ibid., pp. 283–289), which he distinguishes as follows: "A model the elements of which are on the same scale as the phenomena will be called a 'mechanical model'; when the elements of the model are on a different scale we shall be dealing with a 'statistical model'" (ibid., p. 283). Upon examination, it becomes clear that the former is another way of saying norms, jural groupings, and all the other conceptual apparatus of the conscious image of the society, whereas the latter is a statistical summary of the "raw phenomena." Neither the mechanical model nor the statistical model corresponds to the "unconscious model," which is in turn homologous with the social structure that Lévi-Strauss seeks. "Social structure," it will be remembered, "cannot be reduced to the ensemble of the social relations to be described in a given society" and "has nothing to do with empirical reality but with models built up after it" (ibid., p. 279).

The relations of these "models" to one another can now be

seen to correspond, on a higher level, to the interplay between mind and *praxis*. It will be recalled that Lévi-Strauss treats the conscious, or informants', models as transformations, in whole or in part, of both the unconscious model and the objective social reality. The informants' models are not totally illusory. They represent the real situation in part, but at certain critical points they are inversions of that reality. The ethnographer's task is to discover these contradictory relations and to perform a countertransformation on them. The level of empirical reality provided by the folk sociology serves as a base line but it must be transcended; the ethnologist goes beyond it, so to speak, to derive another structure that is at once contradictory of the informant's model and capable of explaining the raw behavioral data gathered in the field. The ethnologist's model, i.e., the social structure, is not, however, wholly derived from the latter information, for it must move to a level of generality that is incongruent with statistical reality. One might say that the ethnologist's model, which corresponds to the unconscious model of the society, stands midway between the conscious model held by the members of the society and the data of actual relationships. It explains both, the first by a conceptual transformation and the second by a transmutation of variation into position. Essential to his entire enterprise is the basic contradiction between idea and act, between the mechanical model derived from informants and the statistical model generated out of the actual observation of behavior, the data of encounters. The structures explain both norm and activity by transcending them, but it is impossible to derive the deeper structure without taking both into meticulous account. Structuralism is, therefore, the quintessential dialectical exercise. It dissolves an apparent unity (i.e., of concept and activity) into opposed elements that continually work against each other and it reconstitutes them into a higher unity while, in the process, transforming both elements. Whether this goal is often reached in structural analysis is open to question, but the method offers the promise.

The structure of the mind is revealed in bits and pieces of culture, and the ethnologist works from these "superstructures" back to the hidden structures of thought and society. This is a procedure that was also used by Freud, for both conscious and unconscious portions of the mind have the common characteristic of being inarticulate regarding themselves. The subject, by definition, cannot express directly what is in his unconscious mind, and any attempt to think about one's own thinking induces instant confusion. The mind is known by its products, whether these be psychological tests, dreams, myths, or fantasies. Both Lévi-Strauss and Freud operate on the premise that the human mind is everywhere much the same and that this similarity lies in certain positive characteristics that will leave their impression upon the symbolic order of culture. The latter, however, is not the free and immediate expression of mental process, for the mind of logic and libido alike must seize upon objects and activities of the external natural or social world. Mind does not make the external world, but rather reworks it. Looked at from the point of view of the culture, mind must be accounted for in determining its form. Most anthropologists would agree that, to the extent that nature is nonmalleable, culture must adapt itself to and be shaped by its natural setting. But by the same reasoning, to the extent that mind is autonomous and nonderivative from culture, culture must adapt to and be shaped by mind. Culture need not be said to spring full-blown from mind any more than from its natural environment, but one can find evidences of its compact with mind throughout its structure, although more in some sectors than in others. This, it seems, is what both Freud and Lévi-Strauss are saying.

However much Lévi-Strauss and Freud differ in the significance that they respectively assign to reason and emotion, they agree in their choice of myth as the optimum subject for the study of psychic processes. Myths, for Freud, were collective daydreams, devices for allowing the mind to express, under the protection of the collectivity, the same material, disguised in the same ways, that it expresses individually under the protection of sleep. Lévi-Strauss also sees the analytic value of myth to lie in its seeming spontaneity and its nonutilitarian character. It is exactly because of the free play and inventiveness of the mind in creating and recreating myths that we are able to infer that the infrastructures discovered in myths reveal an unconscious order in the mind. The structure of the mind becomes imprinted on the myth because "when the mind is left to commune with itself and no longer has to come to terms with objects, it is in a sense reduced to imitating itself as object" (Lévi-Strauss 1969b, p. 10).

Myths are not mind, mechanically projected into culture, but the imitation of mind. They take as their subject matter the concrete facts of life and they tell of man's existential dilemmas in symbolic form, but they do it through a code that at the same time expresses the modalities of the mind. The code is found through the analysis of the positioning of the elements (themes, acts, persons, objects) within the myth and of their signification *relative* to each other. The structure is made manifest to Lévi-Strauss, although there are many anthropologists who do not find it so obvious and verifiable, in the redundancy of the sequences of the myth. It is this replication of the order of the myth, which is found in the presentation of antinomies and their resolutions, that supposedly makes the structure of the myth evident to the native listeners as well. In so doing, it makes the myth "good to think" because the structure corresponds to that of the mind.

Lévi-Strauss first announced his mythology project in 1955 in an article entitled "The Structural Study of Myth." Strategically, he chose the Oedipus myth for his first analysis, producing the surprising conclusion that, "The myth has to do with the inability for a culture which holds the belief that mankind is autochthonous, . . . to find a satisfactory transition between this theory and the knowledge that human beings are actually born from the union of man and woman" (Lévi-Strauss 1963a, p. 216). He does this by reducing the myth to a series of unitary signs that can be grouped for homology and juxtaposed in oppositions. From this operation emerges a series of signs bespeaking man's birth from himself, as opposed to other signs in denial of this thesis. The Oedipal story, much as in Freud's interpretation, is an attempt to resolve this contradiction, for Oedipus's union with Jocasta is a project whereby the son also becomes the father. Myths sort out the contradictions and oppositions of the world but they also make an attempt to reunify them and establish continuity.

The mythology venture becomes clearer with the 1958 publication of "La Geste d'Asdiwal" (Lévi-Strauss 1958), which was translated and republished under the editorship of Edmund Leach (1967). In this analysis of a Tsimshian myth, Lévi-Strauss refutes Boas's contention that mythology is a recounting of the culture of a people:

The myth is certainly related to given (empirical) facts, but not as a *re-presentation* of them. The relationship is of a dialectical kind, and the institutions described in the myths can be the very opposite of the real institutions. This will always be the case when the myth is trying to present a negative truth. [Lévi-Strauss 1967, p. 29]

The negativity of myths is illustrated by the fact that the representation of patrilineal descent and matrilocal residence in the myth are actually inversions of Tsimshian norms. From this, Lévi-Strauss feels confident to state:

Mythical speculation about types of residence which are exclusively patrilocal or matrilocal do not therefore have anything to do with the reality of the structure of Tsimshian society, but rather with its inherent possibilities and its latent potentialities. Such speculations, in the last analysis, do not seek to depict what is real, but to justify the shortcomings of reality, since the extreme positions are only *imagined* in order to show that they are *untenable*. This step, which is fitting for mythical thought, implies an admission (but in the veiled language of the myth) that the social facts when thus examined are marred by an insurmountable contradiction which, like the hero of the myth, Tsimshian society cannot understand and prefers to forget. [Ibid., p. 30]

The reality of Tsimshian society is neither the neat matrilocality and patrilineality of the myth nor the equally tidy patrilocality and matrilineality of the normative system. Rather, it is a conflict between the paternal and maternal principles, which the myth appears to balance out by inverting the rules. The implication is clear that the norms are mythic too, which is consistent with Lévi-Strauss's earlier interpretation of conscious models.

In his analyses of the Oedipus and Asdiwal myths, Lévi-Strauss showed a progressive interest with the variant forms of the myths, a preoccupation that culminated in the three volume *Mythologiques* (*Le Cru et le Cuit,* 1964; *Du Miel aux Cendres,* 1966; and *L'Origine des Manières de Table,* 1968b). The organization of these volumes was announced in the conclusion of "La Geste d'Asdiwal":

Thus we arrive at a fundamental property of mythical thought, other examples of which might well be sought elsewhere. When a mythical schema is transmitted from one population to another, and there exist differences of language, social organization or way of life which make the myth difficult to communicate, it begins to become impoverished and confused. But one can find a limiting situation in which instead of being finally obliterated by losing all its outlines, the myth is inverted and regains part of its precision. [Lévi-Strauss 1967, p. 42]

Lévi-Strauss pursues the permutations that take place in myth in *Le Cru et le Cuit,* taking as his geographic area of empirical concern the South American rain forests. The 187 myths considered are from societies that are presumed to be historically interconnected and that live in a world of common objects, an "established semantic environment" (1969b, p. 8). It is this unity that allows myths from different societies to be treated as variants of each other in a process in which "small but numerous communities . . . express their different originalities by manipulating the resources of a dialectical system of contrasts and correlations within the framework of a common conception of the world." [Ibid.]

His method is to start with a single Bororo myth, the "key myth" and to trace it ever outward to others through showing how one inverts the signs of the other, but occasionally falling back on the key myth, or intermediate ones, when the signs used in the latter correspond to those of the myth being analyzed. This allows both his argument and the geographical extent of his investigation to close upon itself. He finds the critical interpretive clues to myths first analyzed in the transformations of later ones. Thus, through a series of shifts of signs, he proceeds to analyze sixty-three myths before finally establishing to his satisfaction that his original key myth refers to the origin of fire, although this was not manifest within it. Indeed, the original Bororo myth is a reversal of this theme, which is found in a series of Gê myths "which view culinary operations as mediatory activities between heaven and earth, life and death, nature and society" (ibid., pp. 64–65). Thus, the title of *The Raw and the Cooked* refers to this recurrent opposition, which is a statement of man's transcendence of nature and the dialectic between the cultural and natural orders expressed in the idiom of cooking, by which natural (raw) products become cultural (cooked) through man's control over fire.

Each myth or each set of myths analyzed contains an internal dialectic of its own. It poses certain signs or elements that stand in opposition to each other, and introduces a third mediating factor. They pose the contradictions of life and then resolve them. The oppositions are not evident at first glance (nor even after prolonged and careful scrutiny, according to Lévi-Strauss's critics), for the signs are only symbolic of underlying oppositions of which they are the denotata. As an example, the second of the Bororo myths that he analyzes contains a passage in which the hero's son changes into a bird and then transforms the father into a *jatoba* tree, in revenge of the hero's murder of the boy's mother. The hero, burdened by his tree form, wanders about the then dry world, creating water at each place where he rests, the *jatoba* tree shrinking in the process. The contents of the myth immediately suggest form to the author, for the son's transformation into a bird becomes symbolic of a celestial status, while the father, rooted to the earth, signifies the terrestrial. The creation of water, where none had existed before, introduces the mediating element between earth and sky and at the same time resolves another disjunction. This was the hero's burial of his slain wife in the earth, contrary to the Bororo custom of disposal of the dead in rivers, which resulted in a breach "between the social world and the supernatural world, between the dead and the living" (ibid., p. 58). The hero, now free of the tree and having become a culture hero, went among the people and gave them adornments; the adornment of the body elevates man above the animal and makes him a social person. Ornamentation can also be said to mediate the opposition between nature and culture.

Myths may be compared to musical scores, the sounds of which have no significance except in their relation to environing sounds, which set them off. So it is with mythology. Lévi-Strauss asserts that he is not concerned with *meaning* in the interpretation of mythology, in the sense in which absolute meanings have been sought by the Jungians and Freudians, or even in the restricted sense of the historically derived meanings of the Dumezil school. The same symbol may have different meanings in different contexts. Vomiting, for example, may represent either a shift from culture to nature or from nature to culture (ibid., p. 135), and structural analysis must examine each element as a sign and not as a value. This purity is not always maintained by Lévi-Strauss, and numerous examples could be adduced of the assignment of absolute value to a sign (e.g., noise equals disjunction). Moreover, in each set of symbols under examination, an initial decision must be made about meaning, whether absolute or subjective to the society, before the other, relative, meanings may be assigned. But, in theory, the orchestration of myths is a dialectical one, and the only moral that they contain is that the realms of mind, culture, and nature are in contradiction with each other and, internally, with themselves:

And if it is now asked to what final meaning these mutually significative meanings are referring—since in the last resort and in their totality they must refer to something—the only reply to emerge from this study is that myths signify the mind that evolves them by making use of the world of which it is itself a part. Thus there is a simultaneous production of myths themselves, by the mind that generates them and, by the myths, of an image of the world which is already inherent in the structure of the mind. [Ibid., p. 341]

The full dimension of Lévi-Strauss's commitment to the study of what Hegel called "objective spirit," the modalities of the mind projected into the world as a special kind of reality, is tellingly revealed in his equation of nature: culture :: continuous: discrete.[5] The latter opposition may be found between noise and language or, on a higher level, between profane discourse and the sacred discourse of song, chant, and myth (ibid., p. 28). At first reading, it would seem that Lévi-Strauss is referring to the imposition of syntax upon sound, whereby it becomes language and cultural. So he is, but this is only one expression of something at a deeper level. This becomes clear in the subsequent analysis of two Bororo myths, which leads, by a path too involved to spell out here, to the conclusion: "It would therefore seem that the two myths, taken together, refer to three domains, each of which was originally continuous, but into which discontinuity had to be introduced *in order that each*

[5] This should be read: the relationship between nature and culture is as the relationship between continuous and discrete.

might be conceptualized" (ibid., p. 52, my italics). The transition from nature to culture is, then, accomplished through the process of objectification, and we are back to Hegel. But this was to be expected, for the opposition of spirit and nature is basic to Hegel, as were those of the universal and the particular, the finite and the infinite, the real and the ideal. Spirit tends toward the universal and is opposed to the external, finite character of the natural world but it seizes upon this finitude to objectify itself and carry out its work, just as it creates finitude and externality out of the impressions of the senses. This is what Lévi-Strauss means when he says that we do not think *about* nature but *with* it and through it.

His mythological trilogy has taken Lévi-Strauss into a world of "superstructure" far removed from human action into a dimension of thought for its own sake, into a pleasure principle of the intellect. But he started off as a student of kinship, and it is on this aspect of Lévi-Strauss that we will conclude our discussion. *The Elementary Structures of Kinship* is certainly the most reviewed, written about, and discussed book in contemporary anthropology. It has also been one of the least read, although the publication of the second French edition and its translation into English should correct this disparity. The book's theme is grand in scope and dazzling in execution, however restricted it may be in subject matter. It shows a capacity for seeing a universe in a sand speck and all of evolution in a moment. Although its publication launched "structuralism," it was its capstone and climax, and the development of the theory may thus be seen as continuous, but reversed. It is for this reason that I discuss it last.

Lévi-Strauss's central problem is the paradox posed by man as an animal and man as an antianimal, the bearer of culture. It asks how he carries out his nature while denying it, how he weaves delicate illusions and fabricates rules that he does not understand but that prevent him from slipping back into a world from which he has alienated himself. It is a vision of man who employs the metaphor of nature, as in myths, and satisfies the imperatives of nature as the means of transcending it and proclaiming his freedom from it. Lévi-Strauss's theme states in the métier of science what has been intuited in art. In his novel *Sexus,* Henry Miller says that the emulation of coitus in fertility rites lifts reproduction out of biological chaos and symbolically presents it as a distinctively human activity that transcends nature (Miller 1965, p. 602). It is through group activity that sex becomes more than sex. The preoccupation with heroic sexual exploits so characteristic of Miller's works has another theme: Human sexuality goes beyond the mere animal act by virtue of its very intensity. Man uses the idiom of nature to express his independence of it.

The point of departure in most kinship studies is the group, the jurally recognized aggregate of people that stands as a unity and carries out many of the workaday activities of ordinary life. Kin groups require marriage as a means of self-perpetuation, and they define orderly procedures for the procurement of marriage partners and the disposition of their own women to other groups. But in the literature of functionalism, marriage is at best another variable, along with descent and residence, that defines the structure of the group. More commonly, marriage is regarded as contingent to these structures and follows from them. Lévi-Strauss does not quite reverse these priorities but dissolves them. Marriage is not just another thing among things related to one another. It stands in total opposition to the ties of incorporation that unite the members of a group, while being at the same time a necessary part of their existence. One might say that marriage is the negativity of kin-group bonds. They are the opposite facets of the same reality, for their mutual definition of each other's existence is a resolution of the antithesis between man and nature.

Underlying marriage is the more general injunction of exogamy, which in turn is based on the institutionalization of the incest taboo. Lévi-Strauss echoes Freud in regarding the incest taboo as the primary rule of social life and its basis, a thesis later made respectable to orthodox sociology by Parsons. Lévi-Strauss hints at an evolutionary reversal in the emergence of the incest taboo. In contrast to the instinctively derived order of the societies of lower forms of life, primate social behavior is remarkably unstructured: "it seems as if the great apes, having broken away from a specific pattern of behavior, were unable to re-establish a norm on any new plane" (Lévi-Strauss 1969a, p. 8). Their mating patterns are only loosely governed by any natural and social order, and range from involution to randomness. "The natural realm recognizes only indivision and appropriation, and their chance admixture," he writes (ibid., p. 490). Sterility and immoderation, which can be anthropomorphized as incest and promiscuity, are the polar extremes of social relationships in nature. The incest taboo mediates these extremities, producing two results. First, the taboo is normative, and therefore cultural, and it is pan-human, and therefore natural. As both a universal rule and the initial form of group intervention and renunciation, it is the *primary rule* in social life from which other rules are derivative. Second, the incest taboo has both negative and positive aspects. By stating the category within which one cannot mate, it implies an opposed category within which one may or should. Thus, the incest prohibition departs from the natural order by denying involution and at the same time denying randomization of mating.

By resolving an opposition in the natural order, the regulation of incest endows sexuality with a cultural nature: "The prohibition of incest is not merely a prohibition . . . because in prohibiting it also orders. Like exogamy, which is its widened social application, the prohibition of incest is a rule of reciprocity" (ibid., p. 51). The renunciation of a woman results in her being offered and, inasmuch as the same logic prevails among others, it converts the renouncer into a potential recipient. The natural act of mating is thereby transformed into the social act of exchange, or "considered from the most general viewpoint, the incest prohibition expresses the transition from the natural fact of consanguinity to the cultural fact of alliance" (ibid., p. 30). The antinomy of culture and nature is mediated in the incest taboo, and their relationship is not one of static opposition but of dialectical unity:

The prohibition of incest is in origin neither purely cultural nor purely natural, nor is it a composite mixture of elements from both nature and culture. It is the fundamental step because of which, by which, but above all in which, the transition from nature to culture is accomplished. In one sense, it belongs to nature, for it is a general condition of culture. Consequently, we should not be surprised that its formal characteristic, universality, has been taken from nature. However, in another sense, it is already culture, exercising and imposing its rule on phenomena which are initially not subject to it. . . .

But this union is neither static nor arbitrary, and as soon as it comes into being, the whole situation is completely changed. Indeed, it is less a union than a transformation or transition. Before it, culture is still non-existent; with it nature's sovereignty over man is ended. The prohibition of incest is where nature transcends itself. It sparks the formation of a new and more complex type of structure and is superimposed upon the simpler structures of physical life through integration, just as these themselves are superimposed upon the simpler structures of animal life. It brings about and is in itself the advent of a new order. [Ibid., pp. 24–25]

Lévi-Strauss's analysis of marriage forms as modes of exchange follows in the tradition of Marcel Mauss. Women and goods travel along the same paths of reciprocal exchange in primitive societies, although in opposite directions, but women are "the supreme gift." George Bernard Shaw's *Man and Superman* conveyed the message that the basic human relationship was between a mother and her son, relegating the husband to the task of providing the sustenance for this pair and, as an afterthought, for himself. Women were the perpetuators of the natural order, which Shaw considered the serious business of life, while men were kept happy with their lot by being given culture as a plaything. Where Shaw saw men as pawns, Lévi-Strauss sees women as objects of exchange, but otherwise they are in fair agreement. Women have the unique status of duality. They are part of culture, indeed, for they have a social value and are the subject of rules, but they are also part of nature in that they give birth to those who exchange them. Marriage, which elevates women from biological stimulant to cultural sign, is society's continual restatement of the evolution of man:

Its [reciprocal exchange] rôle in primitive society is essential because it embraces material objects, social values and women. But while in the case of merchandise this role has progressively diminished in importance in favor of other means of acquisition, as far as women are concerned, reciprocity has on the contrary maintained its fundamental function, on the one hand because women are the most precious possession . . . , but above all because women are not primarily a sign of social value, but a natural stimulant; and the stimulant of the only instinct the satisfaction of which can be deferred, and consequently the only one for which, in the act of exchange, and through the awareness of reciprocity, the transformation from the stimulant to the sign can take place, and, defining by this fundamental process the transformation from nature to culture, assume the character of an institution. [Ibid., pp. 62–63]

The simplest form of reciprocal exchange of women is in cross-cousin marriage. Lévi-Strauss postulates two groups coming together, one of them giving a woman, for a net loss, to the net gain of the other. Lévi-Strauss's logic is involved, but stated in barest terms, the imbalance can only be redressed by returning a daughter of this union to the wife-giving group or one of the wife-receiver's sisters to the wife givers. A father and his sons, by the giving of their sisters or daughters, have the right to receive in turn the sisters or daughters of those men to whom they were given. The marriage of a man is a gain, that of his sister a loss, and brothers and sisters thus stand opposed to each other. The most direct redress is through two bride-seekers exchanging their sisters, which automatically makes their children into cross cousins. If the exchange is to be delayed one generation, the man who gives his sister may take a daughter of her union for his son, and this too is cross-cousin marriage. All the simplest exchanges that seek to reinstate a balance between men who give their women and those who take them thus conform to the equation of cross-cousin marriage. Brothers and sisters, mothers and sons, and fathers and daughters are thus opposed to each other, and this opposition is expressed in the radical transformations of social relationships that occur when one crosses sex lines in tracing kinship: "In a very great number of societies there are consequences, ranging from a mere difference in terminology to a transformation in the whole system of rights and duties, following from the fact that there is or is not a change of sex in passing from the direct line to the collateral line" (ibid., p. 128).

Lévi-Strauss builds upon the elementary oppositions set in motion by exchange to derive the more complex structures with which his book deals, but this would take us far beyond the scope of our study. In its basic forms reciprocity binds people together but it also divides them. Marriage regulation acquires coherence "only in so far as it is incorporated in a certain system of antithetical relationships, the role of which is to establish inclusions by means of exclusions, and vice versa, because this is precisely the one means of establishing reciprocity, which is the reason for the whole undertaking" (ibid., p. 114). Man thinks "of biological relationships as systems of oppositions": wife owners and owned women, women given and women taken, alliance and consanguinity are only some of these binary categories (ibid., p. 136). These oppositions have been thought by some to derive from duality in social organization, the splitting of society into two intermarrying kin groups. Lévi-Strauss, however, reverses the order and sees such groups to arise from opposition and its corollary of exchange. The dialectical process lies at a deeper level of structure than groupings, and

Lévi-Strauss surmises that: ". . . duality, alternation, opposition and symmetry, whether expressed in definite forms or imprecise forms, are not so much matters to be explained, as basic and immediate data of mental and social reality which should be the starting point of any attempt at explanation" (ibid., p. 136). We have returned to thought.

One of the key tenets of all dialectical philosophies is that there is a human psyche that has certain inherent and universal characteristics and that is an active element in man's history and not a mere passive receptor of an external world. Lévi-Strauss, following this tradition, finds three universal mental structures: ". . . the exigency of the rule as a rule, the notion of reciprocity regarded as the most immediate form of integrating the opposition between the self and others; and finally, the synthetic nature of the gift, i.e., that the agreed transfer of a valuable from one individual to another makes these individuals into partners, and adds a new quality to the valuable transferred" (ibid., p. 84). The first of the structures concerns the dialectic of the individual and the society, manifested in the intrusion of the collectivity into mating. This intrusion converts the simple dyadic relationship of mating into the triadic one (the society and its surrogates are the third element) of marriage. The other two are also dialectical in nature. Reciprocity and the gift reunite on a higher order the self-other, or we-they, contradiction. The mind, then, works dialectically. Social structures do not spring full-blown from the mind, for they are far more complex than the mental structures, but they are built upon the latter. It is for this reason that, as Lévi-Strauss reduces his social structures to ever more basic and parsimonious statements, they approach the simplicity of the categories of mind. In this way, social structures in their barest outlines can be seen as homologous with unconscious models.

This brings us once again to a matter that was raised in reference to Freud's view of personality as becoming rather than being. We are at home with Lévi-Strauss's social structures as long as they deal with models of the Kariera system or even long cycle versus short cycle modes of generalized exchange. But it is in his ultimate transformations, at the level of the deeper structural reality toward which he continually and often faultily gropes, that we tend to lose his train of thought. It is at this level that we leave the world of things and positions and enter the dialectical movement, which destroys things and positions. Causality and functionalism—the same thing really— speak in the latter language, and it is in this idiom that social scientists speak. Lévi-Strauss's structuralism attempted, not always successfully, the study of *process and becoming*. It cannot be said that either mind or action had priority in the beginning. The sensuous world was an essential ingredient in objectifying and realizing the dialectical propensities of the mind, and these, in turn, were essential to the formulation and articulation of oppositional social relationships. Both mind and reality operate in a dialectical fashion, each having its own locus and needs, but, in the first place, the elementary kinship structures were set and fixed by their interplay.

Lévi-Strauss's later writings concentrated on "superstructures," the ideational and symbolic realm, and thereby ignored the dynamic of the process, which must remain the interplay of consciousness and activity. It has become a frozen dialectic that, never having had a sense of history, has even lost its sense of movement. His oppositions have been widely criticized for being just that and no more. K. O. L. Burridge writes: "Lévi-Strauss ignores Hegel's insistence that a contrary should be a contradiction, and he leaves out of account whether what is contrary, or a contradiction, in one culture is necessarily so in another" (Burridge 1967, p. 112). He goes on to give an example: " 'Life' and 'Death' are certainly 'contraries.' But in what sense are they necessarily 'contradictions?' By 'contradictions' we normally refer, surely, to goal directed activities, or on-going processes, which effectively and simultaneously negate each other" (ibid.). Considered merely as signs, as Lévi-Strauss does in his later writings, "life" and "death" are antonyms only, but it is impossible to think seriously about life without considering death as an essential part of it. Hegel states his position more clearly himself: ". . . the true view of the matter is that life, as life, involves the germ of death, and that the finite, being radically self-contradictory, involves its own self-suppression" (Hegel 1892, p. 148). To Hegel, the opposed elements do not negate each other in a simple mutual cancellation process but as an essential part of their existence. They pass into each other, and in going beyond their limitations they realize their possibilities. This is an appropriate way to think of life and death, and it is also how Lévi-Strauss thought of the incest taboo in his earlier days, when his structures were social ones.

The study of the structure of signs or mental images independent of human activity leads to sterility. To translate the life-death opposition into a contradiction, we must move *from signs to the work of life*. In the final analysis, symbols cannot be understood only in relation to each other, but as an integral part of social, and sensual, activity. It is a paradox upon a paradox that we rediscovered the dialectic by rejecting the final authority of the single garrulous informant only to end in a theory that requires the mind of just one old Indian.

6

Image
and Activity

The basic problem with empiricism is not whether we trust the
evidence of our senses but whether we accept their transmutation into the constructs of the mind. The total tradition of dialectical thought has been to subject ourselves to self-criticism,
to recognize the experienced world as at least somewhat different from the phenomenal one and to seek toward an understanding of both by the acceptance of the mutual interpenetra-
tion of the realm of thought and the realm of activity. For it
is only by recognizing this embeddedness of the objective in our
subjectivities and the corollary subjective reworking of the
external world that we can find forms of order and process that
underlie both mind and action.

Durkheim, a scion of the European philosophical tradition,
saw clearly that there was a gap between the ebb and flow of
events and our objectification of them, but he suspended the
problem by accepting the objects almost at face value as long
as they were collectively perceived. This basic affirmation of
belief in the reality of the subjectively perceived social universe
has become so basic within our social thought that it is now
largely unspoken. The belief has been coupled with the assumption of a universe whose order is based upon fit and function and of a man who is plastic and social. It is a model of

things put together into a machine. The parts conformed to common sense, but common sense should have also told us that our over-all view of social structures did not conform to the reality of a world of change, conflict, and restless life. It allowed us, however, to get on with our work . . . for a while. But, as among any group of believers, there have been scattered numbers of iconoclasts and an even greater number who have had a lingering doubt that occasionally came to the surface.

The foremost of the modern iconoclasts is, of course, Claude Lévi-Strauss, followed irregularly and uncertainly by the chief of the doubters, Edmund Leach. Leach came to anthropology from a background in hard technology and was further schooled in the equally hard tradition of British anthropology. His work has used the methods of the latter group to arrive at the conclusions of the dialecticians, and the total pattern of his writings represents a drift away from positivism. His direction is vividly illustrated in a recent publication in which he writes of the problem of the relationship between our language and the naturalistic conception of society. He rejects the Durkheimian view of the social universe as reducible to things, and he challenges the common assumption that positive social ties are natural units of study.

Our language presumes that objects in the world are naturally discrete and separate, and that if they are to be brought together into some kind of "system" this can only be done by "linking them together." This is a mode of thought that is strictly consistent with the atomism which has been dominant in English philosophy for at least a century. But there is nothing intrinsically "natural" about this way of perceiving the world; it would correspond more closely to experience if we spoke of objects and entities as becoming separate only when they are torn apart . . . A great deal may flow from this simple inversion of ideas. It may be, for example, that conventional anthropology is at fault in thinking that the central problem of kinship studies is to show "how individuals are linked together by relationships," for such a formulation implies that it is conceivable that individuals should *not* be linked together by relationships. [Leach 1967a, p. 129]

A systematic philosopher would not be satisfied by Leach's phraseology, but the elements of the dialectic are present in the statement. The world of phenomena is continuous, and the human mind, aided and abetted by language, breaks it up into discrete objects. Our choice in considering these objects as the essence of experience is an arbitrary and a false one. We believe in a universe of separate and independent things that become somehow related to each other, but we could just as profitably, perhaps more so, look upon reality as continuous and study the means by which it becomes fragmented.

This is not just a semantic trick on Leach's part. He goes on to demonstrate that the Kachin look upon what we call "social relationships" as social distinctions. Brothers are *distinguished* from each other as "brothers" (ibid., p. 136). Their unity, it would seem, is assumed, and it is their separateness that must be glossed. The Kachin are "theorists" in that they "start off with formal models and work down to the facts of the case," as opposed to the empiricists who reverse the procedure (ibid., p. 125). To state it another way, the "ethnoscience" (the study of native modes of classification) of the Kachin tends to be dialectical and not positive. All that is needed to complete a dialectical world view is the conceptualization of distinctions as contradictions that beg mediation, and Leach's ethnography is replete with appropriate examples. In short, dialectics are immanent in the ethnography and not just in the ethnographer.

Leach's respect for the facts, and his inverse use of them, his adherence to certain aspects of the empirical tradition and his dialectical reasoning, suggest that the impasse of contemporary social anthropology is not insoluble. Heterodox though my presentation has been, I am not calling for the scrapping of a century of the best social-science research that has been done —that is, the literature of social anthropology. What is called for is a reorientation of research to new questions, emergent from new perspectives, and a critical re-examination of past data and theories. As I suggested earlier, the new perspectives (quite old ones, really) were the result of a qualitative and quantitative improvement in data collection, and empiricism in the narrowest sense of meticulous observation is not in question. But we must *think* about the data more. There is a common refrain that Simmel, Freud, Lévi-Strauss, and Goffman were or are quite brilliant fellows, but that they give us no method by which we can follow them and replicate their results. The missing intervening link is *thought*. No science can offer a fixed set of rules that automatically leads to discovery. This is true of the experimental sciences as well, for at every point along the way, from experimental design to writing the results, scientific intuitiveness and imagination are called upon.[1] This is even more valid in the social sciences, in which we study a refractory object that thinks about himself, and about the scientist. But the one characteristic of social anthropology that makes it adaptive to its subject matter, and that also makes it an amiable way of life, is its eclecticism. New advances do not require that the old be thrown out but only that it be modified and reincorporated. This will certainly be the impact of contemporary structuralism upon social science, although structural-functionalism will cease to be its integrating principle.

The Eclectic Dialectic

One of the more interesting conversions to the Lévi-Straussian point of view in recent years has been that of David M. Schneider of the University of Chicago, who started his career as a student of Talcott Parsons and had come to be one of the most influential proponents of structural-functionalism in the United States. Like most such transformations, Schneider's change of mind came as a result of opposition, in this case in the form of a prolonged debate with Rodney Needham, in which Schneider, with George Homans, attacked Lévi-Strauss's kin-

[1] James Watson's engrossing story of the solving of the molecular structure of DNA, recounted in his *The Double Helix,* is a vivid example of the role of creative intelligence in science.

ship theory (Homans and Schneider 1955) and Needham purported to defend it (Needham 1962). That Schneider came to embrace structuralism and Needham was roundly criticized by Lévi-Strauss himself (Lévi-Strauss 1969a, is one of those reversals that Hegel loved.

The first published indication of Schneider's defection to structuralism came in an essay entitled "Some Muddles in the Models" (Schneider 1965). In it, he came down squarely on the side of the "alliance" theorists (i.e., the Lévi-Straussians as opposed to the British functionalists), stipulating a quasimathematical opposition between marriage and descent (ibid., p. 57). Beyond this, Schneider attempted a systematic differentiation of "the segment as a conceptual entity from its concrete counterpart as a group" (ibid., p. 75), which is a first and fatal step in the disarticulation of society as a part of the natural world. In an echo of Lévi-Strauss's increasing involvement in images rather than activities, he concluded on the note that: "Alliance theory as a theory is capable of dealing with the symbol system as a system apart from, yet related to, the network of social relations" (ibid., p. 78).

The latter passage was also a harbinger of Schneider's brilliant book *American Kinship: A Cultural Account* (1968). The work is not a study of the American family but of the ideology of American kinship. As Schneider states, "This book is concerned with the definition of the units and rules, the culture of American kinship; it is not concerned with the patterns of behavior as formulated from systematic observations of each of its actual occurrences" (ibid., p. 6). Norms are norms, he says, whether or not anybody at all follows them as models of action, which is at once the correct Durkheimian position and a note of doubt as to whether the norms are constraints. But the premise also takes Schneider into the realm of pure symbol, studied without reference to action, although he promises to combine the two at a future date. Kinship norms are, however, juxtaposed to another lower level of phenomena, that of the natural order. Schneider had long taken issue with Marion Levy's definition of kinship as determined "by orientation to the facts of biological relatedness and cohabitation" (Levy 1952, p. 203), a formulation that is at once obvious, common sense, and wrong. He reverses Levy to say, "Kinship is *not* a theory about biology; but biology serves to formulate a theory about kinship" (Schneider 1968, p. 115). The secret of kinship is that it resolves a contradiction within the natural order, that between man and nature, by imposing human rationality in the form of law (ibid., p. 109). The norms of kinship are the means by which man transcends nature while remaining within it, for in America the family is considered to be both a natural unit and a moral unit. This echoes Lévi-Strauss's discussion of the family (1956) without the element of its centripetal pull back toward nature and away from society.

Family and kinship, then, go beyond human sexuality. They mediate a basic contradiction within nature, but they set up a series of subcontradictions. Among these are the antitheses between the respective norms of conduct for work and family, which is resolved by friendship, and the opposition of home and place of work, which is mediated by the vacation. These things are said to characterize American kinship, but we assume that with certain substantive substitutions the polarities and mediators would be universally found. The opposition, in this instance of family and work, whether phrased in terms of substance or of code, is an opposition, in Parsons' terms, of affect versus affective neutrality, particularism versus universalism, and diffuseness versus specificity. The essence of the *norms* of kinship stands out in these contrasts, for they are not just a form of solidarity but the *very model* of it in human relationships. There is such a thing as kinship after all, despite the fact that most kinship ties can be found to have economic and political contents. Kinship is love.

Schneider finds diffuse love to be central to the norms depicting sexuality:

They symbolize diffuse, enduring solidarity. They symbolize those kinds of interpersonal relations which human beings as biological beings *must* have if they are to be born and grow up. They symbolize trust, but a special kind of trust which is not contingent and which does not depend on reciprocity. They stand for the fact that birth survives death, and that solidarity *is* enduring. And they stand for the fact that man can create, by his own act and as an act of will, and is not simply an object of nature's mindless mercy. [Schneider 1968, p. 116, italics his]

Thus, by a circuitous route, Schneider has come back to the positive and attributional characteristics of kinship, which are not biological but diffusely social.

The cynical American reading these words about sex and kinship in America will scoff at Schneider's conclusions as being unrealistic and representative of the worst sort of *schmaltz* that Americans disseminate about the family. He will be right, but he would be wrong to criticize the author, for his was a "cultural account," concerned with the contradictions of the symbolic realm. It omits the procrustean and deadly struggle of the sexes, the wrenching of the young from the frantic embrace of the parents, the family as the very seedbed and model for social conflict, competitiveness, and ambivalence. Now this is the very point about the ideology of the family, on one hand, and the conduct and emotions generated within it, on the other. The family is at one and the same time both ideal and real, and it is dependent for its survival upon the inversion of the two. The ideology makes the struggle possible, for the struggle is transformed and life is depicted as whole by the ideology. The ties of the family are indeed enduring and noncontingent, as the norms would have it, but, as a most perceptive sophomore once wrote during an examination, the family is the only social unit whose function is to break up. It must seem to hold together as a model for future families, but it must destroy itself as a condition for the maturation of the young.

Simmel raised two points that can supplement our discussion

of sex and marriage. In the first of these, he notes that the variety of the forms of marriage defy simple typologies and he comes to the surprising conclusion that marriage can best be defined negatively, by what it is not. And what it is not is the *purely* sexual union:

Whatever marriage is, it is always and everywhere more than sexual intercourse. However divergent the directions may be in which marriage transcends sexual intercourse, the fact that it transcends it at all makes marriage what it is. [Simmel 1950, p. 132n]

Marriage is universally concerned with sex, but it is more than sex. This sets up another paradox, for human sexuality, I would maintain, goes beyond simple mating by virtue of its intensity.

It is common to think of animal nature as being oriented toward excess and satiation, as opposed to the moderation and delayed gratification of the human condition. But man, more than any other animal, is concerned with sex season-in and season-out, day-in and day-out. We cannot be sure what goes on inside the heads of animals, as they cannot tell us, but it is most probable that sex is only an immediate and sporadic pre-occupation with them, rather than having the continuous and multiple qualities of immediacy, prospect, and retrospect. The latter is true only of humans, and human sex is further em-bellished with a rich symbolism and a remarkable polymor-phism of expression. Not only do humans think about sex, but they also indulge in it more than, at least, the other primates. The indulgence far transcends the requirements of biological urgency or species perpetuation, making it appropriate to speak of diffuse, intense sexuality as human, and not animal nature. Human sexuality transcends simple sex by being supererogatory; pushed to its limits, sex becomes more than sex. It is something else: the very negation of the animal impulse. That it serves to express solidarity, to temporarily shatter the isolation of the self, would be Schneider's solution to the paradox, but I would venture the guess that it also divides. Balzac characterized sex as "the loneliest act," and Freud commented on the fact that this most intense expression of Eros is immediately followed by the death of the self. More than any other act, sex is a transformation experience, belonging to the extensive category of alterations of identity and state of being that are central to the dialectical movements of individual lives.

The contrast of union and separation brings us to the second of Simmel's comments on marriage. Marriage, as all married people are aware, is at once a very personal and a very public affair. Its celebration ideally takes place at a ceremony, its consummation in closely guarded privacy. Simmel states this in terms of the polarity of the general and the particular that he finds universally expressed in the sexual act:

On the one hand, sexual intercourse is the most intimate and personal process, but on the other hand, it is absolutely general, absorbing the very personality in the service of the species and in the universal organic claim of nature. The psychological secret of this act lies in its double character of being both wholly personal and wholly impersonal. [Ibid., p. 131n]

Sex, then, can be regarded as a particular kind of merging into a more general thesis, in this case the universality of nature. But it is also possible to look upon particular marriages as essential elements of a general division that is both social and natural—the dichotomy of the sexes.

There are three aspects of marriage that are consummately interesting: universality, permanence, and exclusiveness. By the first, I mean that marriage is recognized as a norm in all societies. The father role may be ephemeral among the Nayar, but Nayar girls are, if not in fact, jurally married. And in certain parts of the West Indies, the rate of consensual union may be much higher than that of legal marriage, but marriage is still a very integral part of the culture. It might be said that the people are not just unmarried, they are *non*married, a situation that is defined by the norm. Moreover, no matter how great the cultural differences between societies may be, marriage is cross-culturally understood, and honored, in all. It took a long time before Mexican divorces were respected in the courts of New York State, but there was never any doubt about the validity of Mexican marriages. And every ethnographer who has taken his wife to even the most exotic field situation has found their marriage to be valid and to define a series of his and her statuses.

Even more curious are the expectations of permanence and exclusiveness that are almost universally normative in marriage. Trial marriages indeed exist in some societies, but this state is one of transition. When full marital status is conferred, the partners and the wider society entertain fond hopes that it is a bond until death. This is certainly true in American society, where one out of three marriages ends in divorce, and it is true of my Tuareg informants in Africa, where the divorce rate is much higher. Realists in both American and Tuareg society know that marriages have a high mortality rate and they may express this in doubts about the stability of other people's marriages or, less frequently, their own. But they know that this is contrary to the value system. Exclusiveness of the *right* of sexual access is another norm that is commonly honored only in the breach. This right is defended with varying degrees of vigor in different societies, but even among the most adulterous of the world's peoples, discretion goes hand in hand with sexual valor.

This poses a series of contradictions between action and norm that can be resolved by looking upon marriage as a relation between Man and Woman and not just a contract between a man and a woman (or their kin groups). When a man gets married, he thinks that he is marrying a woman, but a bit of reflection on his altered status reveals that he has entered into a state of antimarriage with all women. By defining a tie to one woman, he has defined a status toward all other women: he is ceremonially separated from them. The union of the particular begets the schism of the general, and marriage turns out to be the means par excellence of sexual opposition. The existence of this opposition, in turn, makes marriage a union of opposites and is one of the bases of the mutual attraction of the sexes and a reason why marriage is so commonly an institutionalized means, following Schneider, for regaining a lost solidarity and unity. And it is perhaps because of this that the institution of marriage has become more important in exactly those societies where alternate means of sexual separation have been lost. We no longer have bull-roarers to sort out the boys from the girls—just weddings.

These variations on a theme by David Schneider may serve to illustrate the push of the dialectic toward uncovering the contradictions of social life and the tendency by which any thesis will, when pressed to its conclusions, transform itself. The direction of the process is toward the more general, toward the underlying transformational structures that we find in Lévi-Strauss. Moving back to a more empirical mood, I would like to recall some ethnological work in which I have been involved that will serve as further illustration. In 1959, Leonard Kasdan and I published an analysis of patrilateral parallel cousin (father's brother's child) marriage among the Arab Bedouin (Murphy and Kasdan 1959). The positive inspiration of the article was, diffusely, Lévi-Strauss, although it drew a negative impetus from Meyer Fortes's essay "The Structure of Unilineal Descent Groups" (1953). In the latter publication, Fortes included the Bedouin within a typology, drawn largely from African material, of patrilineal and exogamic descent groups, which appeared to us as a misplacement because of Bedouin endogamy. The motivation to investigate Bedouin social structure more closely was strengthened by Lévi-Strauss's masterful analysis of cross-cousin marriage, and we proceeded on the assumption that further knowledge could emerge from the study of the negative case.

Stated most summarily, our analysis concluded that the encystment of Arab descent groups through in-marriage allowed massive fission within them. Each small lineage segment was a social world unto itself, related to other groups only through common descent expressed in genealogy and through political confederation and occasional marital alliances. Furthermore, the fact that both one's mother and father came ideally from the same descent group made these groups *de facto* bilateral, an observation that is valid for all endogamy and that was not original to our paper. Our procedure was very similar to that of Lévi-Strauss. We took the informant's conscious model of patrilineality and father's brother's daughter marriage and made a mechanical model of it in which we assumed the marriage preference to be universally observed. It is not, of course, but the correspondence between norm and behavior is nonetheless one of the strongest that one can find in the realm of marriage. In any event, we were interested in the properties of the system, its ultimate tendencies, and this is the way one uses models; they are not the ethnography. The tendency of the mechanical model was to produce *concrete* social groups, as opposed to the cultural constructs, in which people were indeed related to each other quite bilaterally. Practice, then, contradicted ideology.

A number of scholars (cf. Patai 1965) took issue with our paper because of an impression that we were stating the Arabs to be jurally bilateral and not at all patrilineal. After all, if the Arabs think they are patrilineal, then they are patrilineal, went the argument. This failure to distinguish the ideology of kinship from its practical activity is common among anthropologists, even among those who would not give such easy credence, for example, to the political ideologies of complex societies. Moreover, there would seem to be a wide, although unthought and unspoken, agreement among social scientists with Simmel's and Marx's view that complex societies are more "opaque" than simple ones. Although this is probably true and confirmable by empirical research, abundant evidence on hand reveals that there are also massive gaps between ideology and reality in primitive societies. The critique, however, impelled us to re-examine parallel cousin marriage more thoroughly.

Our first paper on parallel cousin marriage only explored the structural consequences of the practice, but the second one (Murphy and Kasdan 1967) sought an understanding of the roots of the custom itself. We found this to lie within the *ideology* of patrilineality, which is of so great a force among the Bedouin that the agnatic units maintain rights of both disposition and access over their women. The father may give his daughter in marriage, but his brother's son has first right to her. This led us to our conclusion:

This brings us finally to a great contradiction within Arab society. The very strength of its patrilineal ideology is consistent with the exercise of so complete a control over the reproductive capacity of women that they are kept within their descent groups. This, by the process of encystment of lineal segments and through the introduction of affinity into the supposedly solidary bonds of incorporation, actually resulted in weakening the corporate nature of the agnatic units. It further tended to blur their boundaries, for the definitional function of exogamy is lacking and the maintenance functions of oppositional alliance to other groups through marriage has been turned on itself. Moreover the ancestry of the mother and father merge after two or more generations. This produces a latent bilateral structure that is the very antithesis of the patrilineal ideology. [Ibid., p. 13]

Patrilineality, then, is a conscious model that does not represent the structure of concrete collectivities and activities, but it is an important part of the process by which the latter structure becomes what it is. This brings us to a point of great importance. *Values may be incongruent with actions, but they are never irrelevant to them.* The ardent pursuit of the ideal has a habit of begetting its own contradiction, according to folk wisdom, and this is good anthropology as well.

Norms, it was said, are both cognitive and motivational, but they are primarily cognitive. Most social theorists agree that norms arise out of interaction and are, somehow, constructs of the action situation. As such, they may be either accurately perceptive or erroneously refractive, but they derive from the interplay of activity and consciousness. If this theorem is accepted, as it has been in this book, then why does not the underlying bilaterality of the Bedouin in time destroy patrilineality? One way of preventing this is through blind spots in the normative system. In the present example, the Bedouin maintain the ideology of patrilineality through the suppression of female names in their genealogies. This artifice eliminates all ties through women beyond the second degree of kinship and ideally represents the descent group as monolithically agnatic. Emrys Peters reports an exception to this practice among the Cyrenaican Bedouin, who follow the pattern of parallel cousin marriage but who also often establish alliances with other lineages by means of mother's brother's daughter marriage (Peters 1960, p. 44). Interestingly, the names of these linking women are maintained in the genealogies. This is so because they are nodes within the structure and also because they come from outside the patrilineage.

Exogamic patrilineal societies have a much easier time abiding women, or at least the memory of them, than do the Arabs. Joan Vincent shows that among the Teso of Uganda some of the most important economic and residential ties between families are established through their women (Vincent 1968). They are formally patrilineal, but the husbands of two sisters often farm together and cooperate in other ways. The reasons for this are perhaps to be found in the situation of social change among these people, whereby agnatic units have been undercut by the Western economy. This leads to the speculation that, when the corporate ties of patrilineality are subject to attrition, the negative side of the descent system is left. The latter can be stated simply: Patrilineal societies are composed of segments that maintain their interstitial ties through women. (Matrilineal ones, of course, are the reverse.) Women are not just "exchanged," as in Lévi-Strauss; they are the connective tissue of the social whole. The male is the significant connective link only *within* patrilineal *segments*. In patrilineal *societies,* the female is the pivotal figure. This little inversion has ramifications that could be profitably explored by ethnographers, preferably female ones, and it was first essayed in an overtly humorous, but covertly serious, paper by the anthropologist Nancy Tanner when she was a graduate student. Taking off on a theme from the Minankabau of Sumatra, she analyzed the role of the woman in patrilineal societies as an infiltrator of other lineages and a subverter of the loyalties of their sons. It was a lovely conspiracy theory, reminiscent of science fiction stories that reveal women to be secret Martians, but an incisive example of the insights to be obtained from a reversal of the obvious. When we treat women as "signs," as does Lévi-Strauss, then we can see them as items being exchanged within a communication system, but when they are treated as active people, they are the substance as well as the source of social life.[2]

Returning to the empirical métier, let us look at the functions of genealogical manipulation among the Tuareg. It will be recalled from Chapter 4 that the Tuareg marry all categories of cousin, but avow a preference for the mother's brother's daughter. Moreover, a majority of my informants claimed that they actually married a cousin of this class. In each case of a verbally

[2] More careful attention to action rather than norm can result in another inversion of Lévi-Strauss. One of the accomplishments of "alliance theory" has been the reduction of ties of "complementary filiation" into an antidescent category. By this logic, the mother's brother and even the mother may be viewed as affines in a patrilineal society. This has resulted in a curious reversal of ethnography, for in almost all societies, the status of "mater" derives immediately from the woman's function as genitress. That is, the woman who bears a child is its legal mother, whether or not she is married. On the other hand, it is almost universally true that the genitor of a child only becomes the "pater" through marriage. Fatherhood is, therefore, a legal fiction, and the father and his kin are the true in-laws. The natural family unit, then, is the mother and her children, which fits well with later Freudian theory.

reported mother's brother's daughter marriage, I went back to the previously collected genealogies to verify the link. Very rarely, I would find that the man had indeed married a first degree cross-cousin, but in most cases, no linking relatives could be found between the informant and his wife. "But we are children of cross-cousins," the informant would commonly reply. This raised a complication, for the genealogies were only about three generations deep, and the connecting links were often missing at the second generation ascending, where one looks for second-cousin ties. When I would tell the informant that I still could not find the relationship, the reply was that he could not remember the names of people dead so long ago and that maybe, after all, he and his wife were children of children of cross-cousins. At this point, the genealogies failed completely. What is happening here is very simple. The genealogies are *teleologically* inadequate for tracing relationships. Once either ethnographer or informant gets beyond first cousins, the links cannot be exactly specified, and any female can be called a mother's brother's daughter, provided that she agrees to accept the term and the elders ratify the relationship. To the young Tuareg, a mother's brother's daughter is a girl of his local group toward whom he is attracted.

This situation is related to a further anomaly presented by the system of kinship nomenclature. The endogamic Tuareg have Iroquois cousin terms; that is, parallel cousins are called by the same term as brother and sister and cross-cousins are designated by different words. This is a contradiction by all standards of structural-functionalism, but it is one that does not bother the Tuareg much. As in many other groups, they often marry girls who stand as "sisters" toward them, but they simply do not call them "sisters." If you ask a Tuareg by what kinship term he calls a relative, he will say: "None. I call him by his name." The terms are not used much, and when they are used it is as a deliberate attempt to evoke an appropriate response. Thus, if a man calls a girl *tububastchi* (my cross-cousin), it is to express a romantic interest in her. And, since the absence of deep genealogies make all collateral relationships beyond the first degree amorphous, he is in a position to call almost any young lady of his group *tububastchi*. Marital alliances among the Tuareg are involuted, but the idiom in which they express them is of a neat and binary kind. The symbolic system divides the social realm into a "we" and "they" that is not so divided in social reality. Or as I stated it in a fuller discussion of Tuareg kinship: "It is an intraverted social system that speaks in the language of extraversion; while perpetuating its own endogamy, it denies it" (Murphy 1967, p. 170). This is the paradox that Lévi-Strauss discovered within the moiety systems of Brazilian Indians that led him to ask: "Why do societies affected by a high degree of endogamy so urgently need to mystify themselves and see themselves as governed by exogamous institutions, classical in form, of whose existence they have no direct knowledge?" (Lévi-Strauss 1963a, p. 131)

One of the first articles written by Clifford Geertz of the Institute for Advanced Study was an analysis of a funeral in Java in which he showed key discontinuities between the social order and the system of ritual symbolism (Geertz 1957). The essay had a dual purpose. First, it served to illustrate to anthropologists the utility of the Parsonian distinction between the cultural and the social; second, it showed that conflict between the two could result from social change. In his Javanese example, the form of the funeral was incongruent with the substance of social relationships because of change in the latter and a lag in the former. Lag phenomena are familiar to anthropologists, of course, but they are also a central element in Marxian theory. One of the principal sources of historical contradictions, according to Marxian commentary, arises from the quantitative changes that take place in infrastructures and their eventual clash with the far less resilient superstructures. The conflict between the two becomes embedded in the class struggle, and one of the hallmarks of the true revolution is the total overthrow of the old ideology. Geertz's article suggests, to the contrary, that the two continually grind away at each other, producing the restless movement that is perennially productive of change. Contradictions constantly arise in all areas of life and are just as steadily neutralized by their merger into something new; *structural* change need not take place in huge quantum leaps as the simplistic dialectic of quantity and quality would have it (cf. Simmel 1950, pp. 115–117). On the other hand, very great contradictions in social systems can exist without creating undue disturbance of the body politic or interference in carrying out the duties of social life. Both the Tuareg and the Arabs have lived for centuries with enormous gaps between ideology and social reality, which are essential elements in their way of life. Or, to state it differently, the dialectical movements in structures are at one and the same time *the* structure and its ultimate undoing.

Later publications by Geertz would seem to agree with this view. In an essay on the relationship between teknonymy and genealogical amnesia (the nonknowledge of one's ancestry) in Bali (Geertz, H. and C. 1964), the Geertzes pursue the same area of structural ignorance that has just been reviewed for the Tuareg and Arabs. Teknonymy, the custom by which persons are alluded to by their relationships to other persons (Johnny's father, etc.), has the function in Bali of reducing knowledge of personal names, thereby making genealogy keeping almost impossible. The knowledge of relationships is largely confined to ties through the living, and people are known and socially placed by reference to the names of their descendants and not by those of their ascendants. This has the further result of a general shortening of relationships: the extension of kinship to persons within one's own village and the weakening of ties to other villages. On the other hand, the aristocracy keep rather extensive genealogies, which serve to project their political connections beyond the village. The differences in use of teknonymy among commoners and gentry, then, are functional both to the

maintenance of village cohesion and to the country-wide ascend-
ancy of the upper class. This leads the authors to a conclusion
that parallels our critical comments on Durkheim's social facts
in Chapter 2. They write, "The acceptance of any particular
set of verbal categories and of the concepts embedded in them
tends to preclude the awareness of alternative classifications; a
way of seeing is also a way of not seeing" (ibid., p. 105). Or
to put it another way, any thesis immediately posits its negative.

Geertz's dialectical themes are even more specific in his remarkable monograph *Agricultural Involution* (1963), which
analyzes the history of Indonesian society as the growth of a
vast set of contradictions without essential structural change, a
process of "involution," which he traces to the colonial agricultural economy. These contradictions are contained, he argues, by enormous elasticity in the system of social action,
allowing the actors to thread their way through the culture
rather than conform to its norms:

> The result was an arabesque pattern of life, both reduced and
> elaborated, both enormously complicated and marvelously simple:
> complicated in the diversity, variability, fragility, fluidity, shallow-
> ness and unreliability of interpersonal ties: simple in the meager
> institutional resources by which such ties were organized. The
> quality of everyday existence in a fully involuted Javanese village
> is comparable to that in the other formless human community, the
> American suburb: a richness of social surfaces and a monotonous
> poverty of social substance. [Ibid., p. 103]

To varying degrees, this is the story of social life as every
ethnographer has experienced it. It is the contrast between the
wonderful imagery of the symbolic world of the primitives and
the scruffy everyday existence of their camps and villages, between the lovely complexities of their kinship systems and the
mundane and ordinary quality of their family lives, between
the mystic domains of magic and ritual and the bed-rock prag-
matism of their secular activities. Every good ethnographer

studies particulars to find universals, and the Geertzes are good ethnographers.

One of the nicer examples of the possibly inverse relationship between idea and act is given in *Tonalá* by May N. Diaz (Diaz 1966). Mrs. Diaz addresses herself to one of the great conundrums of authority: holders of positions of authority are commonly treated with such distance and elevated to so high a position that they are removed from contact with their subjects; how then do they exercise the power that ideally belongs to authority? This is the dilemma of the Ibo kings of Onitsha, who were so sacrosanct that they were virtually secluded, and it is probably true of the Papacy as well. One partial solution to the problem is bureaucracy, which was virtually absent among the Ibo and exists in curious form in the Vatican, but there are also micro-authority systems that permeate social life in which the contradiction consistently acts to undercut and temper power. This is the situation of the family in the town of Tonalá, Mexico. As is well known, one of the strongest values in Latin America is that of *machismo,* the pattern of masculine virility, independence, and authority. This value is scrupulously observed within the family, and the father is considered to be a man of important affairs. His proper place is in the street and its places of male congregation, where he talks of matters of political and economic importance, far removed from the petty problems of the household. Accordingly, he is treated with great reserve and respect by the members of his family, an attitude encouraged by the deferential and subservient mother. The father is not bothered with domestic trifles, and the children are especially enjoined to free the father from their minor worries. When they must approach him as the ultimate source of authority, they do so through the intermediary of the mother, who listens to their problem or request, settles it, and says, "Let me talk to your father about it." She is the intermediary between son and father, but she is also the intermediary between father and son. As the holder of the communication link, the filter and purveyor of information, she controls the family. The father has been elevated so far that he has gone right out through the roof, so to speak. Mrs. Diaz says that the remoteness of the father causes the child to see his power as being without responsibility, whereas he sees the mother as the source of responsibility, but without power. But to the ethnographer, it is the mother who has the power and the father who bears the responsibility, for, in the final analysis, the mother makes the decisions for which the child, and the larger community, hold the father responsible.

A final example of the dialectics of social life is found within the very inception and structure of a thesis by Thomas Gregor of Cornell University (Gregor 1969). Gregor's study of the Mehinacu Indians of the Upper Xingú River area of Brazil uses the metaphor of photography to state its problem. He sees most ethnographies as "prints," or "positives," of societies, whereas he attempts to give a picture of Mehinacu society in the form of a "negative." The result is a tapestry of avoidances, nonrelationships, disjunctions of communication, and areas of unpredictability in social relationships. Gregor starts from the implicit assumption that just as one problem of social life is the establishment and maintenance of relationships, another is to keep from falling into them. This is a theme from Simmel, of course, and it is related also to the duality of self-alienation and alienation from others. How to get rid of people, or at least to disengage from certain of them, is a question in all societies, but Gregor chose to study the problem among a small group of fifty-seven people who live in close and visible proximity with one another in their small village and are all genetically interrelated.

When everybody is blood kin to one another in a society, there are two choices available, both of which are a means of negating kinship. The first is to call everybody a kinsman. One simple way of doing this is through a moiety system, which allows the social universe to be divided into two halves and automatically bestows one kinship quality to one half and another to the other. People are either A or B, allowing, of course, for a certain intensification of the relationship in the case of very close kin. But except for the A and B distinction, kinship bestows no special tie except to designate a person as a member of the society. Kinship, per se, by becoming everything, becomes nothing. The other technique for getting rid of potential kinsmen is to deny the relationship. One way of doing this is, again, through genealogical amnesia. Among the Mehinacu, who are bilateral and have neither lineages nor moieties, the poor memory of ancestry makes all kinship ties diffuse and nonspecific. People have a great latitude of situational choice of their kinsmen and the determination of these choices is largely a matter of maximizing personal advantage. Everybody in the village can call everybody else by a kinship term, but the extent of diffuseness and overlapping of kin terms is so great that everybody can call everybody else by at least two terms. This gives considerable space for personal maneuvering, and every marriage is an occasion for reordering relationships by deciding which side of the union will be considered kin and which side affines. The total village, needless to say, does not yield a unified and internally coherent structure of kinship. That is, it does not automatically follow that the man you call "brother" will also call the man you call "brother-in-law" by the latter term. This often results in dissonance, rather than complementarity, of expectations, but this is hardly peculiar to the Mehinacu. Their social system is just a bit more fractured than others, but not that much. The system of Mehinacu kin ties is coherent only from the point of view of the individual. It is his personal "order" and not the social order, a point that we will pick up later in this chapter.

Gregor follows the theme of the negativity of relationships throughout all of Mehinacu social structure with felicitous results. He unveils avoidances that exist below the institutional level, and he analyzes the mechanisms of role segregation and

privacy seeking in a society in which almost all activity is visible. Actually, he does for an entire society what Goffman and
his students have done only for gatherings and encounters, and
he does it from the perspective of the operation of a whole social system. One of his best insights follows Simmel's thoughts
on the "lie" very closely. He sees a basic problem among the
Mehinacu to be that of too much information. Despite all the
ruses and evasions used by the Mehinacu to conceal information about themselves and their activities, there exists a float-
ing reservoir of personal knowledge among them that would be
considered inordinate in even the most gossipy American small
town. The threat posed by this information to the holding and
playing of roles is great, as in the case of the philandering man
who would also be a good husband. Adultery is widely pursued
and desperately furtive, but instantly discovered, in Mehinacu
society. This menaces all marriages. People gossip endlessly
about the peccadilloes of others, and, although they try to keep
it from the spouses of the lovers, they soon also hear the talk.
But then they hear all sorts of talk all the time, for the Mehinacu are as good at lying as they are at adultery and gossip.
Nobody really knows, then, what is true and what is false;
they are given ample doubts and few convictions. Everything
is both true and false, and all information is diluted and adul-
terated.

Now, the very same thing can be said of the way the
Mehinacu bandy about kin terms and ties, and it can be said
about other sectors of their normative system as well. And perhaps this can be said about all social life and all normative
systems, for man lives with this curious mixture of both hard
perception and collective delusion; the cultural images of social
life are not all clear reflection nor all absolute refraction, but
a mixture of the two that reduces it all to shadow. It is this
quality of culture that has inspired the dialectical doubt in the
given truth of this world. Dialectical thought is not the inven-

tion of the Sophists, passed on to us by a mechanical idealism through Plato and Hegel and Marx, and so on, but the perception of existential contradiction.

The literature of anthropology yields endless examples of the contradictory nature of social life, but those I have presented in this book should suffice as simple illustrations. If we were to turn to contemporary industrial society, the increase of pertinent data would be astronomical, but this would introduce special problems that would require another volume. Let me just throw out one thought for perusal. We live in a time of curious paradox. The rapid evolution of social complexity is indeed making our society increasingly difficult to comprehend, and we can barely form an image of it, let alone understand it. But at the same time, the development of the social sciences has also made society more accessible to systematic study and has encouraged a popular "objective" attitude about it. If we add to this the fact that the revolution in communications has made vast amounts of social data widely available, through radio, television, and other media, it is plain that we are confronting a situation that has never before existed in human history. The contradictions within our society have been laid bare by communications, which, however faulty, are almost as good as those among the Mehinacu. This has led some to think that we are going back to a kind of tribal existence, but this idea is based upon an ignorance of tribes as well as upon a miscomprehension of modern society. Rather, we are being saturated with information that is indigestible for its sheer quantity but also destructive of the *image of order* that we carry in our minds. Americans are told that they must fight a war in Vietnam to protect freedom, but they then can watch the reality of the war on their television sets.

The public mind has a wonderful capacity for repairing perceived reality to fit its requirements for order. Leon Festinger, a social psychologist, wrote that dissonance between elements in a cognitive system commonly comes under pressure for consistency such that one or both of the contradictory factors are modified to make them more harmonious (Festinger 1957). Thus, in a case in which a black family moved to a white housing project, the residents, faced with a *fait accompli,* shifted their overtly stated opinions toward greater tolerance. Their other choice, of course, would have been to deny the blackness of the newcomer. This is not just an amusing possibility, for it can be accomplished by saying that the new neighbors "aren't like the rest of them." The example of the 1968 Democratic Convention in Chicago is also instructive, for the evidence of the television viewers' senses should have been sufficient to shatter all confidence in the custodians of order. This unpalatable conclusion was evaded by the majority of the public by attributing the violence to the demonstrators. Seemingly, millions of Americans are ready to testify that a horde of savage hippies were assaulting the policemen's clubs with their heads. Edmund Leach writes in *A Runaway World?* (1968a) that people tend to handle behavior that does not fit into the neat categories of meaning by either treating it as "immoral" or ignoring it. They indeed do this, but they also can invert their perceptions.

The gap between value and reality may indeed be greater now than it was in the past, but this is not the critical element. What matters is that the contradictions are more easily perceived today and the breaches less easily healed and mediated. The mood of our age is one of confusion, failure of confidence, and a growing sense of unreality, which are at once its despair and its only hope. But lest it be thought that we are moving rapidly toward social self-awareness, it can only be noted that much of social science, itself, continues to operate with a model of a social order that seeks quiescence. We can see only the oppositions and not their movements. Our norms are being continually and inexorably ground to pieces upon the mill of time, and anthropology and sociology still teach that there is a strain toward their realization in social interaction.

Equilibrium

The theoretical ingredients of the equilibrium concept in structural-functionalism were discussed in Chapter 2 of this book, but a summary review of the idea will perhaps reveal how far away from it we have traveled. Equilibrium does not suggest a model of society that is absolutely fixed and unchanging nor does it merely express the notion that societies have some kind of order and are not continually falling apart. It states, rather, that societies, which are continually subject to disturbances of one kind or another, have a tendency to reassert the integration of their parts so as to yield orderly activity and, commonly, social solidarity. The equilibrium model is said to be a research strategy. It is an "as if" assumption that one makes in order to do analysis. But inasmuch as anything may be assumed and any assumption may yield research results of a kind, it is well to warn that the strategy is only as good as the validity of its premises.

The premises of the equilibrium concept are simple. The most important is that norms and activities are either unitary or tend toward unity. Some social anthropologists fail to make any distinction between the two levels, or kinds, of social reality, and the rest assume a close congruence between them. Thus, when norm and conduct vary widely, two processes are believed to be set in motion. The first is that negative sanctions will bring the conduct back into the permissible range of variation; the second is that, to the extent that the deviation in conduct is general, the norm will readjust to behavioral reality. Norms, however, do not change, according to structural-functionalism, to reflect just any behavior, for the direction and extent of change are conditioned by other norms. That is, the norms, themselves, have an internal consistency and a requirement for mutual complementarity that will operate against the development of any contradictions within the system they form. Change, where it occurs, will be dampened in extent by the strain toward pattern consistency, and it will take forms that are both organically and aesthetically related to their antecedents. The integrated normative system, moreover, is embedded within the motivational apparatus of the actor. As such, it is part of the system of continual social control, for stable activity depends upon shared norms and expectations, a consensus of common values. Finally, the existence of values, which are also internal to the actor, bestows legitimacy upon institutional forms. This, then, is the organic model. Positivism assumes that the experienced world consists of hard facts, but this assumption is not even necessary for a natural science approach. One can quite easily achieve the same results by granting that experience is subjective while operating on the axiom that the total content of our subjectivities is cultural. This complete relativism is the heart of the Parsonian critique of utilitarianism. He simply described a new form of positivism.

The equilibrium assumption has come under severe attack in recent years, bringing forth a trenchant defense of the strategy from none other than Max Gluckman of the University of Manchester. This was somewhat of a surprise, for he, more than any other British anthropologist, has been profoundly influenced by Simmel, who thought that societies survived only by being continually on the run. Moreover, Gluckman's work emphasized opposition, conflict, even rebellion, although it must be noted that he frequently saw these as processes that ultimately contributed to equilibrium and solidarity.

In his critique of the Young Turks (most of whom are in their forties and fifties) who have questioned functionalism, Gluckman takes the tack that everybody resorts to homeostatic models, whether or not he makes a virtue out of it. He accomplishes this by watering down the concept to an "as if" strategy and largely reducing its scope to institutional rather than societal equilibrium. Weber, Marx, Maine, Durkheim, and Tönnies all employed the notion of long periods of stasis, according to Gluckman:

I repeat, they are using a *mode* of approaching history when they use this framework of long periods of relative stasis, to be understood in *as if* equilibriums of structural durations that to a large extent neglect actual historical time in a manner infuriating to many historians; therein they formulate theories of interdependence between social elements. [Gluckman 1968, p. 224]

Gluckman thus reduces equilibrium theory to such a minimal attitude that it requires only the recognition that societies continue. But he does a bit more. By adhering to the model of a society that strains toward internal complementarity and consistency, and yet admitting to steady and progressive change, he becomes a "Big Bang" theorist of social transformation. His departure from the Parsonian "rolling equilibrium" model is concisely expressed in the following passage:

. . . institutional change theoretically could proceed with a constant readjustment of each part to changes in the other parts—in moving, actual equilibrium. This is more likely to occur in parts, rather than in the whole, of a social field. More often there will be a steady change of magnitudes within and between institutions, until there is a sudden and radical transformation of form. All experience indicates this. [Ibid., p. 232]

During the life span of an institution it will tend toward equilibrium, but it also generates its own demise: " . . . an institutional system will tend to develop and hypertrophy along the main lines of its organization until external conditions make it quite impossible for the system to continue to work" (ibid., p. 231). If this is true, we can then ask what was happening to the equilibrium of the *entire system* while these progressive institutional disjunctures were developing. Gluckman would seem to suggest that it hangs together somehow until it all blows up, reducing his entire defense of equilibrium to a very simple dialectic of the sudden transformation of quantity into quality. It is noteworthy that the institutions, themselves, only collapse as a result of contradictions with other institutions—with something *external.* Does the Big Bang within the whole society also become triggered only by external factors? If so, this is a step away from Marx. But even he had trouble with accommodating the great leaps to his materialism.

It is exactly at the point of the radical transformation of society that structural-functionalism fails us, for the analysis of rapid change inevitably becomes narrative. Gluckman states that the delineation of structure is obtained at the expense of empirical richness and detail, a problem that is greatly aggravated when one considers the minutiae of events involved in social change (ibid., p. 234). The studies of institutional structures and of social change are, therefore, antipathetic to one another. Gluckman takes a step toward solving the dilemma, only to deepen it. He writes:

I would rather draw attention to the fact that the separation of institutions from interaction is to a large extent an analytic distinction. For it is *partly* from action and interaction that we build up our abstract structure of institutions; and conversely, in studies of interaction, we are concerned with encapsulations from institutions. Somehow we must try to bring these different types of analyses together. [Ibid., p. 235, italics mine]

This is exactly the problem. Gluckman assumes that the institutions are built up out of behavioral data. They are not. If institutionalization means anything at all, it must be the embedment of the ideal in social action, but this does not mean that the two will fit together, that they are merely complementary to each other.

I believe that Gluckman missed the entire point of the dialectical critique of structural-functionalism. It is exactly the skewing of activity from model and value that is the kernel of the argument. If dialectics operate in social life, they do not do so every century or so, when the peasants take to the hills and the students to the streets. The process is continually operative, and it is even more evident in the microhistorical span of our ethnographies than in history writ large. In fact, one may well criticize the Big Bang theory of history, whether Gluckman's or Marx's, on exactly this basis. The equilibrated order in which Gluckman invests his anthropology and that he attributes, with some justice, to Marx may well be simply the historian's (or anthropologist's) subjective model of the social structure. This has been argued throughout this book, and it is explicit in Leach:

The notion of order is a human notion and psychologically a most necessary one. In order to use our environment and find our way about in it we must credit it with structure and describe it as an ordered system; indeed the selector mechanisms at the back of the retina which translate light and shadow into visual perception predispose us to interpret our observations as order rather than chaos. But the word "relationship" is concerned with the ordering as such, and it entails not human observation but human creation; we do not use words to describe relationships, we create verbal categories which imply relationships, and such verbal categories arise as a consequence of our perceiving the world as an ordered structured system. [Leach 1967a, p. 130]

This follows Leach's earlier statement of the same position in *Political Systems of Highland Burma* (1965), which constituted an empirical demonstration of the thesis that real structures are held together by their inconsistencies. The social structures of the anthropologists may well be, in part, the creations of their own minds and, for the rest, the mental constructs of their informants. This theme is very close to that of sociological phenomenology:

The relationship between the social scientist and the puppet [structural models] he has created reflects to a certain extent an age-old problem of theology and metaphysics, that of the relationship between God and his creatures. The puppet exists and acts merely by the grace of the scientist; it cannot act otherwise than according to the purpose which the scientist's wisdom has determined it to carry out. Nevertheless, it is supposed to act as if it were not determined but could determine itself. A total harmony has been pre-established between the determined consciousness bestowed upon the puppet and the pre-constituted environment within which it is supposed to act freely, to make rational choices and decisions. This harmony is possible only because both, the puppet and its reduced environment, are the creation of the scientist. And by keeping to the principles which guided him, the scientist succeeds, indeed, in discovering within the universe, thus created, the perfect harmony established by himself. [Schutz 1962, p. 47]

This is a devastating paragraph, applying to a wide range of sociological and anthropological theorization, but aimed at the very heart of a system that would seek closure through balance.

There is, of course, some kind of order in society, but the human mind, whether that of the observer or of the participant, also seeks order. It is inherent within the reduction of motion to object, for the very mind that breaks the stream of action into fragments rebuilds the fragments into systems of meaning that allow him to act coherently. But the dilemma is not at all inescapable. It is only necessary to abandon a few of the most cherished assumptions that have led us into this theoretical cul-de-sac in order to see society as process and to distinguish related but not at all complementary forms of order that lie in mind, culture, and activity. Each level manifests contradiction just as much as harmony, counterpoint more than congruence. And between them are inversions, distortions, and opposition.

The theoretician's search for order leads him to believe that the tendency of the world is to break out of these contradictions, as did Hegel and Marx, but it is better theory to believe, as did Freud and Simmel, that this alienation of man defines his humanity and his social life. We can go back to the great revolutions of history and ask: Did they really take place? Did orders having some degree of equilibrium really break up, or was the stasis the historian's creation? Did the new order, whatever it was, depart from the old in the structure of human relationships, activities, and aggregations, or were they primarily revolutions

of the ideational realm? Does revolution produce basic, qualitative changes that reverberate throughout the entire fabric of
society, or is radical change largely confined to selected institutional spheres? Change does proceed in leaps, sometimes
through a series of events that we choose to call revolutions.
These are dialectical movements, but they are not total, nor
can they be easily reduced to a mechanical equation by which
quantity turns into quality.

Let us look, for example, at the cities, the factories, and the
farms of the Soviet Union and compare its everyday life with
that of the United States. They are different, of course, but are
not the two societies less different than they were in 1912? We
see a vast polarity—this is how our minds work—but would an
Andaman Islander? Let us look at both societies in 1912 and in
1970. Are their paths convergent, as some would say, or are
they merely parallel? If revolution is the defining and necessary
form of dialectical process, then how did our histories follow
each other so closely? After all, the United States had no revolution in that period. Or did it? We have undergone an enormous upheaval that has transformed our countryside and cities,
the fabric of our social relationships, and, some would argue,
our very state of consciousness. The pace of change has been
so rapid that the child in each of us has become a stranger to
his adulthood. We can well ask not only where is equilibrium
but where is revolution? Was Marx, just as much as Durkheim,
ultimately a student of the ideal?

Our error, perhaps, has been in seeing the antithesis of order
to be disorder, the latter conceptualized as violent turmoil. I
would suggest that this is an ideal polarity that may not be
empirically useful. It can only be hypothesized at this point that
an equally instructive polarity could be made between system
and entropy, or activity and torpor. It should be asked, with
Radcliffe-Brown, whether religion alleviates anxiety or promotes
it. And does the family provide security for the child, or does
it actually function to inculcate anxieties that can be socially

capitalized? Lévi-Strauss has written in a number of contexts that attention should be paid to those situations in which order breaks down completely as ideal laboratories for the study of rules. The evidence thus far indicates that every effort is made by the stricken populace to continue mundane activity as if nothing had happened. And where this is not possible, they apparently do not go on rampages— they simply sit and stare.

In the final analysis, we may well ask not what are the roots of stability, but what are the roots of activity. What, indeed, are the social conditions that keep people oriented toward the outer world and impelled to do things— all sorts of things? If society does anything, it is to suck people into its substance and use their energies in its restless movement and in the realization of histories that have no goals. Structure is not fixity and harmony but an abstraction from movement. Surely, the chief danger of our turbulent times is not the popularly held specter of revolution on the streets and campuses. It is, rather, the threat of massive personal withdrawal into private worlds, a flight from corporate illusions into personal fantasy.

Mana and Manners

We have taken a long journey from the reassuring just-so world of contemporary social anthropology, moving from the realm of the directed and the certain into a penumbra of doubt. The given and received truths of culture have been held to be partial, negative, or illusory. Man does not live by them; he lives with them. Having argued the broken and inverted nature of cultural reality, there is the strong impulse to put it all back together again, for we have taken apart more than we have reconstituted. But the aim of this book has been to question an orthodoxy and not to create a new one. Any reformulation will depend upon empirical work—and here I reaffirm my ethnographic faith—but it must be a critical empiricism that takes account of the faulty empiricism of the people we study. It must examine the essential interconnectedness of image and activity, without ever thinking that they are the same.

The process by which man's understanding of his milieu becomes detached from its reality has been explored in different contexts throughout this book and now requires some summation. Most of the processes may be reduced to an underlying dialectical one by which the phenomenal stream becomes segmented into units having form and meaning that can be communicated in a social life. This is Durkheim's central question in *The Rules of the Sociological Method,* but he settled for a suspension of doubt in the naturalism of the perceived world. His "social facts" were consequently one-sided and incomplete, finite and bounded. They suffered from a concreteness that is the very negation of reality, and the current shift in social anthropology to process and to more fluid categories is indicative of the limitations of his ideal world (cf. Bailey 1963, p. 226). Durkheim saw the substance of the social facts to lie in certain essential attributes, but he avoided the further logic that they could only be completely defined beyond their parameters—by what they were not. There is a latent negativity in Durkheim's view of society and its components, but this negativity is characteristic of culture itself, which carries out the same operation as Durkheim's rules. Positivism, at best, sees only one side of reality. Every positive statement that is made infers another contradictory one, and it is only through understanding this oppositional quality of all our categories that we can see the larger framework in which they are lodged. The mind selects only certain characteristics of phenomena as significant; it finds cultural meaning in only a segment of reality; it falsifies the world, at the very least, by omission. Culture, then, turns upon the mind and perpetuates the illusion. It is not enough to say that this selected part of phenomena is all that we must, as anthropologists, worry about, for this would imply that this is all that shapes our lives. Culture is not the total content of our minds or even of our life experience, unless it were to be defined so broadly that it would encompass all social life without limits and thus pass into emptiness.

There are numerous other areas of normative distortion, and disciplinary limitations have constrained me from drawing upon the voluminous evidence of experimental and social psychology. Freud, however, saw culture as mixed with illusion and projection, the sublimated stuff of the unconscious mind. One need not be a libidinal determinist (Freud wasn't) to discover remarkable correspondences between individual fantasy and cultural symbolism. The human psyche takes account of reality, but it manages it through a series of distortions and teleologically selective interpretations of it. Society does not at all spring full-blown out of the psyche, or out of Lévi-Strauss's "mind," but we must admit that many of the unmistakable parallels in culture derive from the pan-human similarity of the mind and of certain aspects of early human experience. Whether one sees man's intelligence as being like a digital computer or as being dark and irrational, it is something that is not wholly determined by culture. Neither mind nor culture are even thinkable without each other, but this does not mean that one is reducible to the other. In the final analysis, culture is a product, the synthesis of mind and action.

Society, as we have depicted it, is not as tidy and transparent as it is to the structural-functionalists, but it is not chaotic either. Its order only lies at a deeper level. It is the very incongruence of our conscious models, and guides for conduct, to the phenomena of social life that makes that life possible. The individual seeks security and order as a condition of his psychological functioning (cf. Leach 1965, pp. ix–xv), but society just as certainly requires tension and flexibility. The individual, therefore, must be predisposed to activity, and, given the uniqueness of every social situation, he must have latitude for action. The norms provide the image of order and fitness; they bind time and activity in the mind, but they cannot be allowed to impede their flow. They also promote the image of value and purpose in a world that is permeated with particularity of interest and indeterminancy of the results of action. Norms have their functions as the scenario of activity. They may indeed constrain, but they can also give freedom of movement. Geertz says that his Javanese village "both clung to the husks of selected established institutions and limbered them internally in such a way as to permit a greater flexibility, a freer play of social relationships within a generally stereotyped framework" (Geertz 1963, p. 103). It is this same kind of latitude of choice that I found in the Tuareg pattern of mother's brother's daughter marriage, and that allowed young men to pursue a host of desirable young ladies in the belief that they conformed to a preferred category. We encountered this theme again in Evans-Pritchard's *Kinship and Marriage Among the Nuer* (1951), in which the author states that it is the very depth of the ideology of patrilineality and the pervasiveness of the model of lineages that allow the Nuer to move about so freely and to honor matrilateral links as much as the agnatic ones. Schneider finds this conclusion to be one of "those special gems of paradoxical obfuscation for which Evans-Pritchard is justly famous" (Schneider 1965, p. 74), but I would rate it as one of the most mordant insights ever to come out of social anthropology. Perhaps Simmel's remark that mutual nonknowledge of others makes interaction possible can be extended to the realm of culture. The perpetuation of social life depends, then, upon the placement of a veneer between its flow and its perception. Culture is an illusion, but, like other illusions, it gives life.

Finally, the very relation between norm and action is contradictory both in form and in content. Norms, as creations of thought that are further thought upon, tend to be formally specific and bounded. They can be verbalized and codified; some are rigidified into law. Despite this *formal* parsimony and discreteness of norms, they are diffuse, multiplex, and unbounded in content. They are generated out of broad ranges of activity and, by virtue of the fact that they are norms, they apply to a wide spectrum of activity. Thus, we are able to articulate the norms, but it is not always so easy to state which norm belongs to exactly which situation. Norms, then, are formally specific and diffuse in content.

Activity has exactly the diametrically opposite quality. Because of the uniqueness and nonrepetitive character of deeds, they are formally diffuse. That is, they are not as articulated, formulated, and bounded as norms, for this would imprison activity and make situational responsiveness impossible. On the other hand, acts are indeed specific in content. Each is discrete and pertinent to the particular social setting. Action, then, is formally diffuse and specific in content.

Activity is sequential in time, continuous, multifaceted, and nonrepetitive; norms are timeless, discontinuous, repetitive, and one-dimensional. Norm and activity seldom meet, and there must always be strain between them. And the nature of man and his existence commonly convert the strain into discontinuity and contradiction. It will be immediately objected that action is indeed given form in social life. This is true, but we cannot ignore the fact that *some* activities are more carefully delineated than others. Much conduct may be amorphous, but other behaviors are quite "formal." They involve rules that are rigidly followed. In short, we should consider the possibility that certain activities are specific in both form and content. And we should also think about whether some norms are diffuse in both form and content. These norms and actions, by partaking of each other's qualities, could serve as mediators of the contradiction between norm and act.

Let us first consider the possible diffuseness of norms. The one element that best meets our criterion is the concept of the sacred. It is amorphous in form, for it is the most unbounded, nebulous, and abstract of ideas. Furthermore, it is diffuse in content, for it is conceived as a force that is suffused throughout the experienced universe. It is for this reason that Durkheim saw the idea of *mana* as the quintessential expression of the sacred. *Mana,* according to the experience of ethnographers, is one of the most difficult of all cultural expressions to describe, and it is difficult to delineate because the informants find it so. It is charged with movement, and it invades anything. Stones, trees, people, gardens, almost any object can have *mana. Mana* is the sphere of activity, force and continuity projected into the dimension of wonder. Characteristically, it is also dangerous and surrounded with taboos or other injunctions that require highly specific forms of behavior.

This last observation brings us directly to actions that are specific in form as well as in content. The two types of activity that meet our criterion are ritual and etiquette, which are really much the same thing. Both are highly specific in content, but they also have a remarkable and highly distinctive specificity of form. One conducts a ritual, or a proper dinner table, in a highly exacting manner, attempting to replicate as nearly as possible antecedent behavior in similar situations. And, like *mana,* etiquette and ritual are dangerous areas, an observation of Simmel that was discussed in Chapter 3. Their violation exposes the inconsistencies of life by breaching the one point at which norm and action meet.

This brings us to a final negation of Durkheim. Ritual and the sacred do not express the solidarity of the social group nor do they symbolize the constraint of its norms upon the individual. Rather, they bridge the contradiction between norm and action and mediate the alienation of man from his fellow man. Etiquette and ritual elevate activity to correspondence with culture, a transition from the particular to the general, just as the notion of *mana* reduces the general to the level of the particular. The breaks within the world are sealed by empty forms. It is thus of consummate importance that rebels against the social order find little response to their verbal challenges to God and capitalism, the two great values of American culture, but can drive their elders into a frenzy by flagrant breaches of manners. As if to illustrate the ultimate absurdity of social life, in 1964, a handful of young students were able to reduce the entire state of California to hysteria by walking about the Berkeley campus with signs stating in bold letters: "FUCK YOU."

Bibliography

BAILEY, F. G. 1963. *Politics and Social Change: Orissa in 1959.* Berkeley: University of California Press.

BARTH, FREDRIK. 1967. On the Study of Social Change. *American Anthropologist* 69: 661–669.

BEAN, SUSAN S. 1970. Two's Company, Three's a Crowd. *American Anthropologist* 72: 562–564.

BOAS, FRANZ. 1928. *Anthropology and Modern Life.* New York: W. W. Norton & Co.

BROWN, NORMAN O. 1959. *Life Against Death: The Psychoanalytic Meaning of History.* New York: Vintage Books, Random House.

BURRIDGE, K. O. L. 1967. Lévi-Strauss and Myth, in E. R. Leach, ed., *The Structural Study of Myth and Totemism.* London: A. S. A. Monograph No. 5, Tavistock Publ.

CARRASCO, PEDRO. 1963. The Locality Referent in Residence Terms. *American Anthropologist* 65: 133–134.

COSER, LEWIS A. 1956. *The Functions of Social Conflict.* New York: The Free Press.

———. 1965. Georg Simmel, in *Georg Simmel.* Edited by Lewis A. Coser. Englewood Cliffs, N. J.: Prentice-Hall.

DAVIS, KINGSLEY. 1959. The Myth of Functional Analysis as a Special Method in Sociology and Anthropology. *American Sociological Review* 24: 757–773.

DIAZ, MAY N. 1966. *Tonalá: Conservatism, Responsibility and Authority in a Mexican Town.* Berkeley: University of California Press.

246 BIBLIOGRAPHY

DURKHEIM, EMILE. 1964. *The Rules of the Sociological Method.* New York: The Free Press.

———. 1965. *The Elementary Forms of the Religious Life.* New York: The Free Press.

——— and MARCEL MAUSS. 1967. *Primitive Classification.* Translation and introduction by R. Needham. Chicago: University of Chicago Press.

EGGAN, FRED. 1966. *The American Indian: Perspectives for the Study of Social Change.* Chicago: Aldine Publishing Co.

ENGELS, F. 1906. *Feuerbach: The Roots of the Socialist Philosophy.* Translated by A. Lewis. Chicago: Charles H. Kerr & Co.

EVANS-PRITCHARD, E. E. 1940. *The Nuer.* London: Oxford University Press.

———. 1951. *Kinship and Marriage Among the Nuer.* London: Oxford University Press.

———. 1965. *Theories of Primitive Religion.* London: Oxford University Press.

FESTINGER, LEON. 1957. *A Theory of Cognitive Dissonance.* Stanford, Calif.: Stanford University Press.

FINDLAY, J. N. 1962. *Hegel: A Re-examination.* New York: Collier Books.

FORTES, MEYER. 1953. The Structure of Unilineal Descent Groups. *American Anthropologist* 55: 17–41.

FREUD, SIGMUND. 1922. *Group Psychology and the Analysis of the Ego.* London: International Psychoanalytic Press.

———. 1938. *The Basic Writings of Sigmund Freud.* Translated and edited by A. A. Brill. New York: Modern Library, Random House.

———. 1962. *Civilization and Its Discontents.* Translated and edited by James Strachey. New York: W. W. Norton & Co.

GEERTZ, CLIFFORD. 1957. Ritual and Social Change: A Javanese Example. *American Anthropologist* 59: 32–54.

———. 1963. *Agricultural Involution: The Processes of Ecological Change in Indonesia.* Berkeley: University of California Press.

———. 1967. The Cerebral Savage. *Encounter* 28, No. 4 (April 1967): 25–32.

GEERTZ, H. and C. 1964. Teknonymy in Bali: Parenthood, Age-Grading and Genealogical Amnesia. *Journal of the Royal Anthropological Institute* 94: 94–108.

GLUCKMAN, MAX. 1968. The Utility of the Equilibrium Model in the Study of Social Change. *American Anthropologist* 70: 219–237.

GOFFMAN, ERVING. 1956. The Nature of Deference and Demeanor. *American Anthropologist* 58: 473–502.

GOLDENWEISER, A. 1936. Loose Ends of a Theory on the Individual Pattern and Involution in Primitive Society, in *Essays in Anthropology Presented to A. L. Kroeber.* Edited by R. Lowie. Berkeley: University of California Press.

GOODENOUGH, W. H. 1965. Yankee Kinship Terminology: A Problem in Componential Analysis. *American Anthropologist* 67: 259–287.

GOULDNER, ALVIN W. 1968. "Disorder and Social Theory." *Science* 162: 247–249.

———. 1970. *The Coming Crisis of Western Sociology.* New York: Basic Books.

GREGOR, THOMAS. 1969. *Roles in a Small Society: A Study of the Mehinacu Indians.* Ph.D. Dissertation. Columbia University.

HARRIS, MARVIN. 1964. *The Nature of Cultural Things.* New York: Random House.

———. 1968. *The Rise of Anthropological Theory: A History of Theories of Culture.* New York: Thomas Y. Crowell.

HEGEL, G. W. F. 1892. *The Logic of Hegel.* Translated from the Encyclopaedia of the Philosophical Sciences by William Wallace. Oxford: The Clarendon Press.

———. 1956. *The Philosophy of History.* New York: Dover Publications.

———. 1959. *Encyclopaedia of Philosophy* (translated and annotated by Gustav Emil Mueller). New York: Philosophical Library.

HERSKOVITS, M. J. and F. S. 1934. *Rebel Destiny: Among the Bush Negroes of Dutch Guiana.* New York: McGraw-Hill.

——— and ———. 1947. *Trinidad Village.* New York: Alfred A. Knopf.

HERTZ, ROBERT. 1960. *Death and the Right Hand.* Translated by R. and C. Needham. New York: The Free Press.

HOMANS, GEORGE and DAVID M. SCHNEIDER. 1955. *Marriage, Authority and Final Causes.* New York: The Free Press.

JAMES, WILLIAM. 1902. *The Varieties of Religious Experience: An Essay in Human Nature.* London: Longmans, Green & Co.

JOHNSON, ALLEN. 1968. *Economics and Dependence on a Plantation in Ceará, Brazil.* Ph.D. Dissertation, Stanford University.

248

BIBLIOGRAPHY

KAUFMANN, WALTER. 1966. *Hegel: A Reinterpretation.* New York: Anchor Books, Doubleday.

KROEBER, A. L. 1917. *Zuni Kin and Clan.* American Museum of Natural History. Anthropological Papers 18: 39–204.

LEACH, EDMUND R. 1961. *Rethinking Anthropology.* London: Athlone Press.

———. 1965. *Political Systems of Highland Burma.* Boston: Beacon Press.

———. 1967a. The Language of Kachin Kinship: Reflections on a Tikopia Model, in *Social Organization: Essays Presented to Raymond Firth.* Edited by M. Freedman. Chicago: Aldine Publ. Co.

——— (ed.). 1967b. *The Structural Study of Myth and Totemism.* A. S. A. Monograph 5, London: Tavistock Publ.

———. 1968a. *A Runaway World?* New York: Oxford University Press.

——— (ed.). 1968b. *Dialectic in Practical Religion.* Cambridge Papers in Social Anthropology No. 5, London: Cambridge University Press.

LEFEBVRE, HENRI. 1969. *The Sociology of Marx.* New York: Vintage Books, Random House.

LÉVI-STRAUSS, CLAUDE. 1949. *Les Structures élémentaires de la Parenté.* Paris: Plon.

———. 1956. The Family, in *Man, Culture and Society.* Edited by H. Shapiro. New York: Oxford University Press.

———. 1958. La Geste d'Asdiwal. *Ecole Pratique des Hautes Etudes, Section des Sciences Religieuses.* Extr. Annuaire 1958–1959: 3–43.

———. 1960. On Manipulated Sociological Models. *Bijdragen tot de taal, Land en Volkenkunde.* Netherlands 116:1.

———. 1963a. *Structural Anthropology.* Translated by C. Jacobson and B. Schoepf. New York: Basic Books.

———. 1963b. *Totemism.* Translated by R. Needham. Boston: Beacon Press.

———. 1963c. The Bear and the Barber. *Journal of the Royal Anthropological Institute* 93: 1–11.

———. 1964. *Mythologiques: Le Cru et le Cuit.* Paris: Plon.

———. 1965. *Tristes Tropiques.* New York: Atheneum.

———. 1966. *Mythologiques: Du Miel aux Cendres.* Paris: Plon.

———. 1967. The Story of Asdiwal, in *The Structural Study of Myth and Totemism.* Edited by E. R. Leach. A. S. A. Monograph 5, London: Tavistock Publ.

————. 1968a. *The Savage Mind.* Chicago: University of Chicago Press.

————. 1968b. *Mythologiques: L'Origine des Manières de Table.* Paris: Plon.

————. 1969a. *The Elementary Structures of Kinship.* Translated by J. H. Bell and J. R. von Sturmer. Edited by R. Needham. Boston: Beacon Press.

————. 1969b. *The Raw and the Cooked.* Translated by J. Weightman. New York: Harper & Row Publishers.

LEVY, MARION. 1952. *The Structure of Society.* Princeton: Princeton University Press.

LEWIS, OSCAR. 1951. *Life in a Mexican Village.* Urbana: University of Illinois Press.

LOWIE, ROBERT H. 1920. *Primitive Society.* New York: Boni and Liveright.

MANDELBAUM, MAURICE H. 1938. *The Problem of Historical Knowledge: An Answer to Relativism.* New York: Liveright.

MARCUSE, HERBERT. 1941. *Reason and Revolution: Hegel and the Rise of Social Theory.* New York: Oxford University Press.

————. 1955. *Eros and Civilization.* Boston: Beacon Press.

MARX, KARL. 1947. *The German Ideology.* New York: International Publishers.

MEAD, GEORGE HERBERT. 1967. *Mind, Self and Society.* Edited by C. W. Morris. Chicago: Phoenix Books, University of Chicago Press.

MILLER, HENRY. 1965. *Sexus.* New York: Grove Press.

MILLS, C. WRIGHT. 1959. *The Sociological Imagination.* New York: Oxford University Press.

MURPHY, ROBERT F. 1957. Intergroup Hostility and Social Cohesion. *American Anthropologist* 59: 1018–1035.

————. 1959. Social Structure and Sex Antagonism. *Southwestern Journal of Anthropology* 15: 89–98.

————. 1960. *Headhunter's Heritage: Social and Economic Change Among the Mundurucú Indians.* Berkeley: University of California Press.

————. 1963. On Zen Marxism: Filiation and Alliance. *Man* 63: 17–19.

————. 1964. Social Distance and the Veil. *American Anthropologist* 66: 1257–1274.

————. 1967. Tuareg Kinship. *American Anthropologist* 69: 163–170.

————. 1970. Basin Ethnography and Ecological Theory. *Languages and Cultures of Western North America*. Edited by E. H. Swanson. Pocatello: The Idaho State University Press.

———— and LEONARD KASDAN. 1959. The Structure of Parallel Cousin Marriage. *American Anthropologist* 61: 17–29.

———— and ————. 1967. Agnation and Endogamy: Some Further Considerations. *Southwestern Journal of Anthropology* 23: 1–14.

NEEDHAM, RODNEY. 1960. The Left Hand of the Mugwe: an Analytical Note of the Structure of Meru Symbolism. *Africa* 20: 20–33.

————. 1962. *Structure and Sentiment*. Chicago: University of Chicago Press.

PARSONS, TALCOTT. 1937. *The Structure of Social Action*. New York: McGraw-Hill.

————. 1951. *The Social System*. New York: The Free Press.

————. 1964. *Social Structure and Personality*. New York: The Free Press.

————. 1966. *Societies: Evolutionary and Comparative Perspectives*. Englewood Cliffs, N. J.: Prentice-Hall.

————, ROBERT F. BALES and collaborators. 1955. *Family, Socialization and Interaction Process*. New York: The Free Press.

———— and EDWARD A. SHILS (eds.). 1951. *Toward a General Theory of Action*. Cambridge: Harvard University Press.

PATAI, RAPHAEL. 1965. The Structure of Endogamous Unilineal Descent Groups. *Southwestern Journal of Anthropology* 21: 325–350.

PETERS, EMRYS. 1960. The Proliferation of Segments in the Lineage of the Bedouin of Cyrenaica. *Journal of the Royal Anthropological Institute* 90: 29–53.

RADCLIFFE-BROWN, A. R. 1952. *Structure and Function in Primitive Society*. New York: The Free Press.

————. 1958. *Method in Social Anthropology*. Edited by M. N. Srinivas. Chicago: University of Chicago Press.

REDFIELD, ROBERT, R. LINTON, and M. HERSKOVITS. 1936. Memorandum on the Study of Acculturation. *American Anthropologist* 38: 149–152.

REDFIELD, ROBERT. 1930. *Tepoztlán, A Mexican Village*. Chicago: University of Chicago Press.

SAHLINS, MARSHALL D. and ELMAN SERVICE. 1960. *Evolution and Culture*. Ann Arbor: University of Michigan Press.

SCHNEIDER, DAVID M. 1965. Some Muddles in the Models, in *The*

Relevance of Models for Social Anthropology. A. S. A. Monograph 1, London: Tavistock Publ.

———. 1968. *American Kinship: A Cultural Account.* Englewood Cliffs, N.J.: Prentice-Hall.

——— and GEORGE HOMANS. 1955. Kinship Terminology and the American Kinship System. *American Anthropologist* 57: 1194–1208.

SCHNEIDER, LOUIS (ed.). 1967. *The Scottish Moralists on Human Nature and Society.* Chicago: University of Chicago Press.

SCHUTZ, ALFRED. 1962. *Collected Papers I: The Problem of Social Reality.* Edited by M. Natanson. The Hague: Martinus Nijhoff.

SERVICE, ELMAN. 1962. *Primitive Social Organization.* New York: Random House.

SIMMEL, GEORG. 1950. *The Sociology of Georg Simmel.* Translated and edited by Kurt H. Wolff. New York: The Free Press.

———. 1968. *The Conflict in Modern Culture and other Essays.* Translated by K. Peter Etzkorn. New York: Teachers College Press.

SSRC (Social Science Research Council Summer Seminar on Acculturation). 1954. Acculturation: An Exploratory Formulation. *American Anthropologist* 56: 973–1002.

STEWARD, JULIAN H. 1938. *Basin-Plateau Aboriginal Sociopolitical Groups.* Washington, D.C.: Bureau of American Ethnology Bull. 120.

———. 1955. *Theory of Culture Change.* Urbana: University of Illinois Press.

STURTEVANT, EDGAR H. 1947. *An Introduction to Linguistic Science.* New Haven: Yale University Press.

VINCENT, JOAN. 1968. *Status and Leadership in an African Community: A Case Study.* Ph.D. Dissertation, Columbia University.

WEINGARTNER, RUDOLPH. 1962. *Experience and Culture.* Middletown, Conn.: Wesleyan University Press.

WILLIAMS, F. E. 1923. The Vailala Madness and the Destruction of Native Ceremonies in the Gulf Division, Territory of Papua. *Anthropological Report* No. 4, Port Moresby.

WRONG, DENNIS. 1961. The Oversocialized Conception of Man. *American Sociological Review* 26: 183–193.

YALMAN, NUR. 1963. On the Purity and Sexuality of Women in the Castes of Malabar and Ceylon. *Journal of the Royal Anthropological Institute* 93: 25–58.

Acknowledgements

Grateful acknowledgement is made to the following publishers for permission to reprint passages from copyrighted publications.

The Sociology of Georg Simmel, by Georg Simmel, translated by Kurt Wolff. The Free Press, 1950. © 1950 by The Free Press. Reprinted by permission of The Macmillan Co.

The Elementary Structures of Kinship, by Claude Lévi-Strauss, translated by J. H. Bell and J. R. von Sturmer, edited by R. Needham. Beacon Press, 1969. © 1969 by Beacon Press. Published first in France under the title *Les Structures élémentaires de la Parenté* in 1949. Reprinted by permission of Beacon Press and Eyre and Spottiswood (Publishers) Ltd.

The Elementary Forms of the Religious Life, by Emile Durkheim. The Free Press, 1965. © 1915 by George Allen and Unwin Ltd. Reprinted by permission of The Macmillan Co. and George Allen and Unwin Ltd.

Index